IMAGES
of America

OLD SYLVAN BEACH AND THE PAVILIONS

I0793051

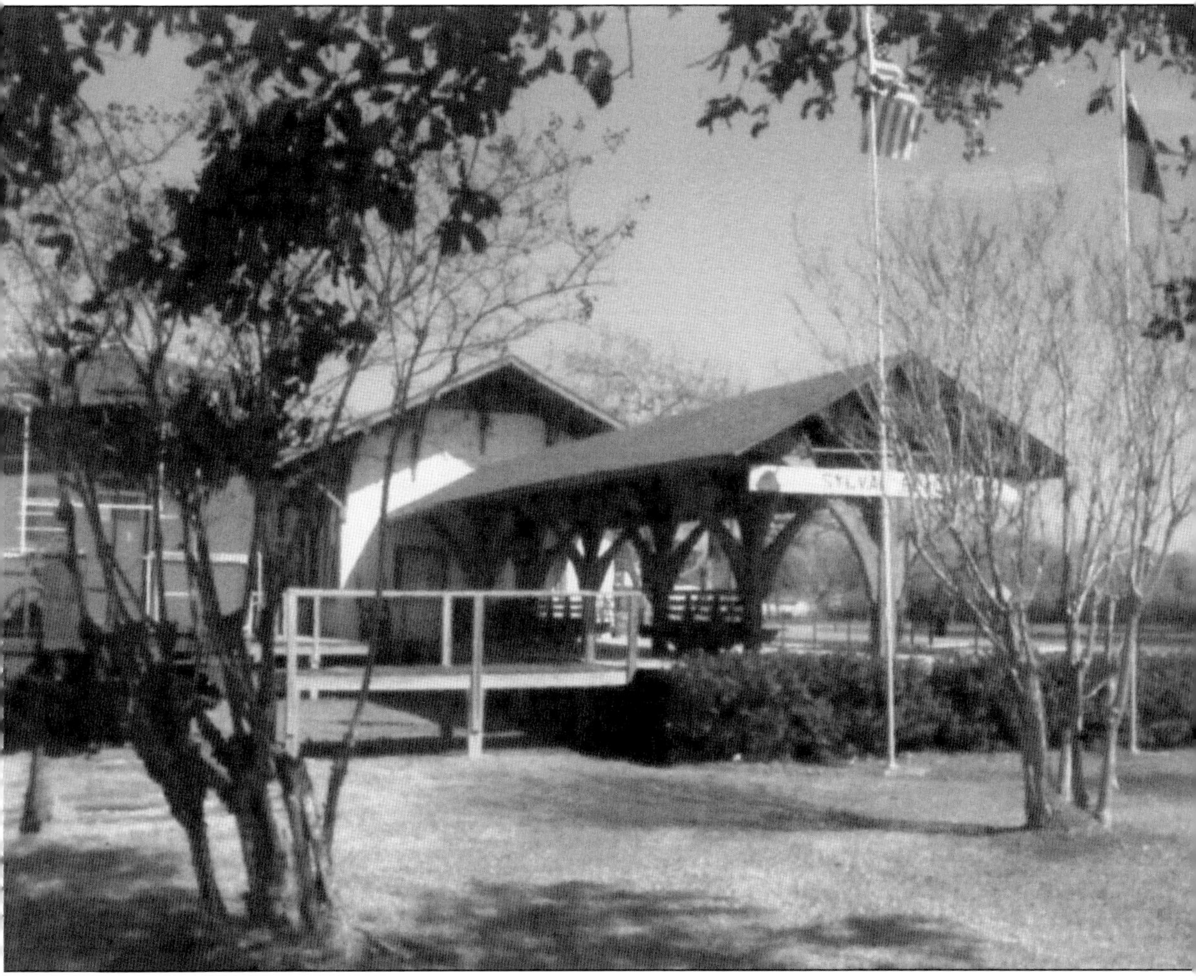

The La Porte Depot (pictured) is the home of the La Porte Bay Area Heritage Society, whose continuing effort to collect and preserve the pictorial history of Sylvan Beach, La Porte, and the Galveston Bay area is invaluable. The overwhelming majority of the images in this book appear courtesy of the society's archives. The vigorous efforts of local preservationists recently culminated in the restoration of the Sylvan Beach Pavilion and the return of this depot to the Sylvan Beach location, where it now serves as the Old Sylvan Beach Depot Museum. (Courtesy of the La Porte Bay Area Heritage Society Museum Archives.)

ON THE COVER: The Sylvan Beach Bathing Beauty Contest started in 1924 under Cecil Sisson's management of the park. This image reportedly shows the first group of young ladies vying for the title of Miss Sylvan Beach; it was the most popular event ever staged at the park. (Courtesy of the La Porte Bay Area Heritage Society Museum Archives.)

IMAGES
of America

OLD SYLVAN BEACH AND THE PAVILIONS

Ann Uloth Malone and Dan Becker

ARCADIA
PUBLISHING

Copyright © 2014 by Ann Uloth Malone and Dan Becker
ISBN 978-1-4671-3207-7

Published by Arcadia Publishing
Charleston, South Carolina

Printed in the United States of America

Library of Congress Control Number: 2013958036

For all general information, please contact Arcadia Publishing:
Telephone 843-853-2070
Fax 843-853-0044
E-mail sales@arcadiapublishing.com
For customer service and orders:
Toll-Free 1-888-313-2665

Visit us on the Internet at www.arcadiapublishing.com

To the memory of my husband, Norman
Malone, who always knew I could
And to my beautiful children and grandchildren—always try
And to my dear friend Dan Becker, who always does the best he can.

—Ann Malone

To the memory of my father, Gabriel Becker, who
is laughing gently as I write these words
And to Mary and Mary, and Ann and Ann, and
Dain and Dain, you know what I mean.

—Dan Becker

Contents

ACKNOWLEDGMENTS

All images appear courtesy of the La Porte Bay Area Heritage Society Museum Archives unless otherwise noted.

INTRODUCTION

We are talking about Sylvan Beach! This book is not an erudite academic historical treatise. No, we are talking about Sylvan Beach, which means we are talking about beautiful women in bikinis, moonlit pavilions and Howard Hughes, the jitterbug and the Charleston, Ray Charles and a train called the "Moonlight Excursion," picnics and carnivals, music and romance, and love and legend.

The unlikely truth is that familiarity and age can make our most beautiful treasures banal if we do not pause to remember, observe, and venerate the events and moments when we first saw or most appreciated a place like Sylvan Beach. For this reason, we ask you to come back with us to Sylvan Beach, to the place where, for over 100 years, Houston and much of Texas came to play and dance, pray and picnic, fall in love, get away from work, bay at the moon, or splash in the bay. La Porte and the land that was to become Sylvan Beach have played host to such Texas heroes and luminaries as Sam Houston, Sidney Sherman, and Ashbel Smith—and, in later days, Howard Hughes, Denton Cooley, Walter Cronkite, and Richard "Racehorse" Haynes. Sylvan Beach is a mere 15 minutes from Houston's Interstate 610; five minutes from the plain on which the Battle of San Jacinto was fought; less than an hour from world-changing oil discoveries like those at Goose Creek, Spindletop, and Sour Lake; and, of course, right next to the entrance to the Houston Ship Channel and the Port of Houston.

La Porte was founded in 1892 with 22 acres of bayfront property set aside for a park that was initially called the Grove or Sylvan Grove. In 1893, La Porte hosted the first party in the park—a Fourth of July celebration at Sylvan Beach. The newly incorporated City of La Porte purchased the land from John Beazley, whose daughter Julia recorded a local legend that the pirate Jean Lafitte had a safe house in the Sylvan Beach area. Texas folklorist J. Frank Dobie includes a version of the Lafitte legend in one of his compilations.

St. Mary's Seminary (and "select boarding school") opened on Sylvan Beach in 1901. After the Sylvan Beach Hotel was damaged by a hurricane in 1900, Bishop Nicholas Gallagher bought it to convert into a dormitory for seminarians. The current St. Mary of the Immaculate Conception Catholic Church at Sylvan Beach was completed in 1927. Andrew Jackson Houston (a son of Sam Houston) taught military science at St. Mary's Seminary. St. Mary's also operated one of the piers that reached out into the bay at Sylvan Beach.

This book will set the stage with a chapter on the popularity it enjoyed, discuss neighbors from Houston and other points inland, and highlight the way various means of traveling to Sylvan Beach both shaped the area and reflected the changes in the world around it. We will look at the park's history through the prism of a camera lens—and that will sometimes say more than words could ever say, but it can also sometimes also be inadequate to convey a moment in time. Nighttime photography is harder to find, so it was difficult to include those long-ago moments many may remember from Sylvan Beach Pavilion, like memories of a summer evening with a full moon hanging over Galveston Bay and a soft breeze coming off the water.

The camera cannot replicate the sounds of old Sylvan Beach—the strains of Harry James's trumpet playing "You Made Me Love You" in the evening at Sylvan Beach or the pervasive call of seabirds in the morning. The good news is that Sylvan Beach is still here, the Sylvan Beach Pavilion has reopened, the Sylvan Beach Festival still happens every April, the girls in the beauty contests are as beautiful as ever, and the people are just as friendly. So, look through these pages; follow us through a century at Sylvan Beach; and, when you have finished, y'all come see us and make some new memories.

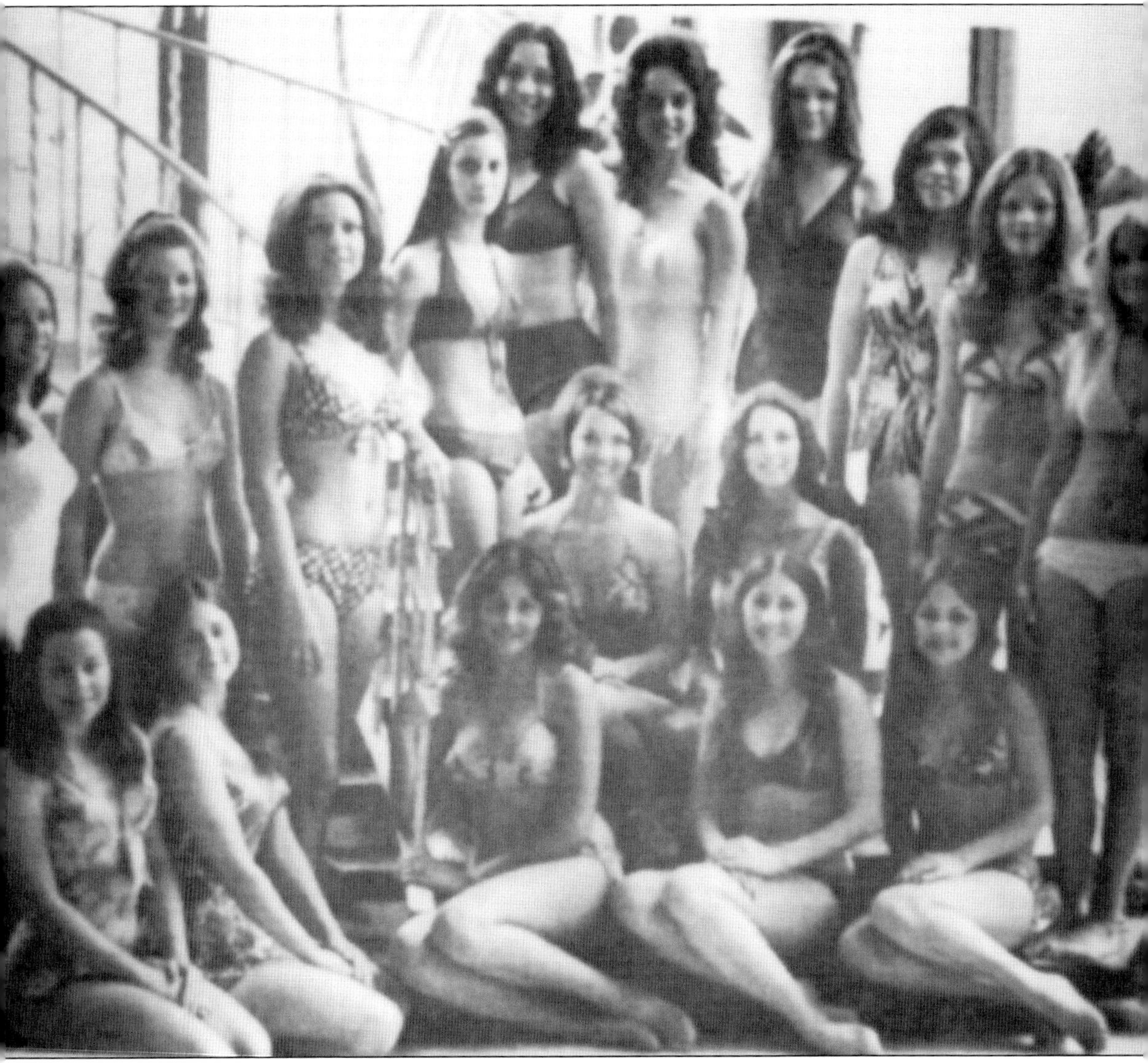

This photograph was taken at the Houston Yacht Club during the 1973 Sylvan Beach beauty contest. The Sylvan Beach beauty contest was affiliated with the Miss Texas Pageant, which fed into the Miss America Pageant. The first Sylvan Beach bathing beauty contest was held in 1924. Pictured here are, from left to right, (first row) Valerie Zarncki, Deborah Fincher, Donna Felscher, Bridget Frankum, and Debbie Roehrick; (second row) Angie Shepherd and Brenda Freed; (third row) Bobbie Norman, Debbie Kressley, Sanid Schroeder, Carol Spier, Becky Ellis, Sandy Tate, Sheryl Standifer, Kippy Payne, Susan Louder, and Holly Goodrich.

One

Sylvan Beach and La Porte

The city of La Porte, where Sylvan Beach lies, was incorporated on August 10, 1892. At the time, Galveston was the largest city in Texas and the commercial center of the state. The great storm of 1900 would deal Galveston a blow from which it would never fully recover, facilitating the ascendance of Galveston's younger inland competitor, the city of Houston. The waning of Galveston's star was accelerated on March 3, 1899, when Congress approved a project to dredge a channel 25 feet deep from the foot of Main Street in Houston to Bolivar Roads in Galveston Bay. Although the project was difficult and performed gradually, it ultimately helped to yield the Houston Ship Channel and the Port of Houston, which would forever replace Galveston as the dominant port in Texas. the channel also fulfilled La Porte's prophetic name by making it indeed "the door" to Texas. The project had been made possible in part because after the channel was cut roughly a mile from Sylvan Beach, Commodore James Morgan's estate had been reimbursed for the channel Morgan had cut across Morgan's Point, allowing the toll chain to finally be lowered.

Early on, before La Porte and Sylvan Beach came into existence, the most practical way to travel to Sylvan Beach was by water. By the mid-1880s, Houston had a dozen steamships and 22 schooners scheduling daily voyages from the foot of Main Street. Eventually, some of them made trips to or stops at Sylvan Beach, including at the Sylvan Hotel, which had its own pier at which visitors could disembark. Then, by 1900 and in increasing numbers each year thereafter, Sylvan Beach received the majority of its visitors from points inland, especially from the rapidly growing city of Houston. The train from Houston to La Porte—the La Porte, Houston & Northern Railroad—arrived in 1895 and added a West La Porte stop (the Sylvan Beach stop) in 1905. Although the train traveled down the bay to Seabrook and on to Galveston, Sylvan Beach was always receiving more visitors by train from Houston than Galveston.

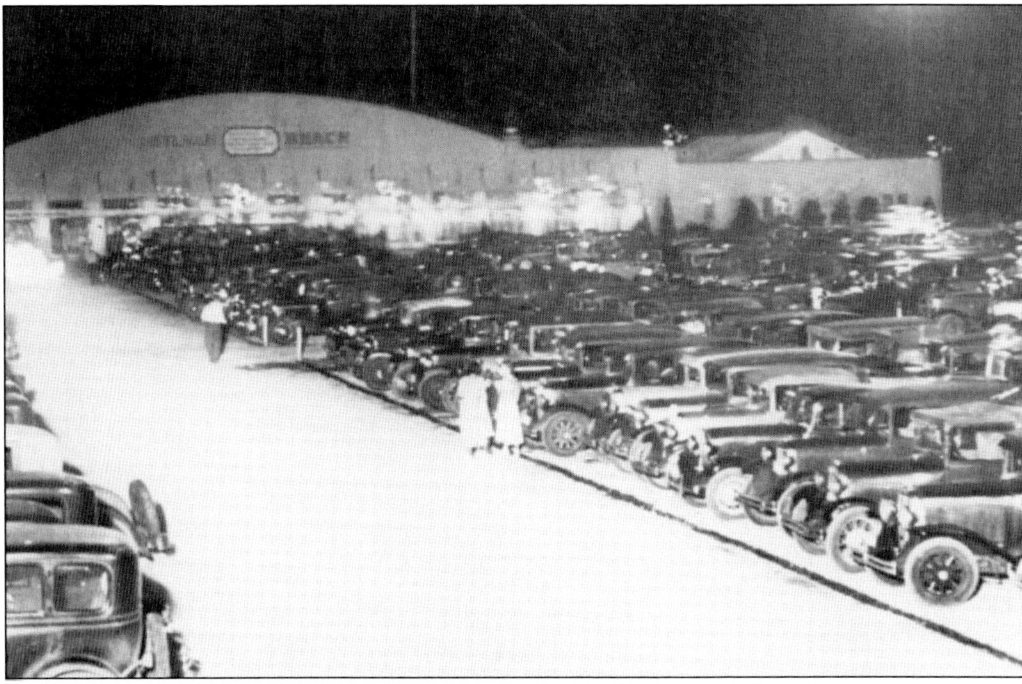

This view of the Sylvan Beach Pavilion at night shows the automobiles of guests who came to enjoy music and dancing. In the early years, rocking chairs were placed around the perimeter of the dance floor. The building's facade and the cars date this photograph to the 1920s.

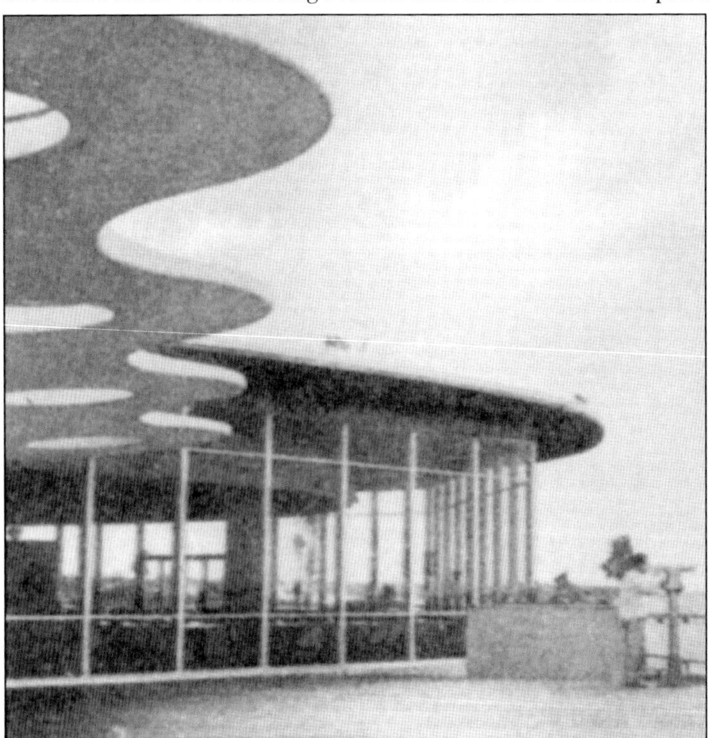

This 1956 image shows the outside deck of the elegant new Harris County Pavilion at Sylvan Beach. The Harris County Commissioner's Court recruited Houston architects Thomas Greacen and Raymond Brogniez to design this new pavilion after the great hurricane in 1943 destroyed its predecessor. Crews finished construction of the pavilion in 1956.

The Park Airplane Ride was one of the rides brought to Sylvan Beach to entice people to visit; the airplane, with cables attached, is visible on the right side of this photograph. From its inception, Sylvan Beach Park was designed and run as an attraction for families.

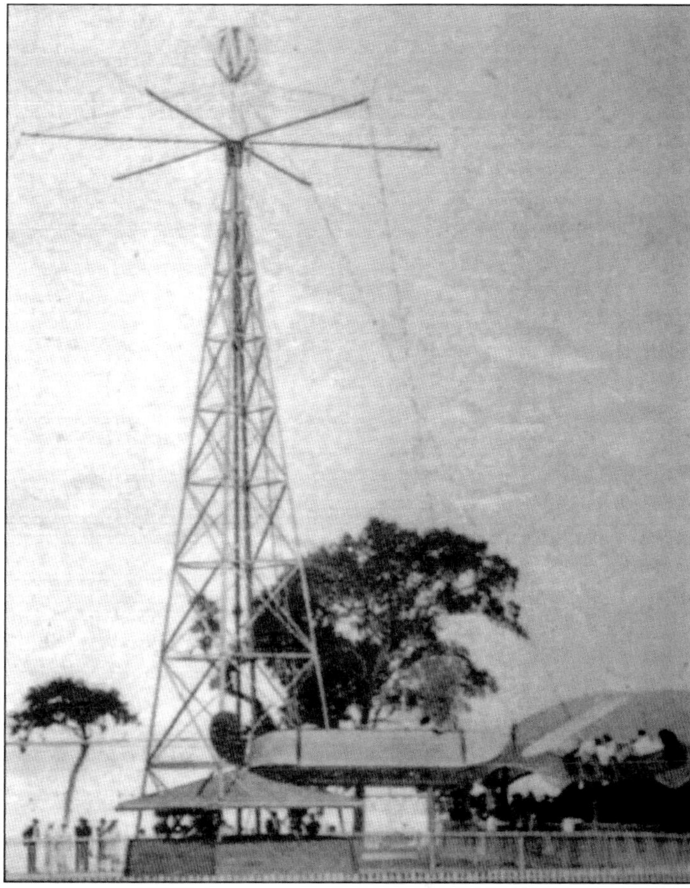

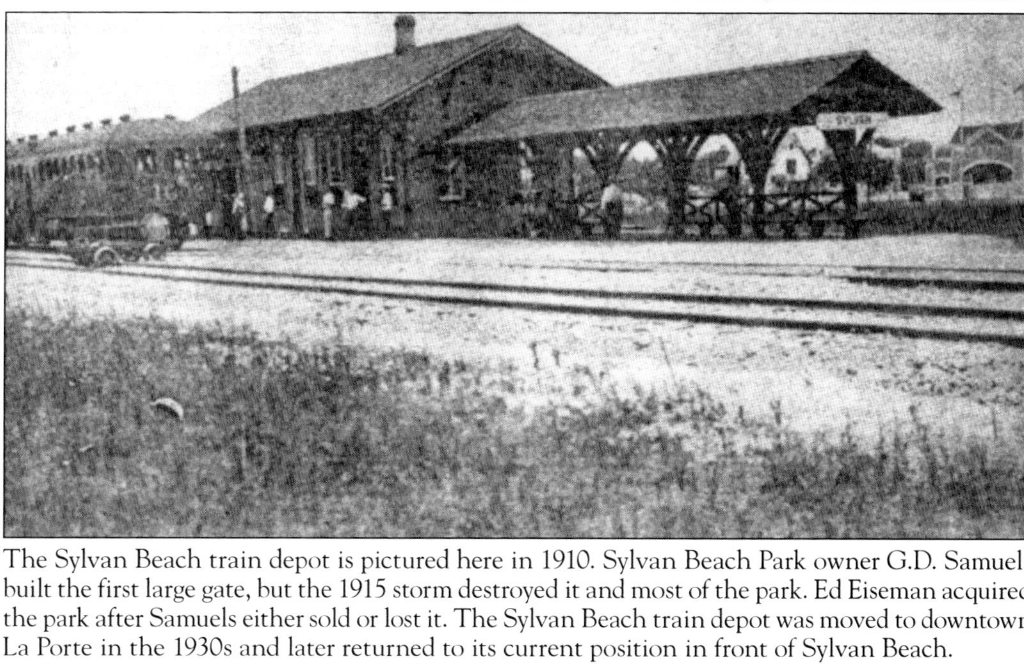

The Sylvan Beach train depot is pictured here in 1910. Sylvan Beach Park owner G.D. Samuels built the first large gate, but the 1915 storm destroyed it and most of the park. Ed Eiseman acquired the park after Samuels either sold or lost it. The Sylvan Beach train depot was moved to downtown La Porte in the 1930s and later returned to its current position in front of Sylvan Beach.

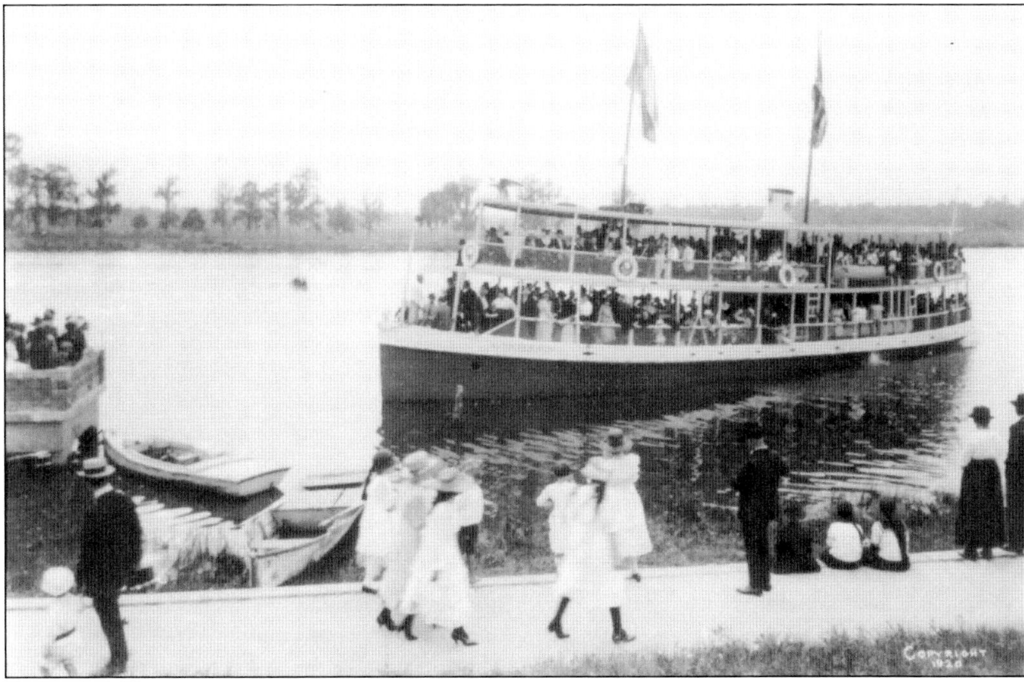

This boat and others like it brought folks from Houston to Sylvan Beach, via Buffalo Bayou, and returned the same day. Houston streetcars would wait for the day-trippers. After train service came to La Porte in 1895, bayou vessels became less integral for passenger traffic to Sylvan Beach.

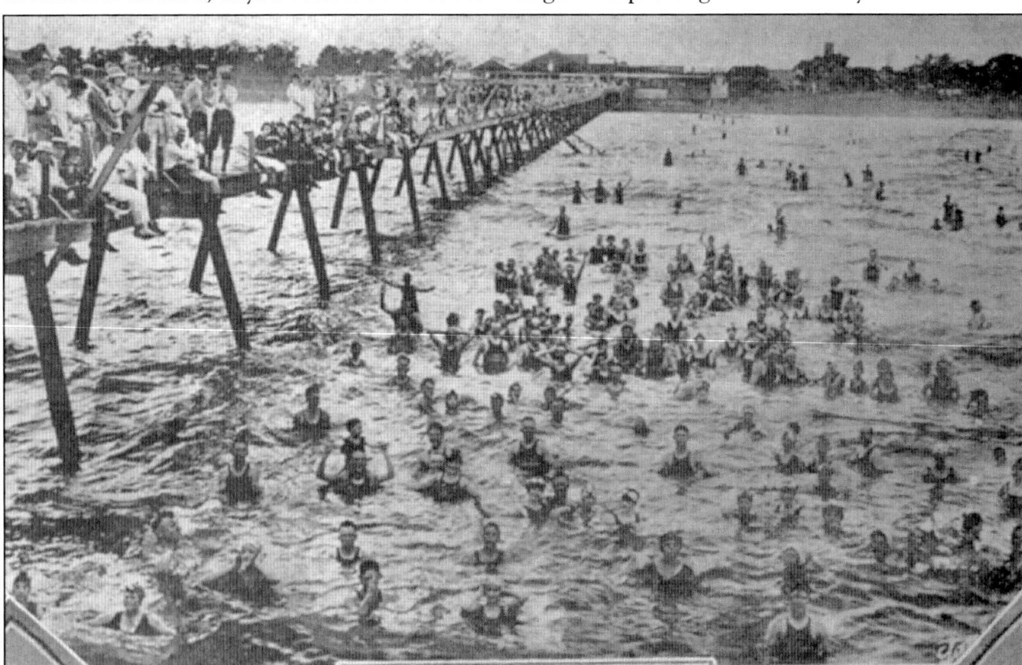

This is how Sylvan Beach Park looked every weekend in the summer when people rented cottages in the area. Sylvan Beach was convenient to Houston, so people could visit often to enjoy a respite from the hot summers.

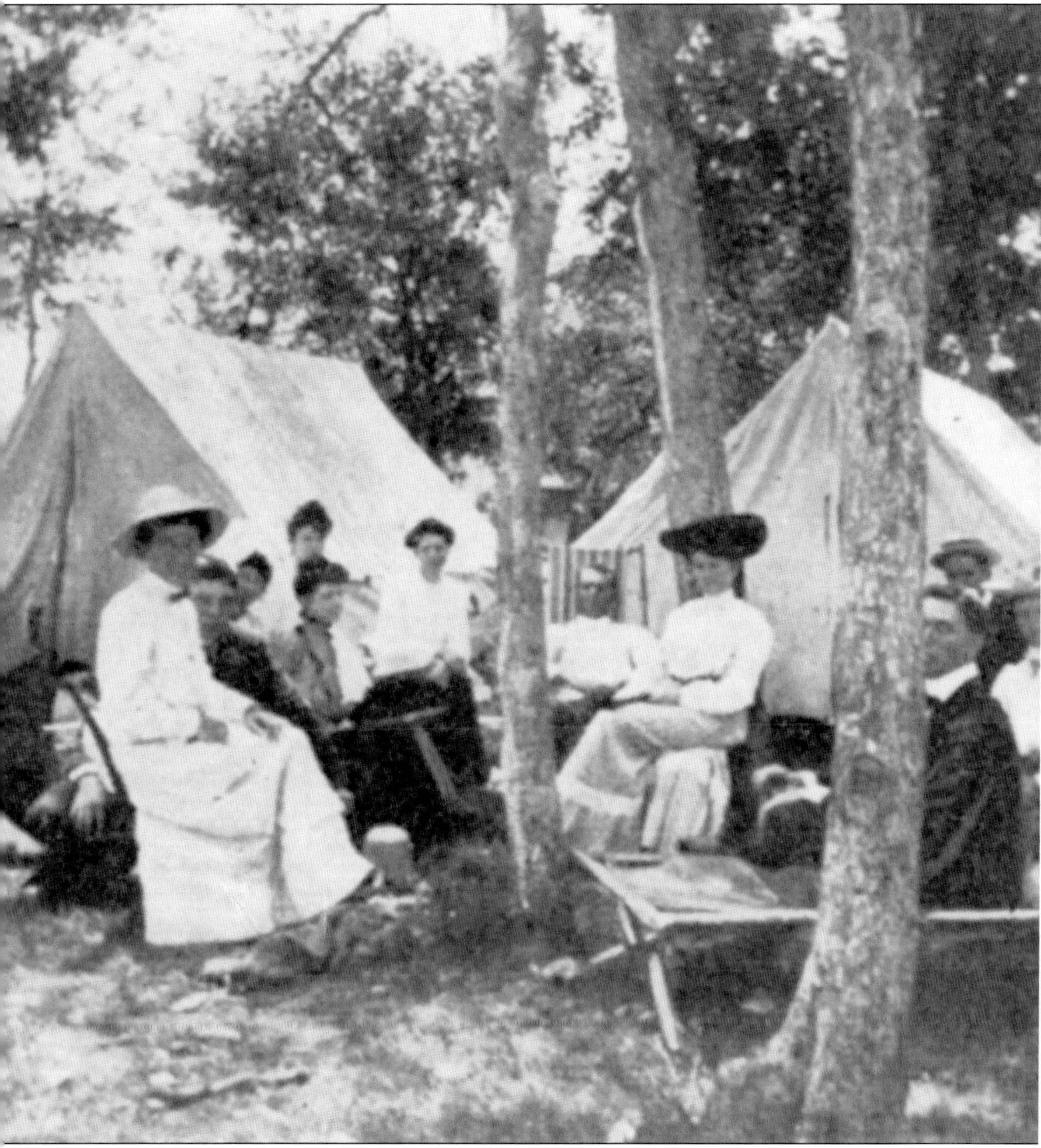

Sylvan Beach Park was always a place for large group picnics. In this c. 1904 image, people are gathered for the last day of a meeting. Picnics today at Sylvan Beach do not look much different other than changes in attire. The current park is somewhat less wooded than it was in 1904.

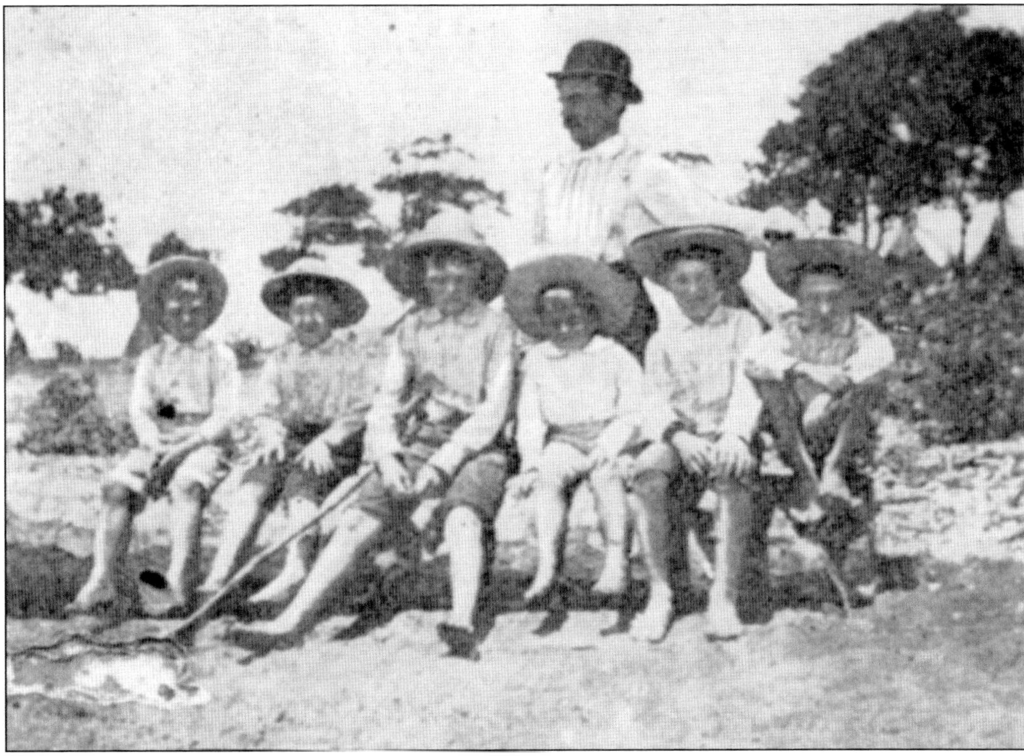

These young boys probably had a great time fishing and crabbing at Sylvan Beach when they visited with the Baptist Young People's Union in 1903. Sylvan Beach Park, especially in its early years, was a venue for many revivals as well as recreational events for various churches.

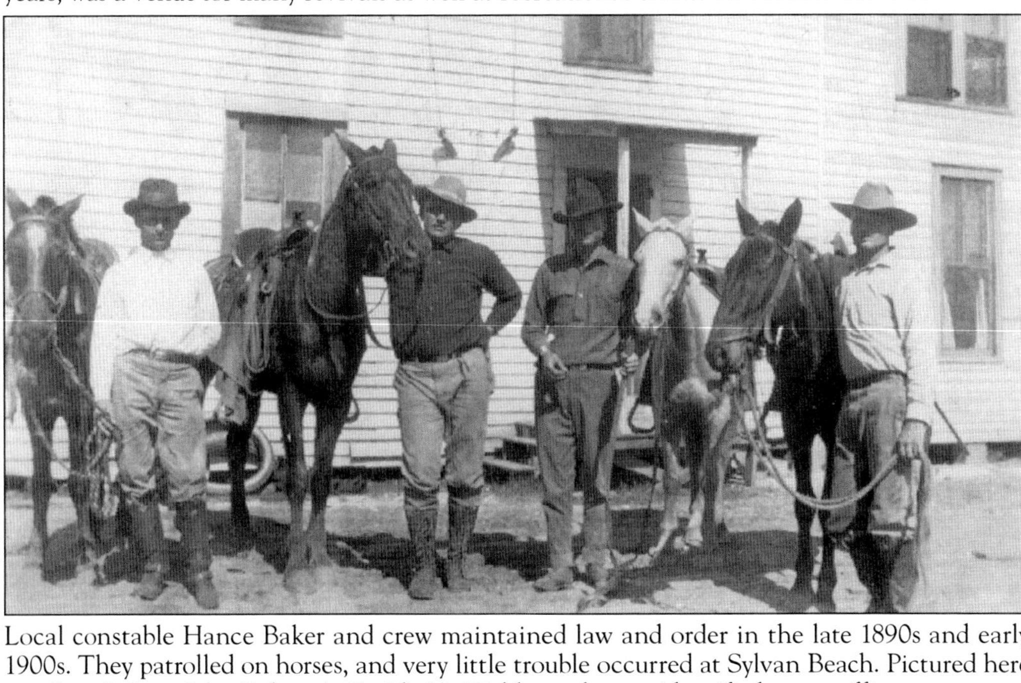

Local constable Hance Baker and crew maintained law and order in the late 1890s and early 1900s. They patrolled on horses, and very little trouble occurred at Sylvan Beach. Pictured here are, from left to right, Baker, A. Smith, H. Nickle, and an unidentified peace officer.

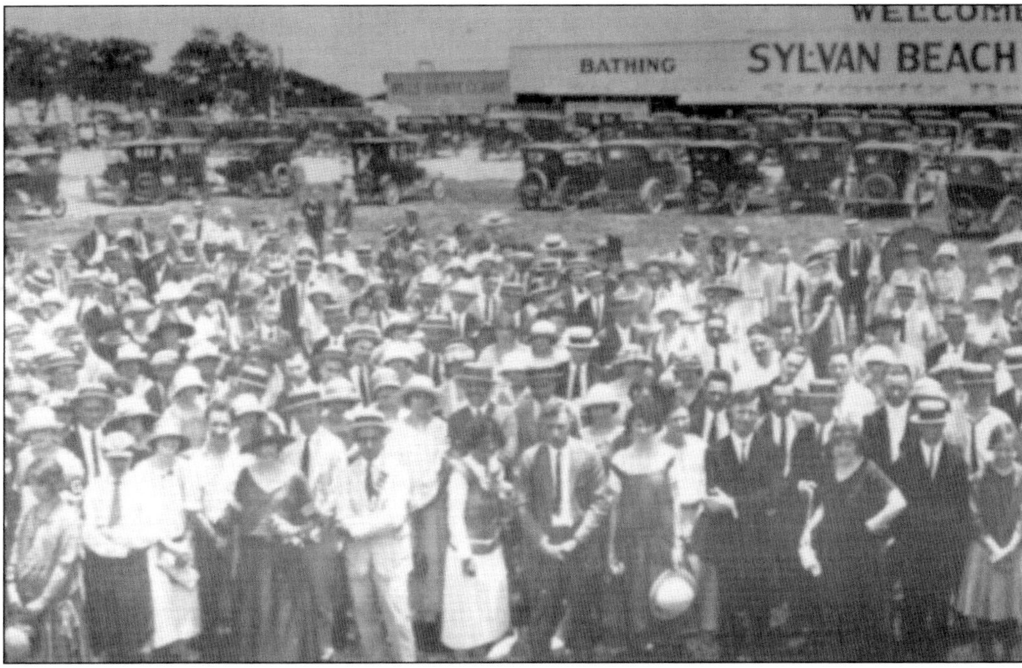

This 1923 crowd at Sylvan Beach Park is at a company picnic. The manager of the park, Cecil Sisson, knew the heads of a number of companies, many of which held picnics at Sylvan Beach. Sponsors helped pay for these events, and the companies would rent the park for the entire day.

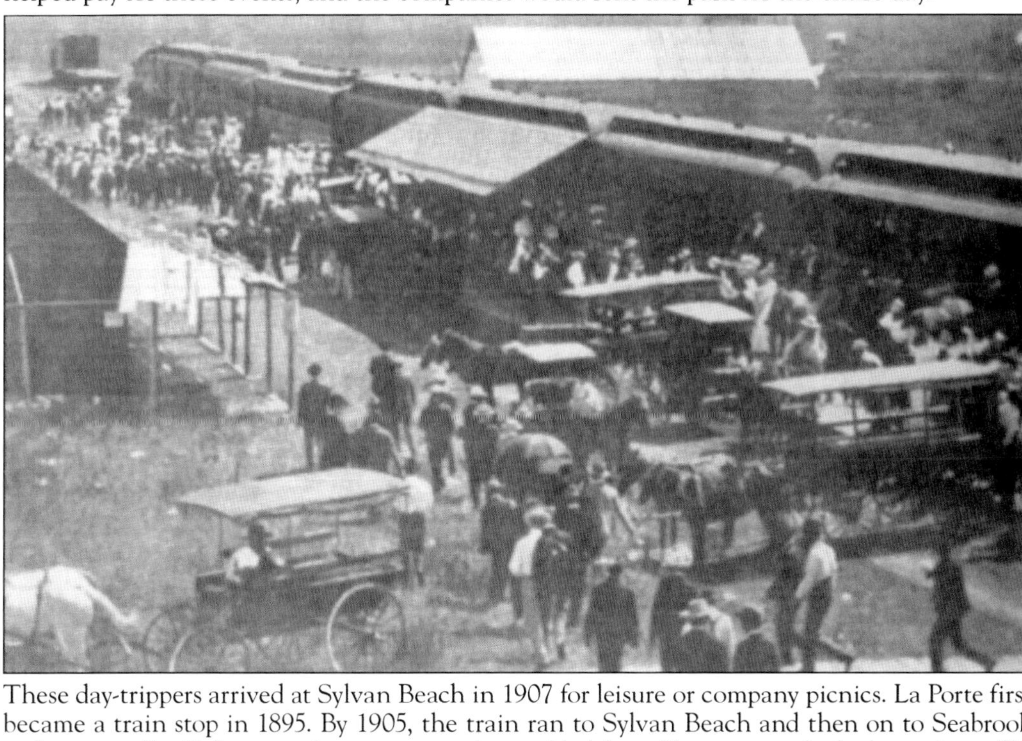
These day-trippers arrived at Sylvan Beach in 1907 for leisure or company picnics. La Porte first became a train stop in 1895. By 1905, the train ran to Sylvan Beach and then on to Seabrook and, eventually, Galveston; the easy access it provided from Houston sparked a boom in traffic coming to the park.

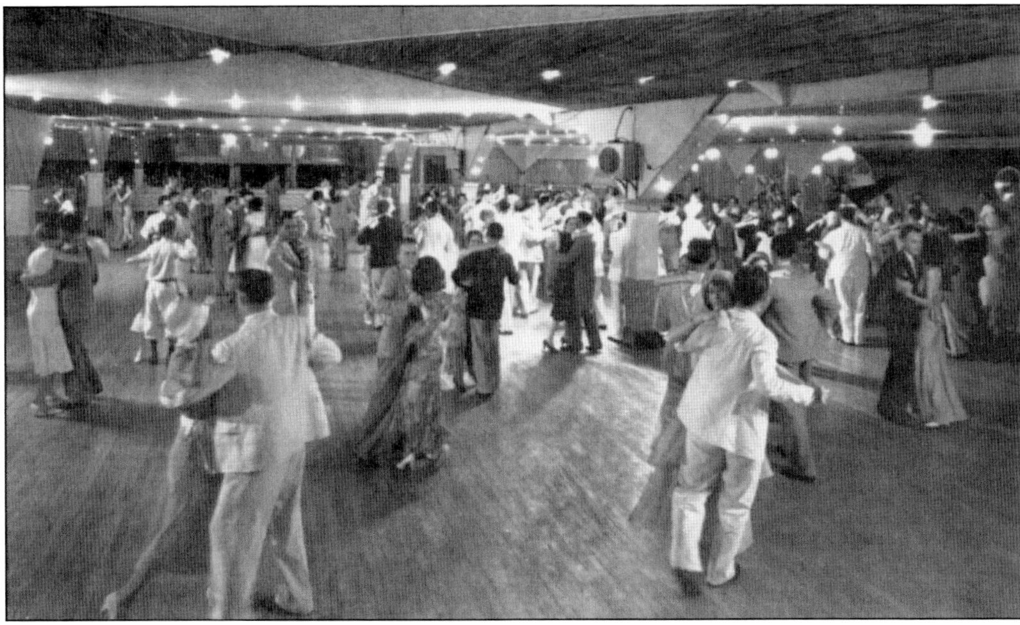

Dancing at Sylvan Beach was always fun. The dance floor, pictured here in the 1930s, was the largest in the South and was made from the wood of other dance halls that had closed. Three thousand visitors could dance on it at once. The venue at Sylvan Beach attracted many greats of the big band era.

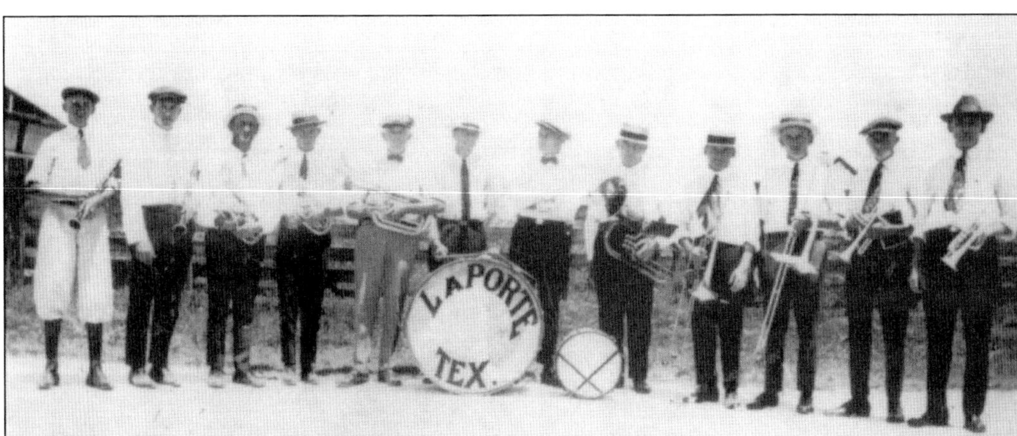

According to Gordon Black, La Porte's local historian, the La Porte Band formed in 1894 to perform at Sylvan Beach Park. At the beginning, few of the members could play instruments and only learned three songs, which, according to local stories, they would play as long as the audience would applaud. Eventually, they enlarged their repertoire and were much loved.

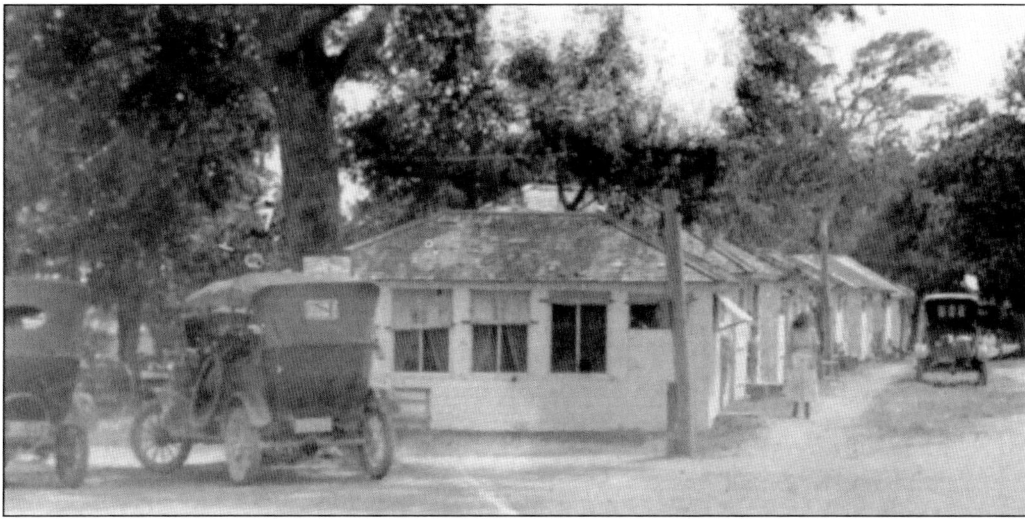

Between 1920 and 1930, Sylvan Beach Park owner G.D. Samuels built cottages available for rent at the park for the weekend or the summer. A savvy marketer, Samuels provided that if a girls' club rented a cottage, the renters did not have to pay.

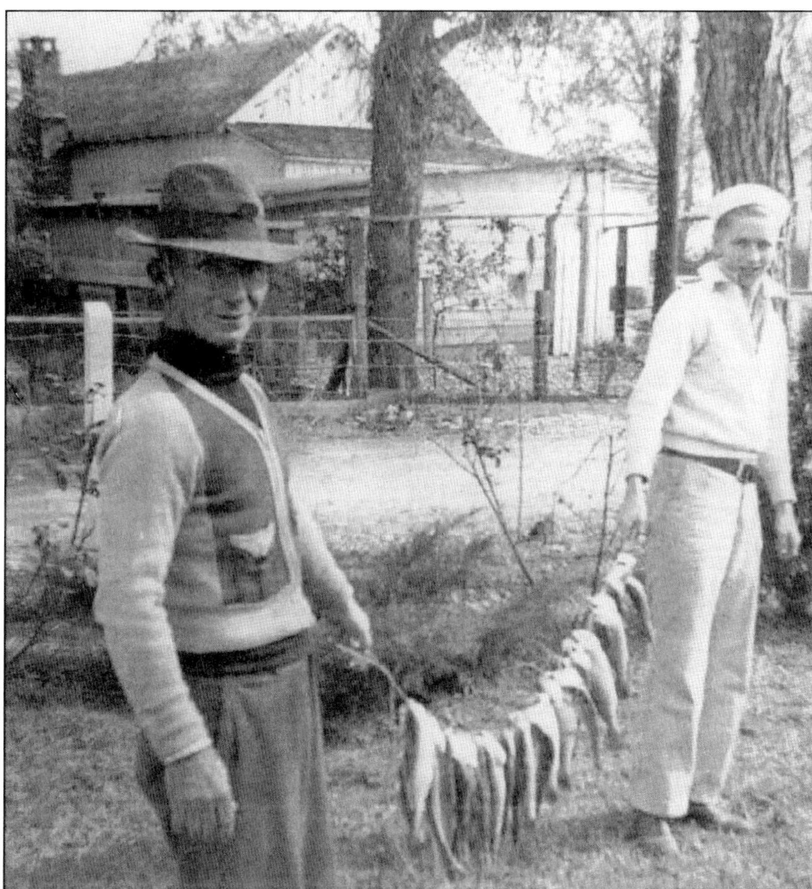

Maxwell Quiett (right) and his father pose with their catch from the bay. Fishing in Galveston Bay was excellent in days past and remains popular today. Many old-timers remember days like this from the 1940s, which was when this photograph was taken.

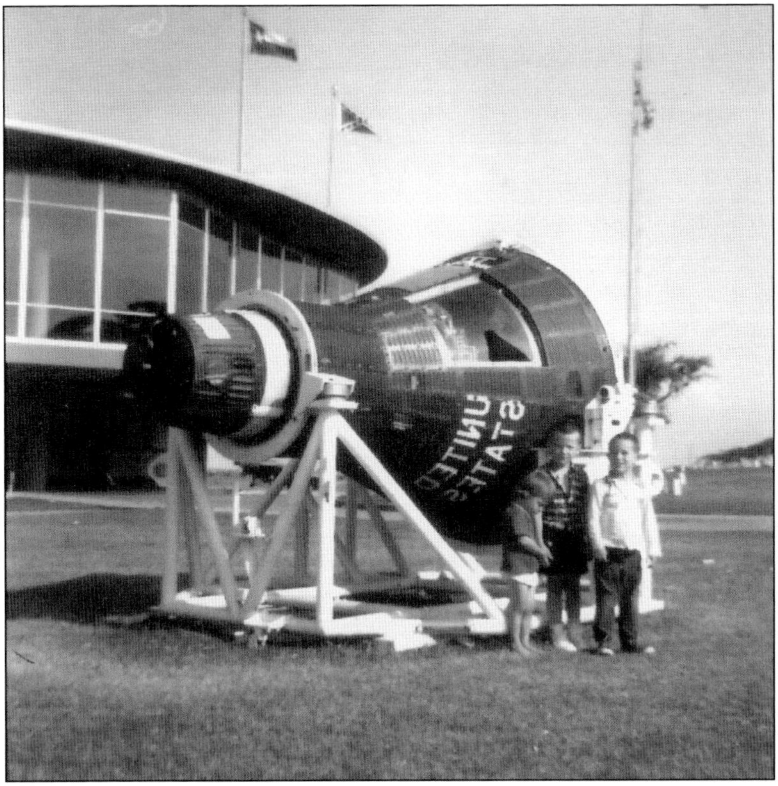

In 1964, Sylvan Beach Park played host to a Mercury space capsule. Here, the Miller children—Debbie Miller (left), Chris Miller (center), and Seth Garner—may be contemplating a future in the space program. Sylvan Beach has served as an exhibit space for a wide variety of displays, including motorcycles, vehicles from World War II, the Vietnam Moving Wall, fireworks, and Bay Day.

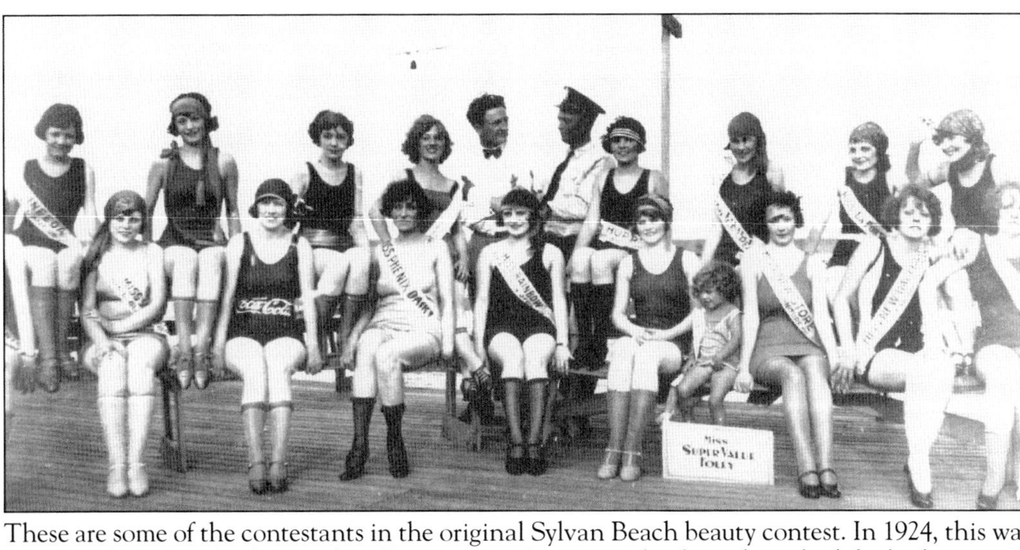

These are some of the contestants in the original Sylvan Beach beauty contest. In 1924, this was still very daring, and Foley Brothers Department Store is said to have furnished the bathing suits. This revue was the beginning of a long tradition at Sylvan Beach.

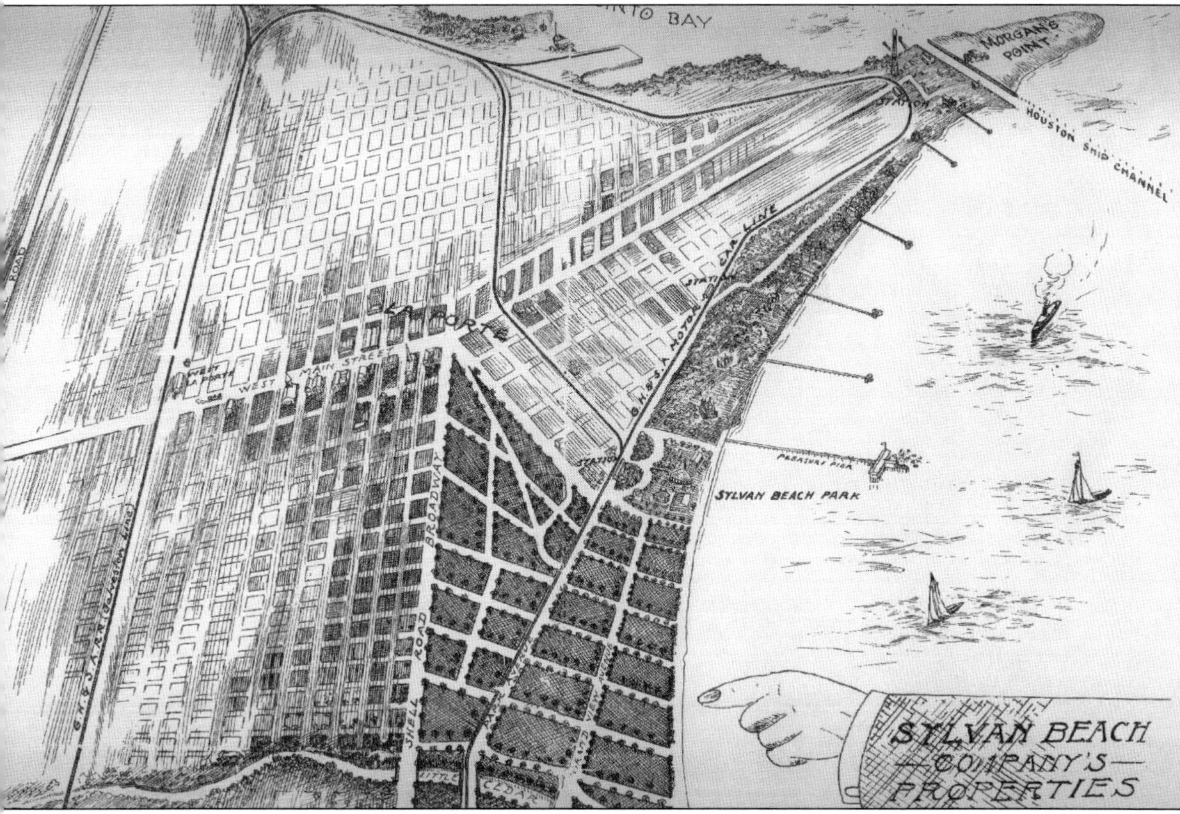

This book is about Sylvan Beach, but it should be noted that a lovely residential subdivision created by the Sylvan Beach Company has grown over the years. The Sylvan Beach Company's promoters advertised in 1914 that the new seaside community would provide "three miles of smiles that will not wash off."

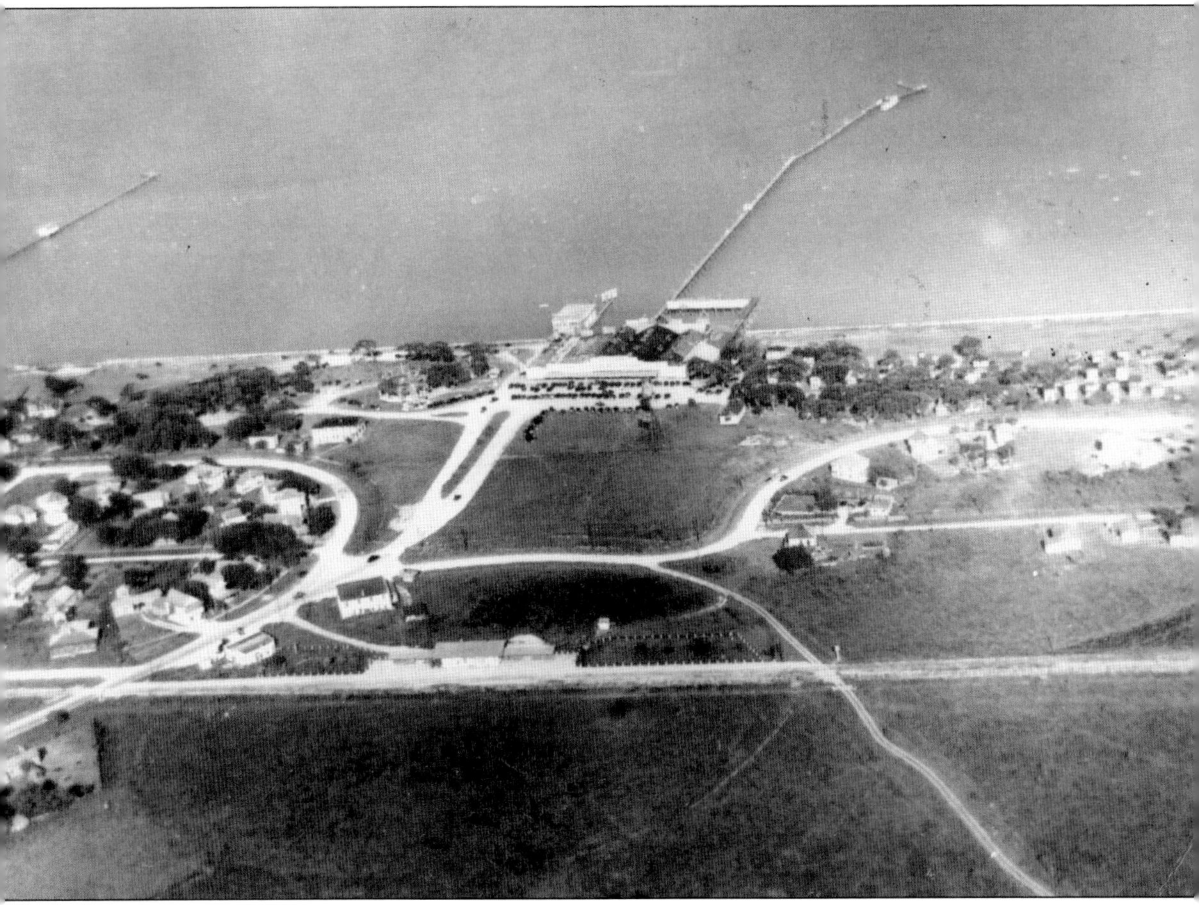

This c. 1930 panoramic aerial view of Sylvan Beach and the surrounding area shows the pier extending into Galveston Bay and, very faintly, the elevated pier for the bathing beauties.

Two

Houston Comes to Sylvan Beach

On January 10, 1901, the Lucas gusher came in at Spindletop. Sour Lake's first gusher arrived in 1903. The Goose Creek Oil Field, in what is now Baytown, was discovered in 1903; the first gusher flowed in 1908, and it grew massively for the next 20 years. Humble Oil did much of the development of the Goose Creek field, and Ross Sterling, the company's president, built his mansion (a near-duplicate of the White House) in Morgan's Point about a mile from Sylvan Beach. The oil led to an economic boom and rapid growth of the workforce in the area.

In this era, Sylvan Beach was a popular destination for picnics and company gatherings hosted by Humble and many other energy companies that operated in the vicinity. Soon, the area along the bays and the Houston Ship Channel and San Jacinto River would transform from rural and woodsy to industrial. Moreover, the oil boom and the expansion of car ownership that accompanied it rapidly and irretrievably changed transportation in the United States and, locally, transit from Houston to Sylvan Beach. In the 1910s and 1920s, Sylvan Beach sometimes saw 10,000 to 20,000 visitors per weekend arriving by car.

Today, millions of residents of the Houston metropolitan area live in a city that is home to the second-largest seaport in the United States but never gaze on the sea—at least not from their city. Most of the land containing access to the Houston Ship Channel and Galveston and Trinity Bays is in the hands of the Port of Houston or private companies in the petrochemical industry. But a whisper of the beauty and grace of a time and place long gone remains just a few miles and a few minutes—if the Houston freeways are merciful—from downtown Houston.

Sitting by a tree on Sylvan Beach, one see the land or the bay much as Sam Houston, Ashbel Smith, Sidney Sherman, Lorenzo de Zavala, David Burnet, and Commodore James Morgan might have (with the exception of Smith, all of these men once reportedly called the bay area home). People can look at the beautiful Sylvan Beach Pavilion and imagine the old pavilion and the Coney Island–like atmosphere where young Walter Cronkite sold hamburgers and young Denton Cooley listened to music, where David Westheimer and Jack Valenti and Richard "Racehorse" Haynes came to dance and date. The pavilion is where Ray Charles entertained enraptured audiences, some of whom had been denied entrance to Sylvan Beach until 1962 because of their skin color. Astronauts from nearby NASA have lived and played at Sylvan Beach, and space capsules have adorned the entrance to the pavilion.

It is a remarkable and beautiful place where visitors can ruminate simultaneously about the past, present, and future of Texas, of Houston, of La Porte, and of the great coastal communities that still know Sylvan Beach and its beautiful pavilion.

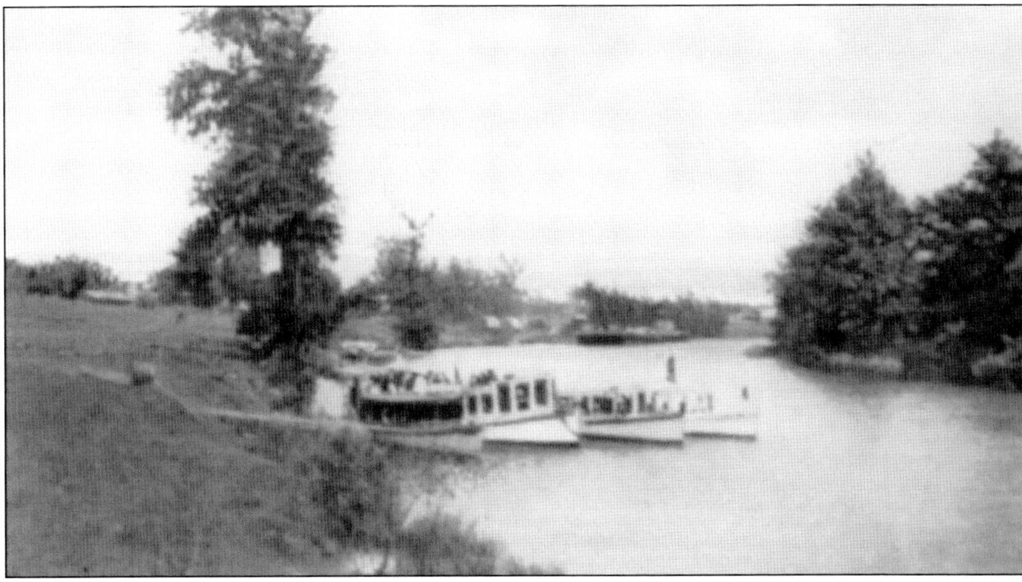

These boats are typical of the ones that ferried people down Buffalo Bayou to activities at Sylvan Beach, especially before trains came to the area. Prior to train service or automobiles, it would take a teamster with a buckboard and horses more than eight hours to make the trip from Houston.

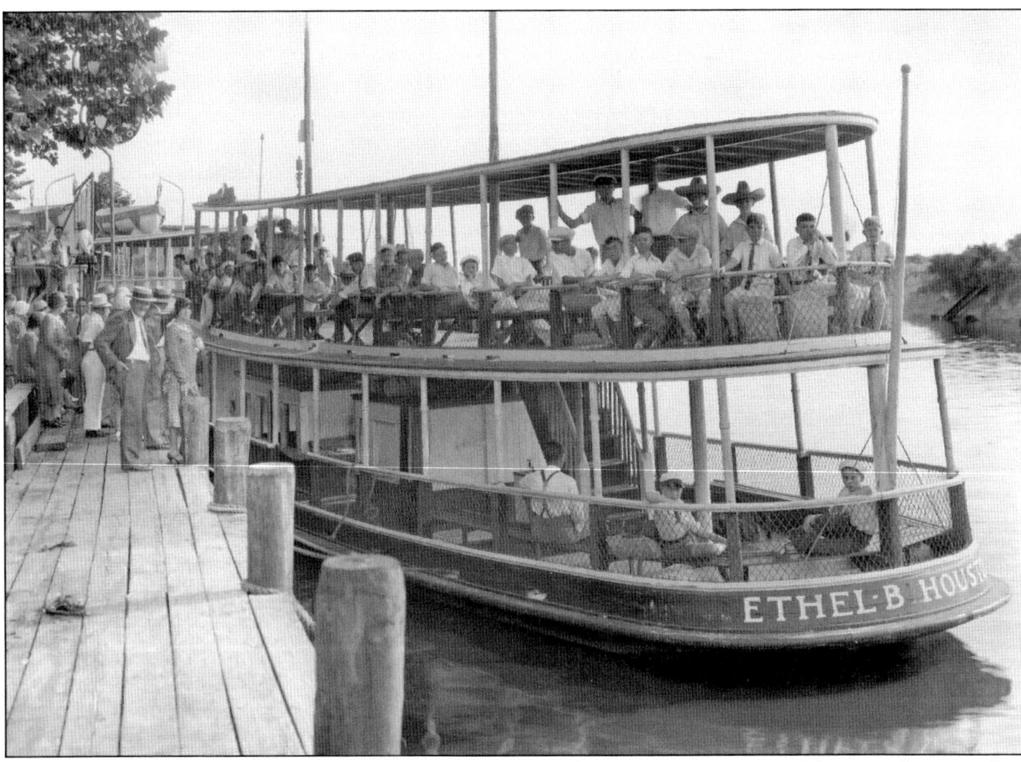

People came on large boats to get to Sylvan Beach Park on excursion trips. Thousands arrived on weekends. Before air-conditioning, Houston was a very warm place in the summer. Many visitors were lured by the promise of a splash in Sylvan Beach's bay.

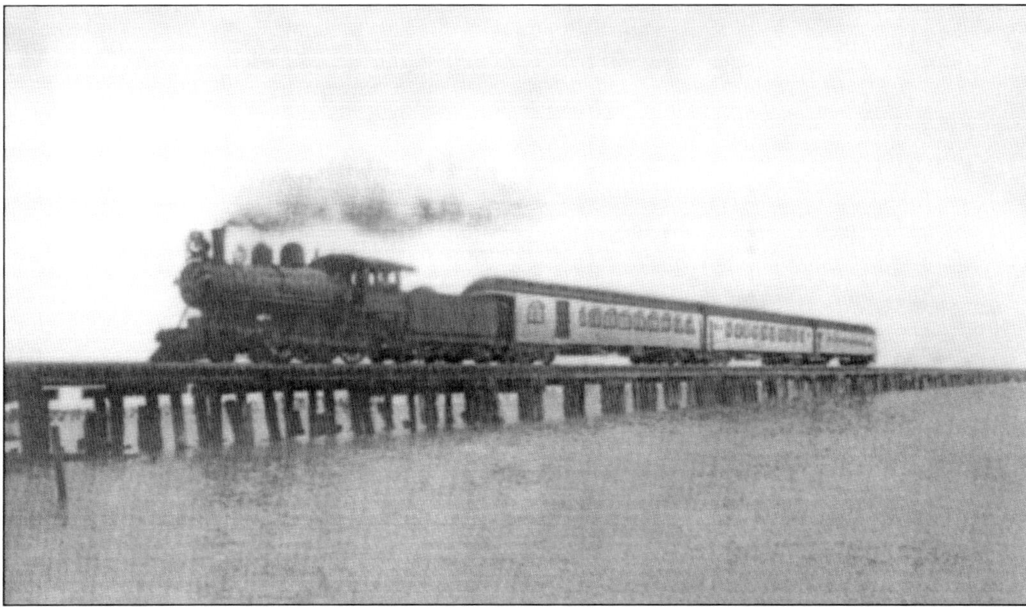

In 1905, trains started stopping at Sylvan Beach before traveling on to Galveston. Visitors from Houston could then catch the train late in the evening to return to their home city. Train service to La Porte arrived in 1895, but the depot and stop at Sylvan Beach did not exist until 1905.

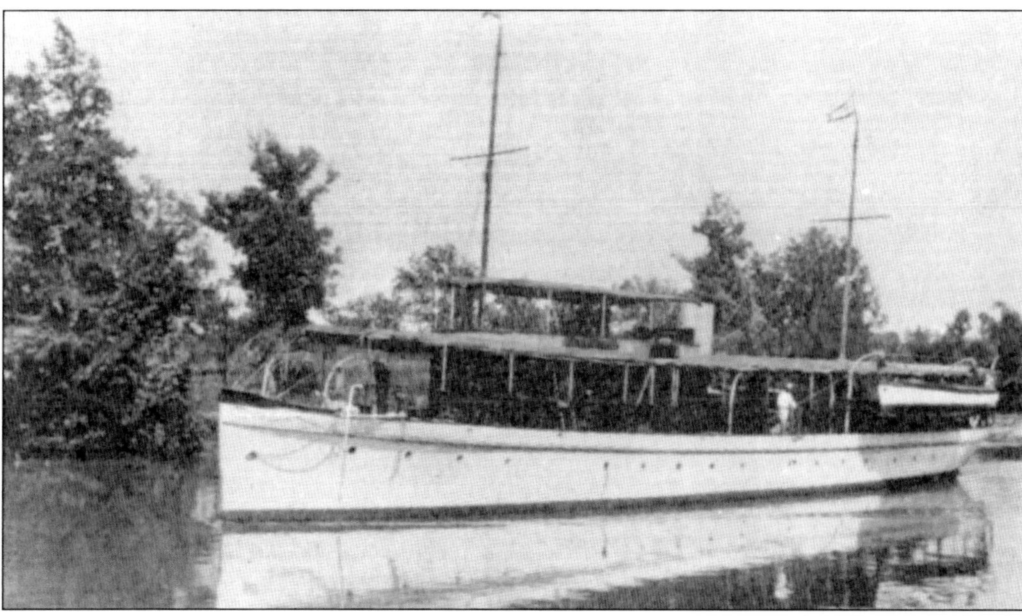

Many types of boats brought people to Sylvan Beach. Boat owners put advertisements in newspapers to keep customers informed of service times. Generally, a vessel with a shallow draft was required to navigate the passage from Houston to La Porte. The Sylvan Hotel had its own pier for arriving passengers.

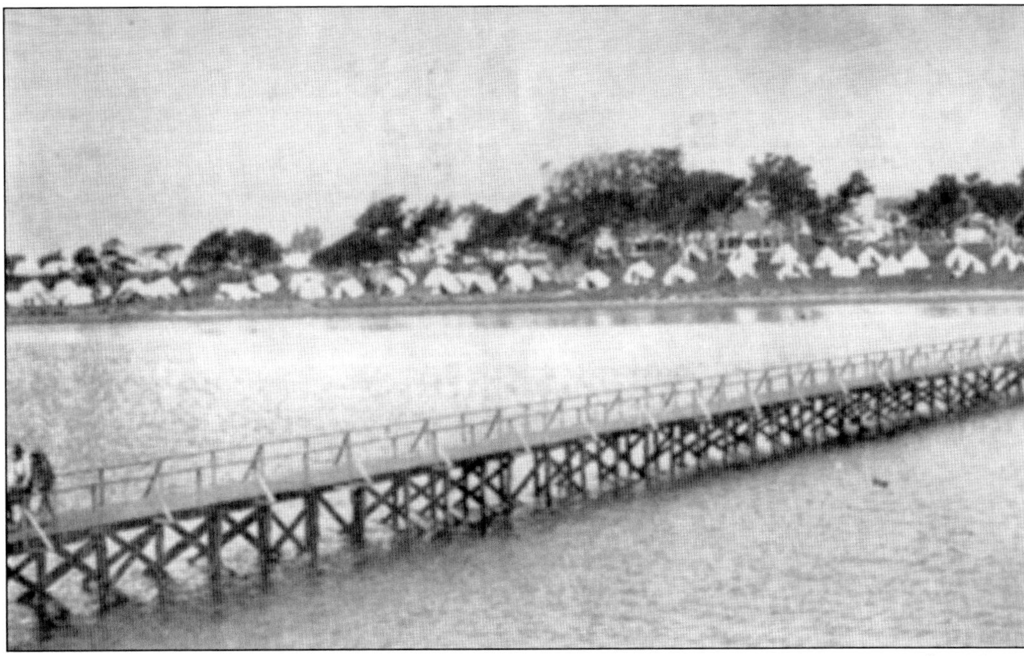

The early pavilion is visible in the background of this image. The Baptist Young People's Union met at Sylvan Beach for several years starting in 1902; special trains would bring them to La Porte. Hackneys were used to transport the conventioneers to Sylvan Beach from the La Porte Depot.

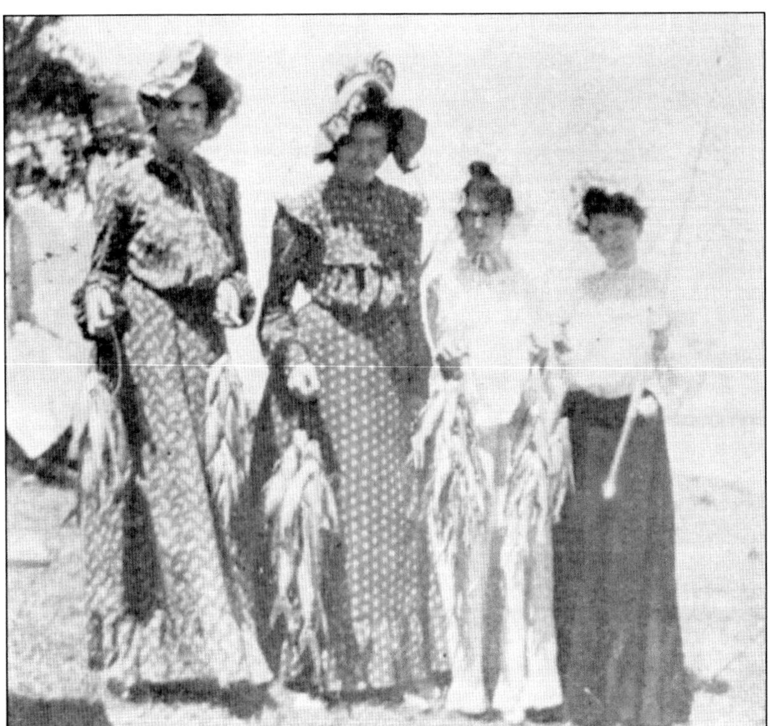

These ladies had a great day fishing, but they had yet to cook and clean the fish. They were with the Baptist Young People's Union. Fishing is still one of the most popular activities at Sylvan Beach. Numerous denominations of church groups have used the site for revivals or recreation.

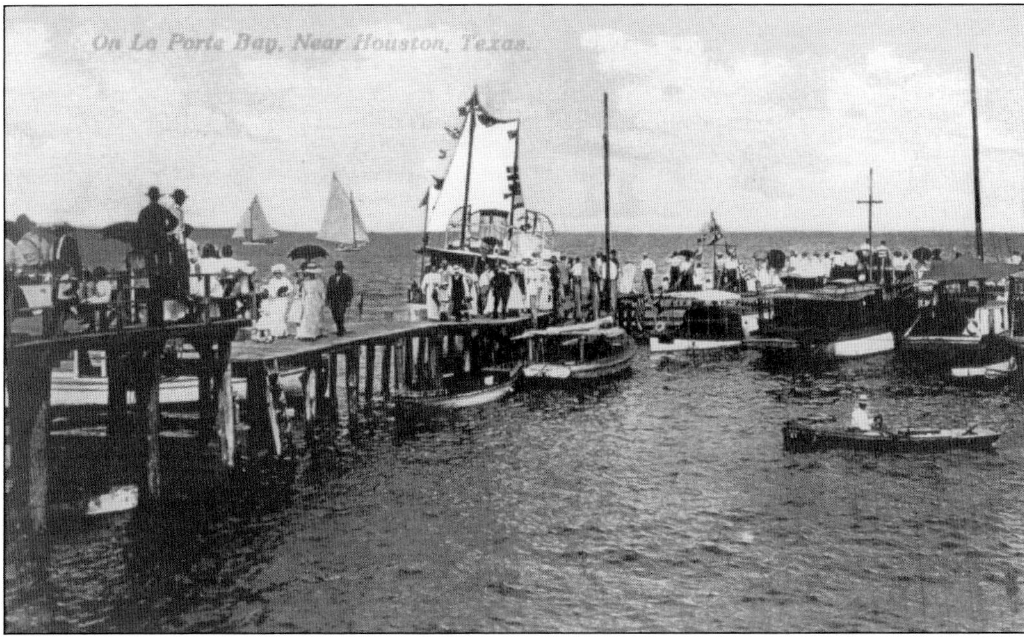

This 1914 photograph shows the busy pier at Sylvan Beach as people arrive for a regatta. Sailing enthusiasts often held races here. Racing on the bay had been popular since the 19th century. Morgan is the namesake for the neighboring community of Morgan's Point. He was a commissioner of the Texas navy and a commandant at Galveston during the Texas Revolution.

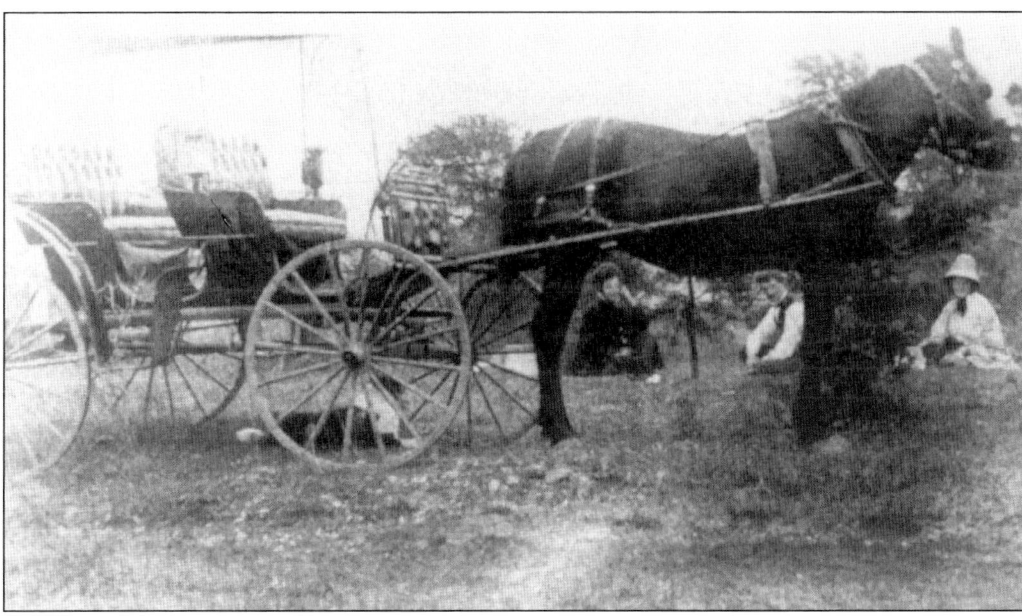

Many different modes of travel brought visitors to Sylvan Beach. Guests arriving by train could hire a hackney, like the one pictured here, for further transport. People came from everywhere to enjoy good times such as swimming, boating, picnicking, and admiring the bay. Sylvan Beach remains a venue devoted to family-friendly entertainment.

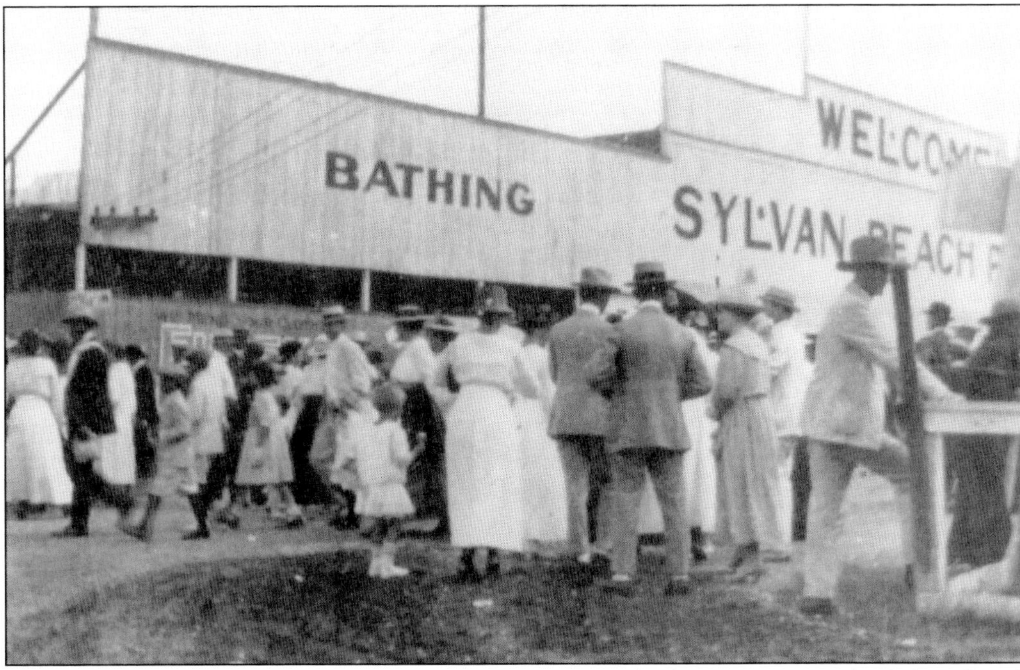

In this c. 1930 photograph, hundreds of people wait outside the entrance to the Sylvan Beach park buildings. The main gate was located near where present-day Fairmont Parkway dead-ends at Bayshore Drive.

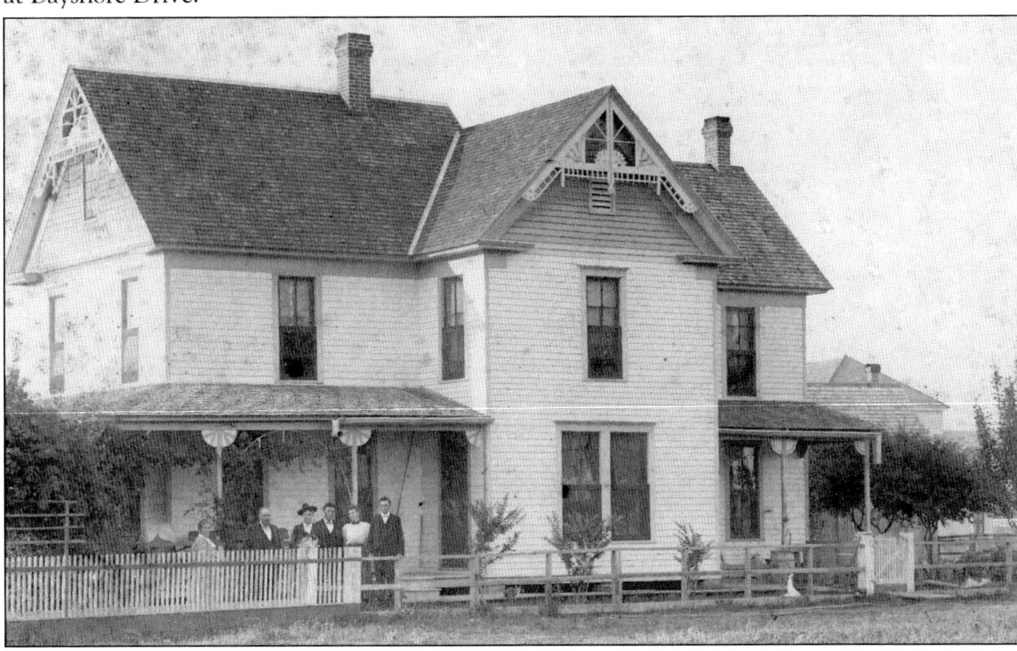

This c. 1890 photograph shows Col. James H. Tennant's Bayshore home near La Porte, Texas, with Tennant at far left. He was the guiding spirit and builder of the La Porte, Houston & Northern Railroad, which was later purchased by Southern Pacific. His energy and capital ensured the building of the railroad, which was a huge factor in the growth of the city. (Courtesy of James B. Tennant.)

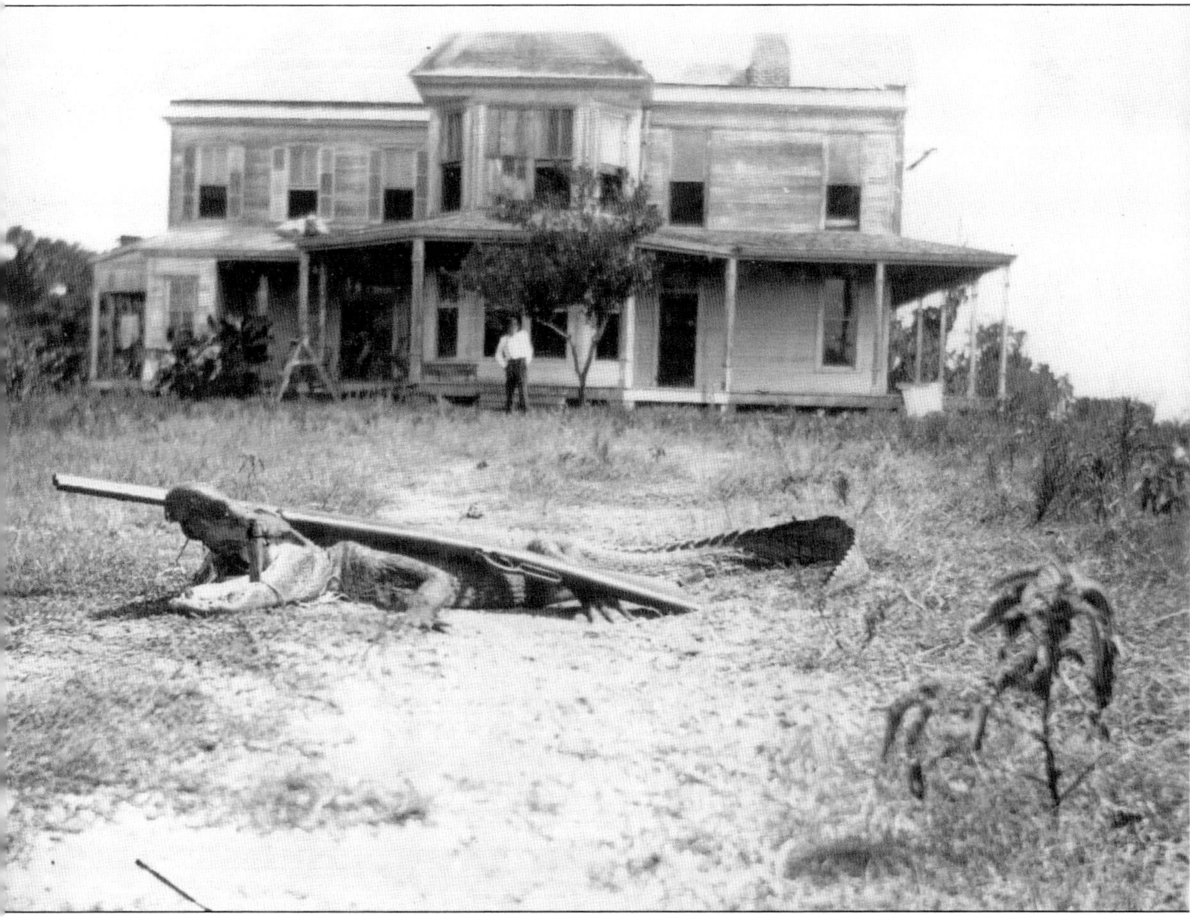

This picture shows construction on a property purchased by Col. James H. Tennant in La Porte, Texas. This structure, nicknamed "Strang Place," was not completed before Tennant's death but would have been a most beautiful addition to the La Porte landscape. This photograph depicts the back of the building and is a fortunate candid photograph of a very large alligator. (Courtesy of James B. Tennant.)

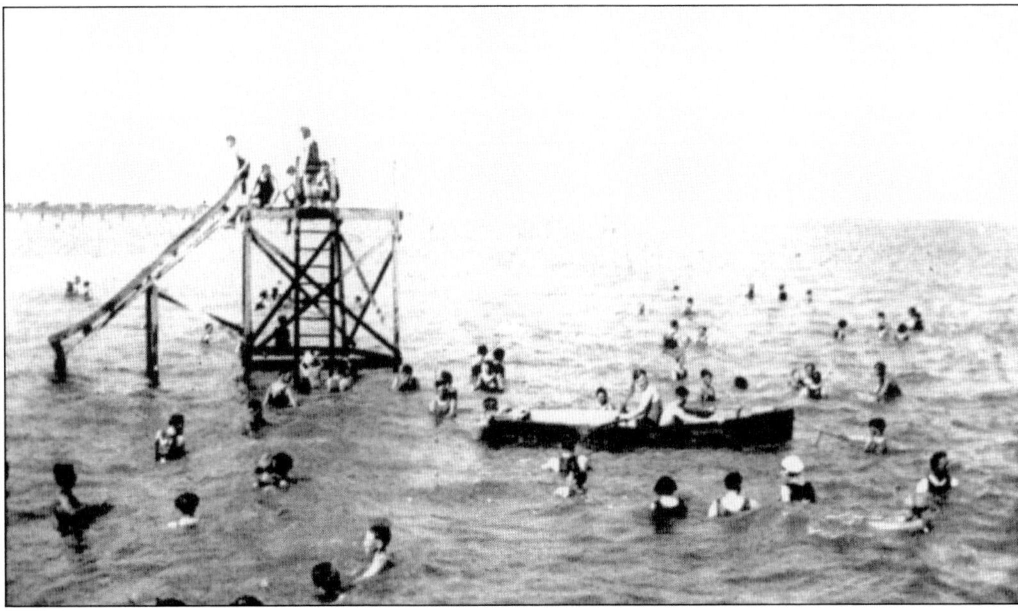

Swimmers of all ages enjoyed the clear and beautiful bay water. Bathing suits could be rented, as could rowboats. The water was shallow, so very few swimming accidents occurred. Then, as now, the bay was a mixture of salt and fresh water.

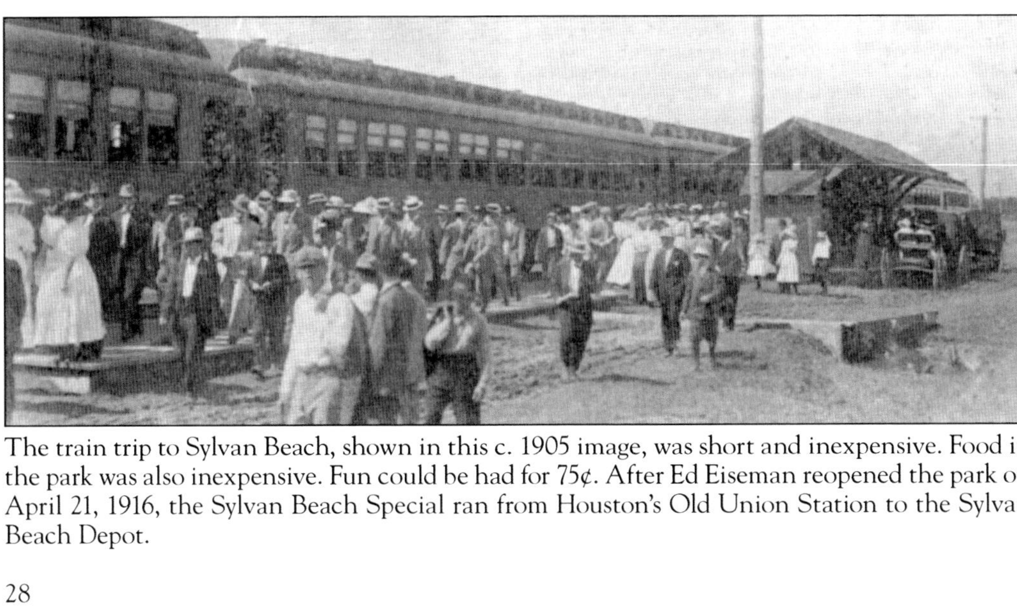

The train trip to Sylvan Beach, shown in this c. 1905 image, was short and inexpensive. Food in the park was also inexpensive. Fun could be had for 75¢. After Ed Eiseman reopened the park on April 21, 1916, the Sylvan Beach Special ran from Houston's Old Union Station to the Sylvan Beach Depot.

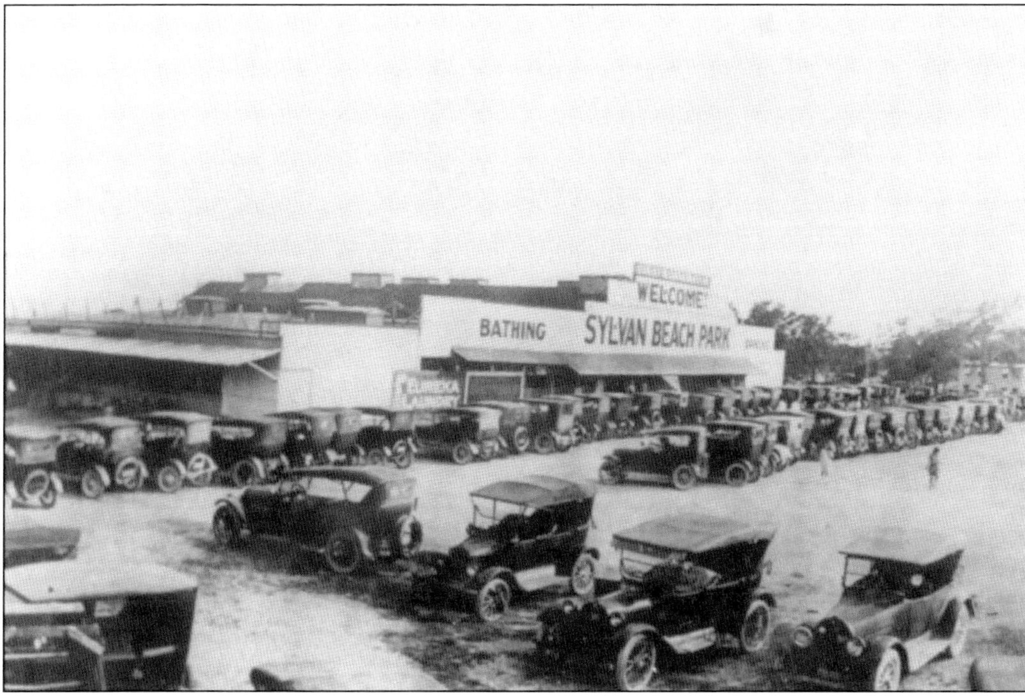

When automobile travel began and roads improved, many visitors chose to come by car rather than by train. This mid-1920s photograph of the crowd at Sylvan Beach captures the beginning of the end of the commuter train, a development in La Porte that mirrored a similar transportation revolution in the rest of the nation.

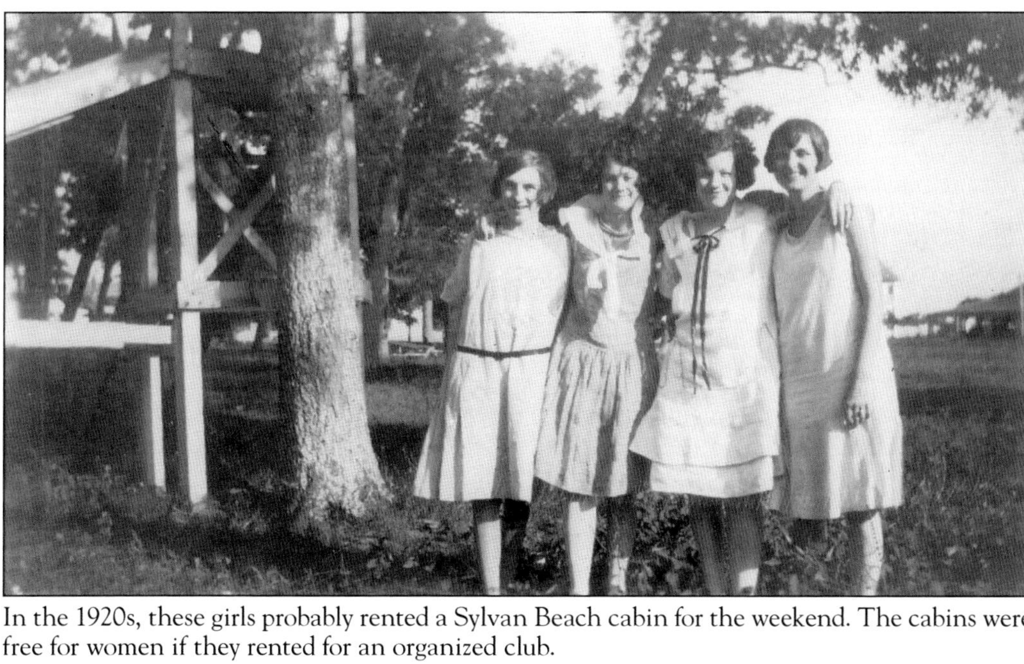

In the 1920s, these girls probably rented a Sylvan Beach cabin for the weekend. The cabins were free for women if they rented for an organized club.

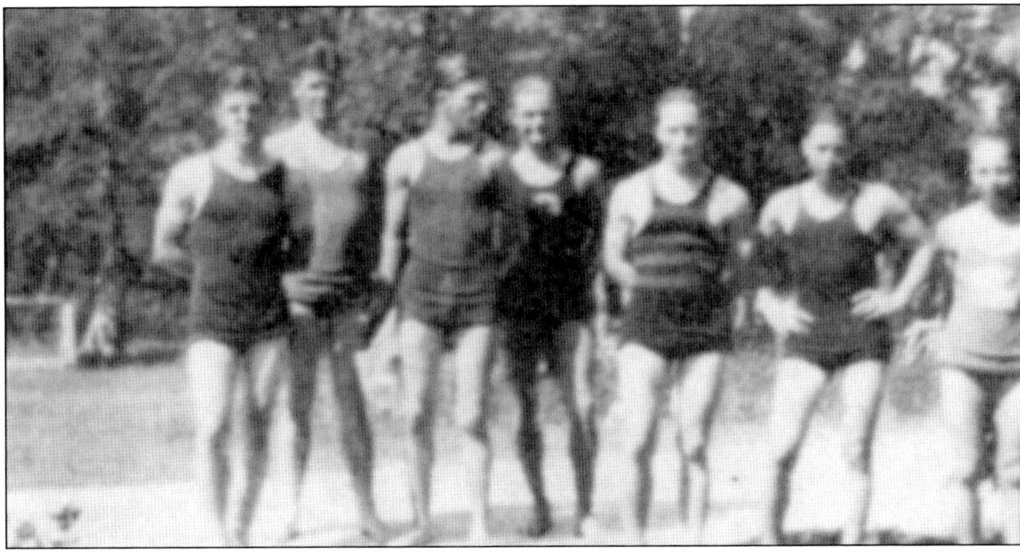

These young men came to Sylvan Beach Park in the 1920s to enjoy swimming, dancing, and boating—and to possibly meet some pretty young girls. Presumably, this is why Ed Eiseman, who purchased the park from G.D. Samuels, continued Samuels' policy of renting cabins to women for free. These young men are from Garfield Street; members of the Guillet, Hermann, and Schellings families still live on Garfield.

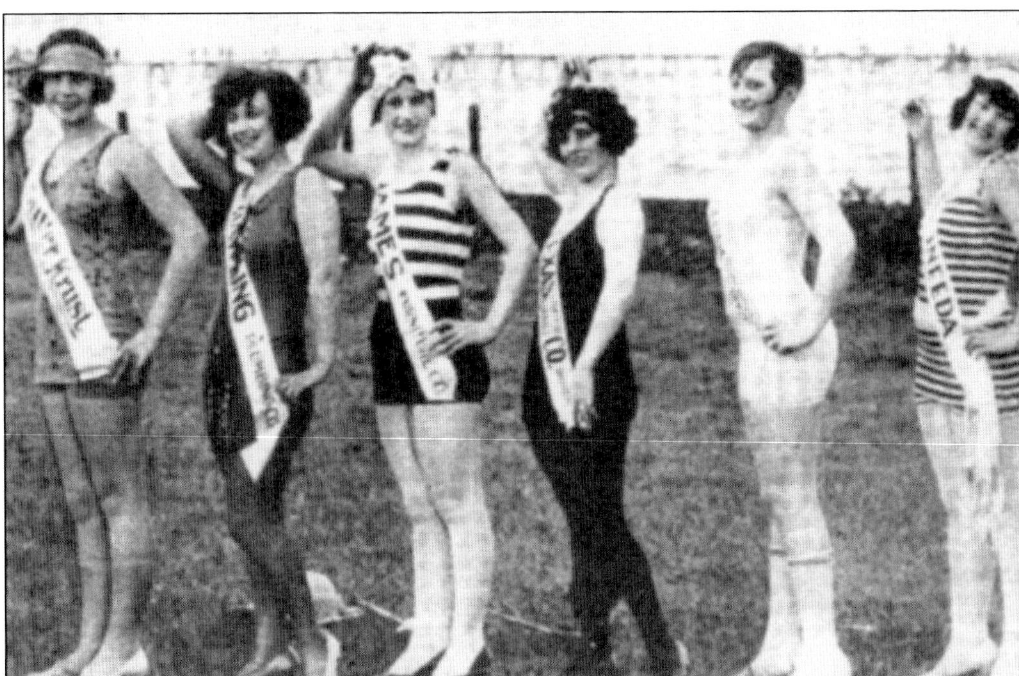

These are some of the girls in a later bathing beauty revue. The girls were always pretty, but the bathing suits improved. Cecil Sisson started this very popular event in 1924. Foley's Dry Goods in Houston became an early sponsor of the beauty contest.

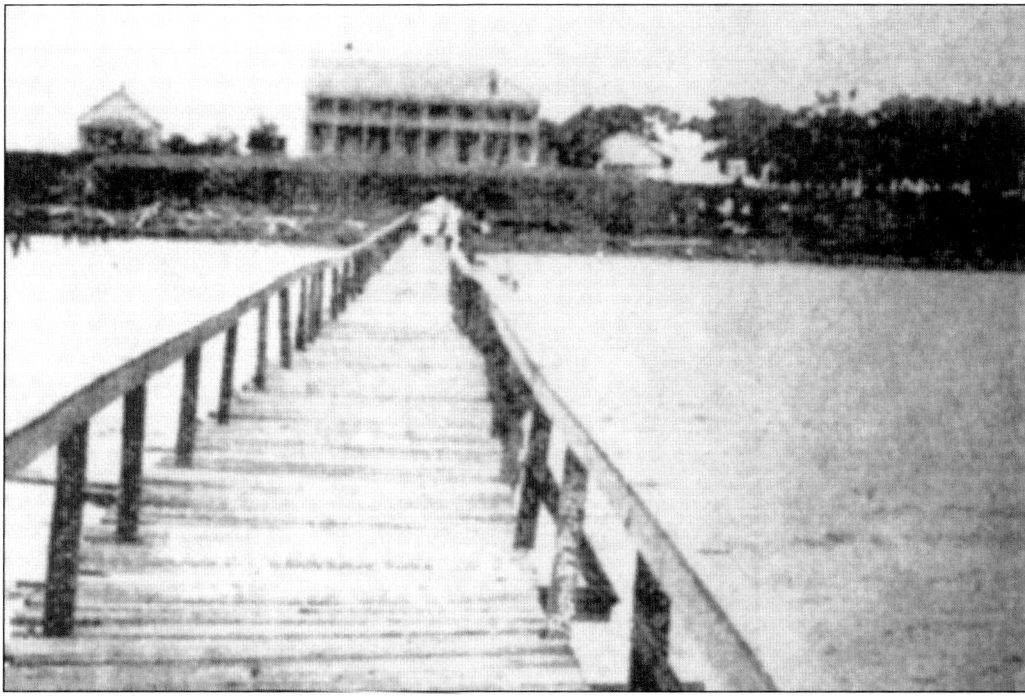

This is a c. 1900 photograph of Bay Shore Park, which was an early competitor of Sylvan Beach. It was owned by John Beazley, who had sold the La Porte city founders the land on which Sylvan Beach now sits. Bay Shore Park was only in business for a couple of years.

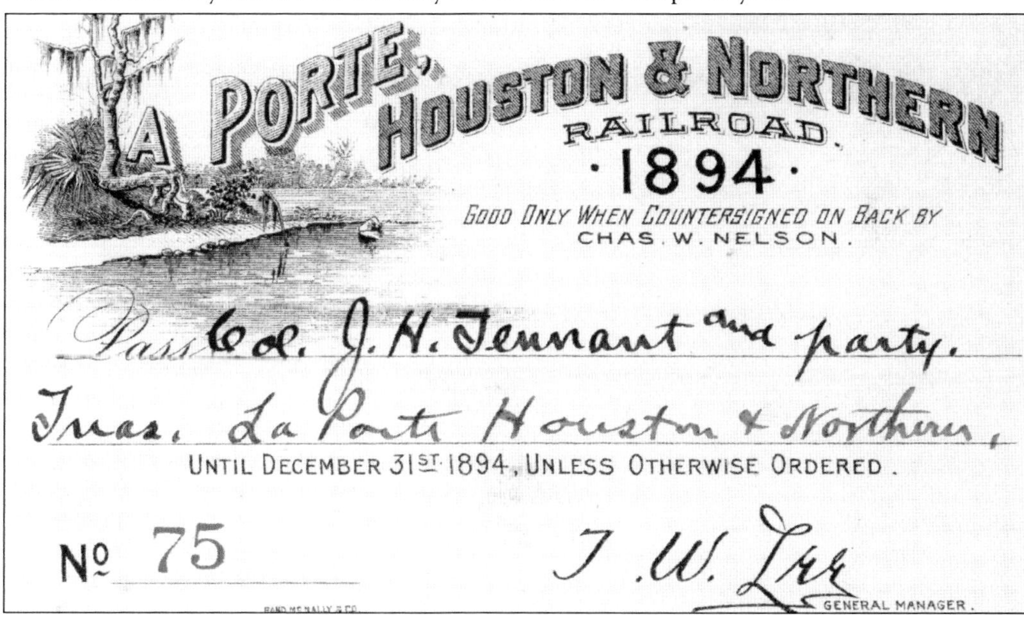

The back of this ticket reads: "The person accepting this pass assumes all risk of accidents, and expressly agrees that the company shall not be liable, under any circumstances, whether by negligence of their agents or otherwise, for any injury to the person, or for any loss or dame to his property while using it. If presented by any other person the individual named thereon, the conductor will take up this pass and collect fare." (Courtesy of James B. Tennant.)

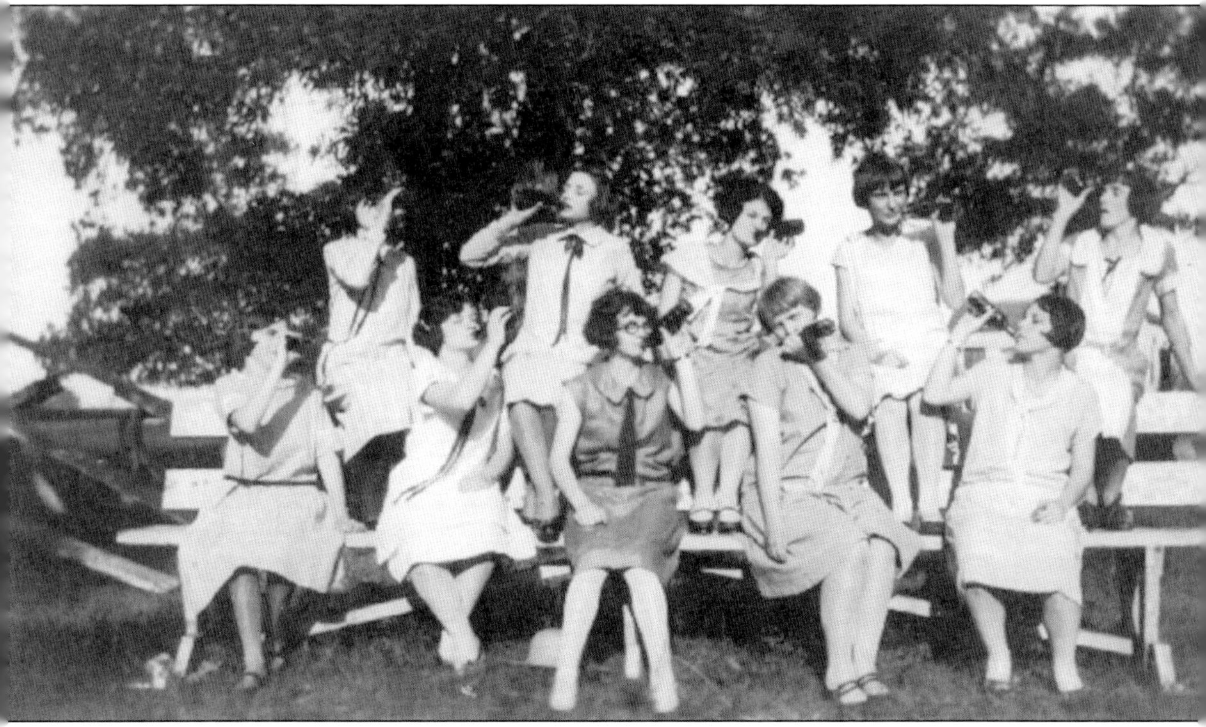

Girls came to Sylvan Beach Park to see and be seen. In the days when "Kodaking" was new, people thought they had to pose and act out. These girls are drinking Coca-Cola from bottles—a promenade along the shoreline was a good way to work up a thirst.

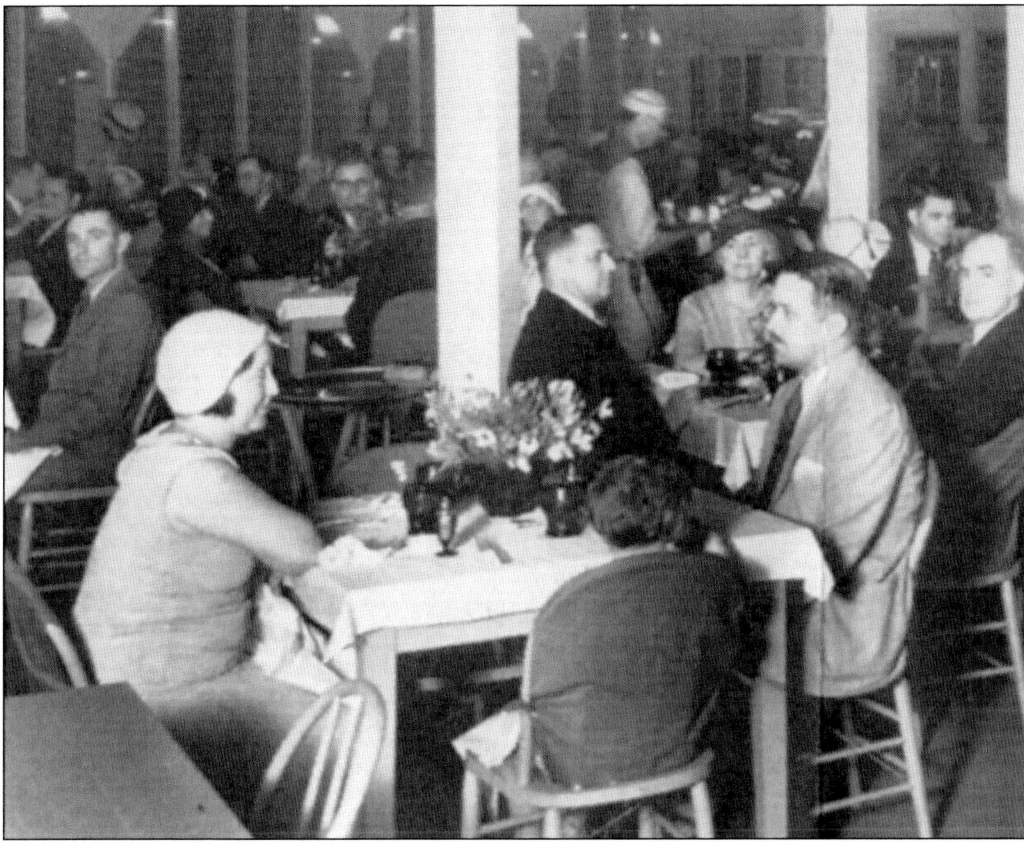

In the 1920s and 1930s, the upscale restaurant at Sylvan Beach Park was very busy, which led to many guests waiting in line. The Goose Creek Oil Field was developed early in the 20th century; meanwhile, the ship channel was growing, and executives and rank and file alike flocked to Sylvan Beach.

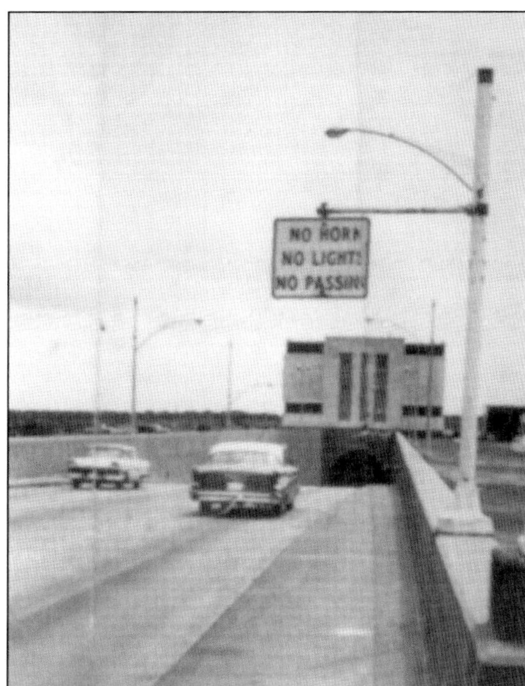

As cars and roads improved, the La Porte–Baytown Tunnel became a reality in 1953. It created a shorter distance from the city to the bay area and Sylvan Beach Park. Various ferries and vessels had previously transported people and sometimes cars across the entrance to the ship channel between La Porte and Baytown.

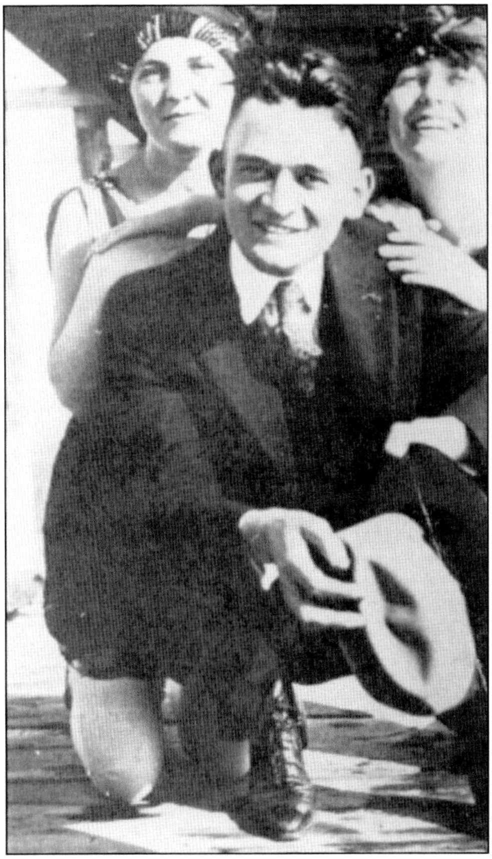

The Sylvan Beach bathhouse and pier were destroyed in a 1915 storm. They were quickly rebuilt and opened for business in 1916 under Ed Eiseman and his son Ed Jr. Ed Jr. is pictured at left with two unknown women.

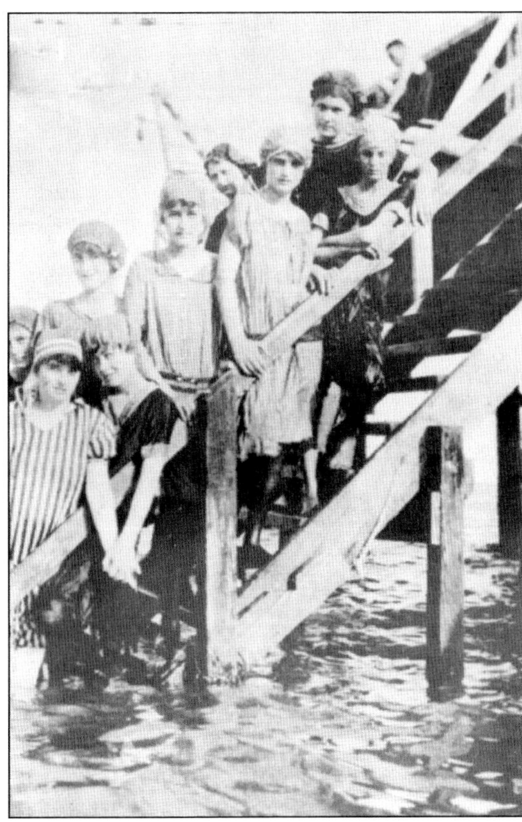

This photograph shows swimmers exiting the bathhouse and stepping directly into the bay water. One Fourth of July, the beach recorded 700 swimmers. Despite how far the pier and bathhouse extended into the bay, the water at the base of the steps was still relatively shallow. There were 100 changing rooms in the bathhouse on the pier.

Three

The Early Years

The parcel of 22 acres set aside for Sylvan Beach was first known as the Grove or Sylvan Grove. Of the many festivals and celebrations that would occur at Sylvan Beach, the first recorded one was held on the Fourth of July in 1893. The Sylvan Hotel had been constructed on Sylvan Beach with its own pier for receiving visitors who arrived via the water from Houston or Galveston. If the Sylvan Hotel had no vacancies, visitors could stay at the Artesian Hotel on Main Street in La Porte.

The images of the first Sylvan Beach Pavilion show an open-air dance pavilion with a small attached structure for bands and musicians. It sits very close to the bay, as does the present pavilion, and is surrounded by trees—hence came the name "Sylvan Grove."

The great hurricane of 1900, which nearly destroyed Galveston, also devastated Sylvan Beach and wrecked the dance pavilion. The Sylvan Hotel was another casualty of the storm, and St. Mary's Seminary later bought the hotel structure for use as a dormitory. The church that was built at St. Mary's in 1908 was designed by renowned Galveston architect Nicholas Clayton. The depression of 1900, combined with title problems and the hurricane that same year, led to litigation between the founders of La Porte and bankers in Galveston. The suit was eventually resolved, with Galveston financiers Adoue and Lobit taking over ownership of Sylvan Beach and then selling to G.D. Samuels, of Houston, in 1909.

After Samuels bought Sylvan Beach, he improved and enlarged the dance pavilion, built a new trademark gateway for the pavilion fence, and constructed numerous cottages for overnight visitors. Historians have suggested that one of the purposes of the fence was to keep stray cattle out of the park, as much of the parkland was still pastoral. Another severe hurricane hit the area in 1915 and again damaged the park, its pavilion, and its cottages. Shortly thereafter, a discouraged Samuels gave up operating Sylvan Beach. His exit marks the end of "the early years" of Sylvan Beach (although this chapter includes a couple of pictures from the next few years after he left).

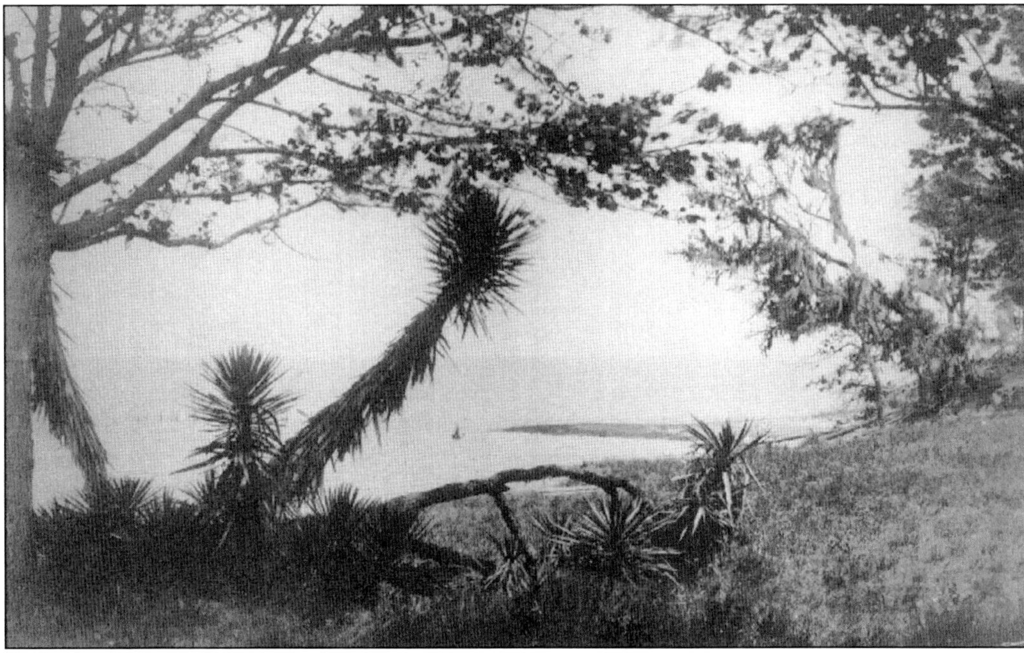

This photograph shows Sylvan Beach much as it must have looked when the land was first set aside by the founders of La Porte. Originally called "the Grove" because of the numerous live oak trees, the area's name was later briefly changed to Sylvan Grove and finally to Sylvan Beach.

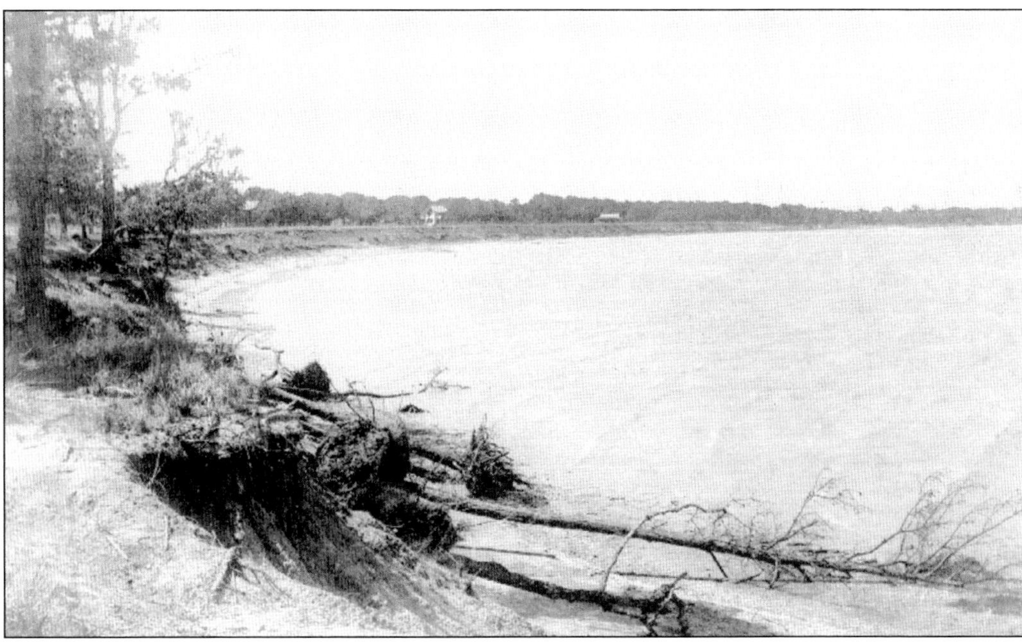

This is the coastline at Sylvan Beach, which is essentially a shallow inlet between the jutting landmasses of Morgan's Point and Red Bluff. Due to erosion and subsidence, the water line now reaches over 100 feet farther into the land than in 1892 (a road visible on old maps is now below the water).

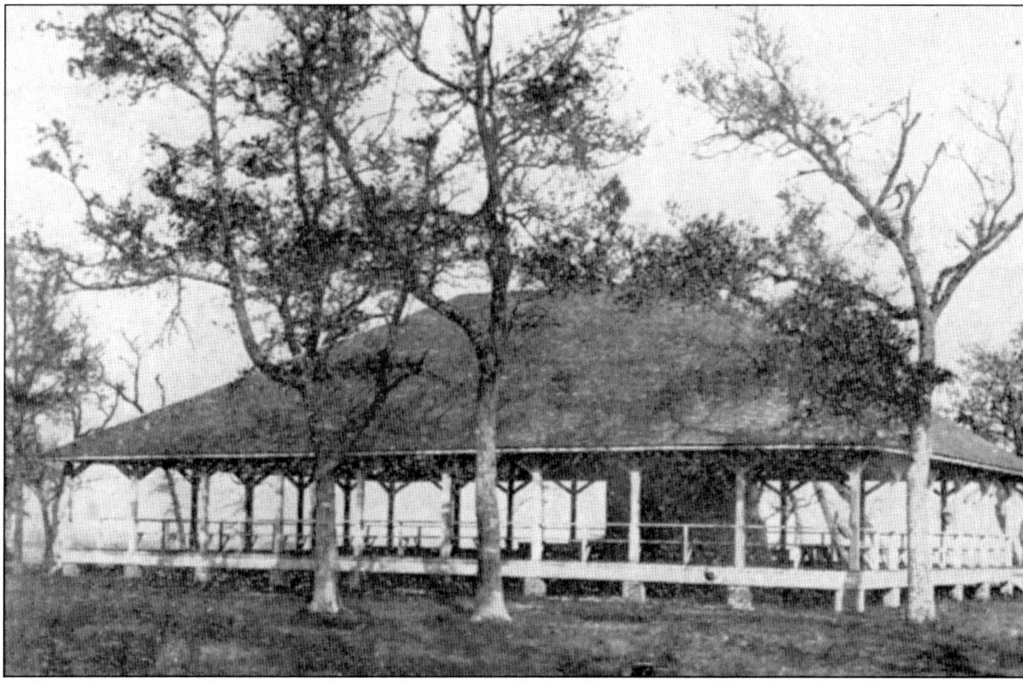

One of the first things the city did was build a pavilion for gatherings and dances. When the Baptist Young People's Union conference was held at Sylvan Beach, the pavilion became a tabernacle; the group met here from 1902 through 1906. This 1893 image is the first photograph of the Sylvan Beach Pavilion and is believed to show the original pavilion. In the early years, if the pavilion was destroyed or damaged by the elements, the replacement constructed was identical.

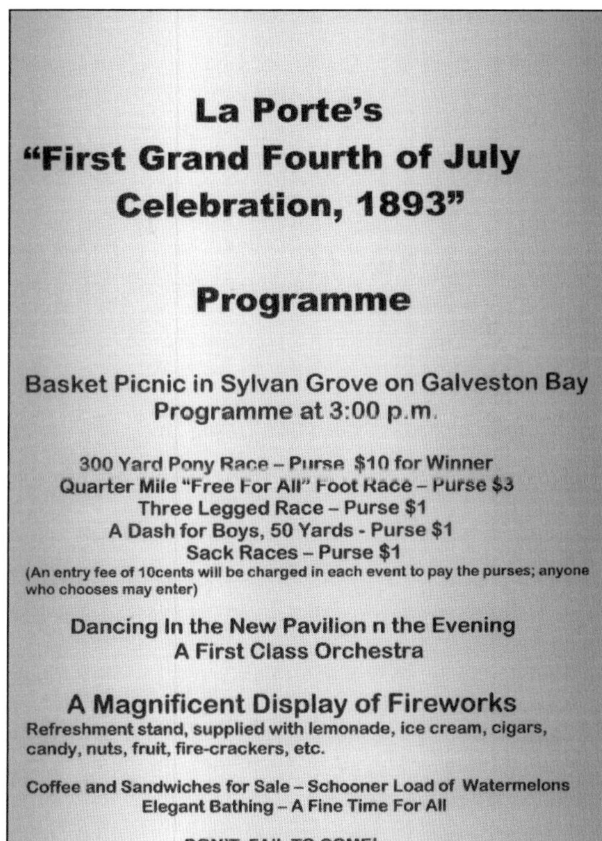

La Porte's
"First Grand Fourth of July Celebration, 1893"

Programme

Basket Picnic in Sylvan Grove on Galveston Bay
Programme at 3:00 p.m.

300 Yard Pony Race – Purse $10 for Winner
Quarter Mile "Free For All" Foot Race – Purse $3
Three Legged Race – Purse $1
A Dash for Boys, 50 Yards - Purse $1
Sack Races – Purse $1
(An entry fee of 10cents will be charged in each event to pay the purses; anyone who chooses may enter)

Dancing In the New Pavilion n the Evening
A First Class Orchestra

A Magnificent Display of Fireworks
Refreshment stand, supplied with lemonade, ice cream, cigars, candy, nuts, fruit, fire-crackers, etc.

Coffee and Sandwiches for Sale – Schooner Load of Watermelons
Elegant Bathing – A Fine Time For All

DON'T FAIL TO COME!

The picnic advertised here was the first recorded activity in the park. These notices were sent everywhere, and people *did* come by boat, horseback, wagon, foot, or train.

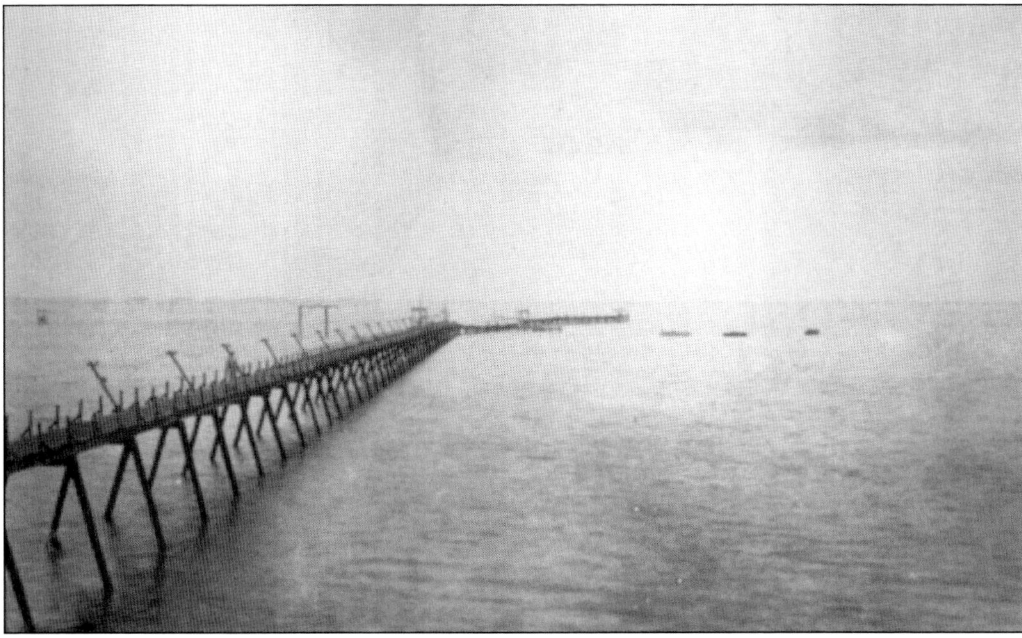

This, said to be the first pier at Sylvan Beach, was built in the 1890s. Before the construction of the pier, visitors to Sylvan Beach rode boats from Houston and disembarked at Morgan's Point (and, later, at the Sylvan Beach Hotel pier), and took hackneys or walked to the final destination. Later, they also could ride the train to Deer Park and then get hackneys to get to the park.

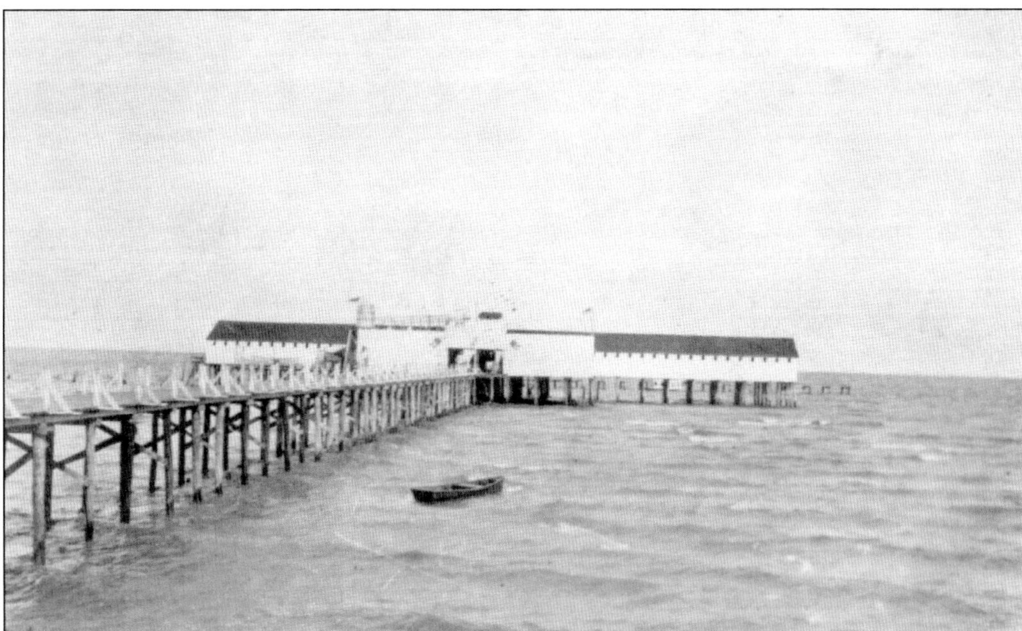

A bathhouse was added to the existing pier sometime before 1900. The pier and bathhouse were damaged sometime between 1900 and 1910 but were, as always, rebuilt. Bathing suits could be rented for 10¢, because not everyone had one. Back then, the rented bathing suit was quite a bit more ponderous than suits sold today.

This is the menu of box lunches available at Sylvan Beach around 1905. A person could take the train to Sylvan Beach, eat lunch, and swim for a round-trip total of $1. An edition of the *La Porte Chronicle* from July 25, 1907, boasts of the Carrollton Hotel, complete with tennis courts, in east La Porte, and the Bay Shore Park near Sylvan Beach, now managed by Dr. John Beazley, who had sold La Porte's founders the land on which Sylvan Beach would be situated.

Box Lunches

No. 1. Twenty Five Cents

Plain or Deviled Ham Sandwich
Cream Cheese Sandwich
Two Hard Boiled Eggs
Potato Chips
Pickle
Cookies

No. 2. Thirty Five Cents

Chicken Salad Sandwich
Pimento Cheese Sandwich
Two Hard Boiled Eggs
Potato Chips
Pickle
Cookies

No. 3. Fifty Cents

Fried Chicken
Bread and Butter Sandwich
Pimento Cheese Sandwich
Potato Salad
Pickle
Slice Cake

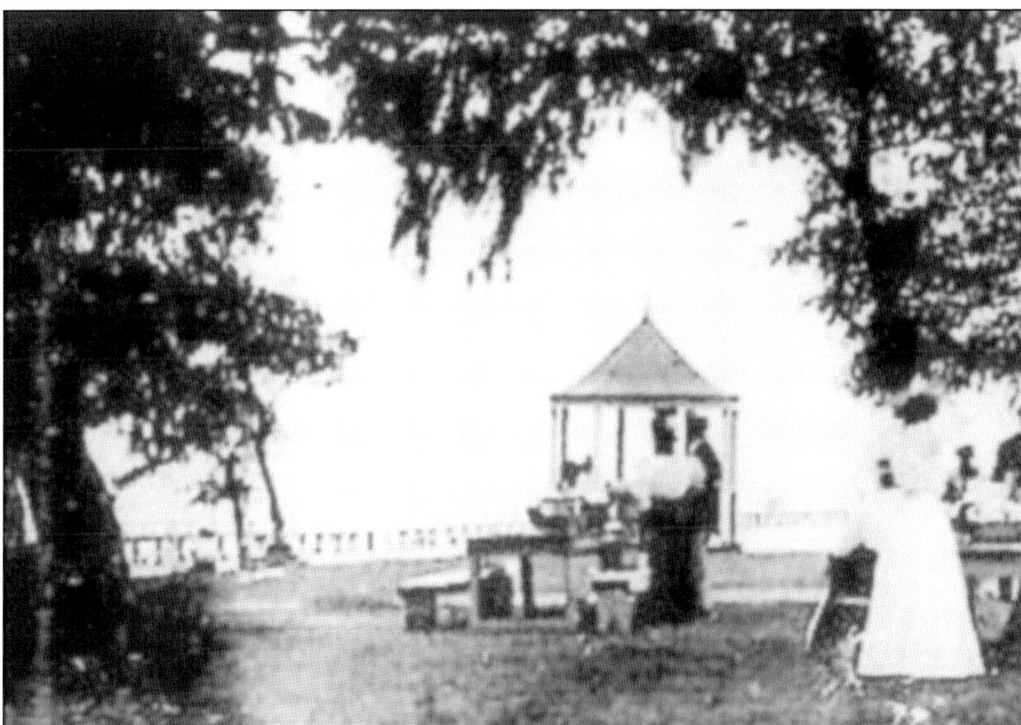

This group was having a picnic in the late 1890s and enjoying the bay breeze. Storms did not keep visitors away for long—as soon as repairs and cleanup were completed, they returned. By this time, wealthy Houstonians had begun to build large summer homes in nearby Morgan's Point, Bayridge, and on the land that would eventually becomes Shoreacres.

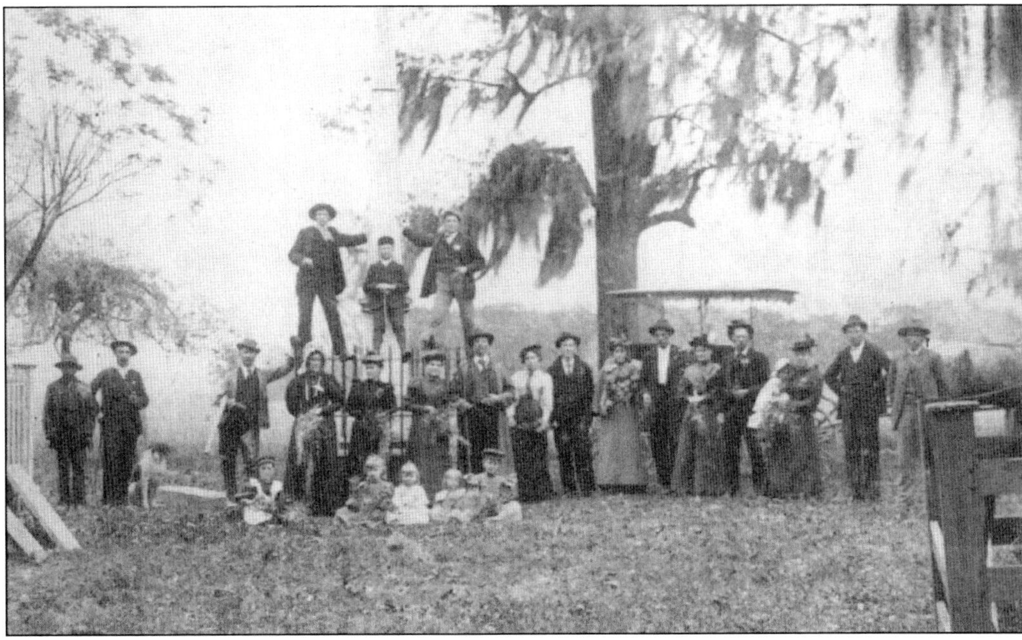

This is what a typical family get-together at Sylvan Beach looked like in the late 19th or early 20th century. The park was routinely used by families and groups who often arrived in buggies. Note the Spanish moss hanging from the tree branches.

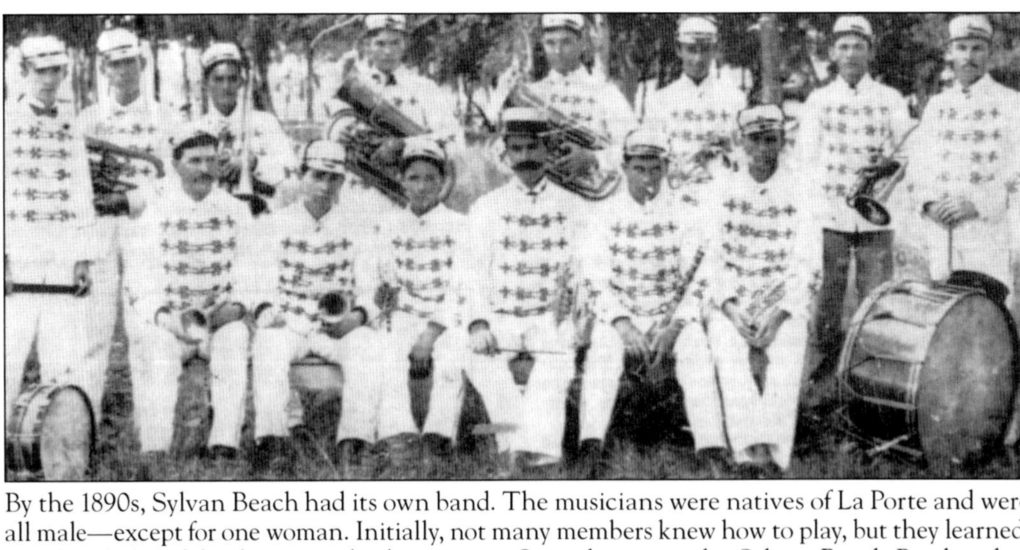

By the 1890s, Sylvan Beach had its own band. The musicians were natives of La Porte and were all male—except for one woman. Initially, not many members knew how to play, but they learned. The band played for dances and other events. Over the years, the Sylvan Beach Pavilion has had several house bands as well as a plethora of local talent from nearby communities. Mickey Gilley, whose famous club, Gilley's, was only a couple of miles down Main Street (aka Spencer Highway), once served as grand marshal of the Sylvan Beach Festival parade.

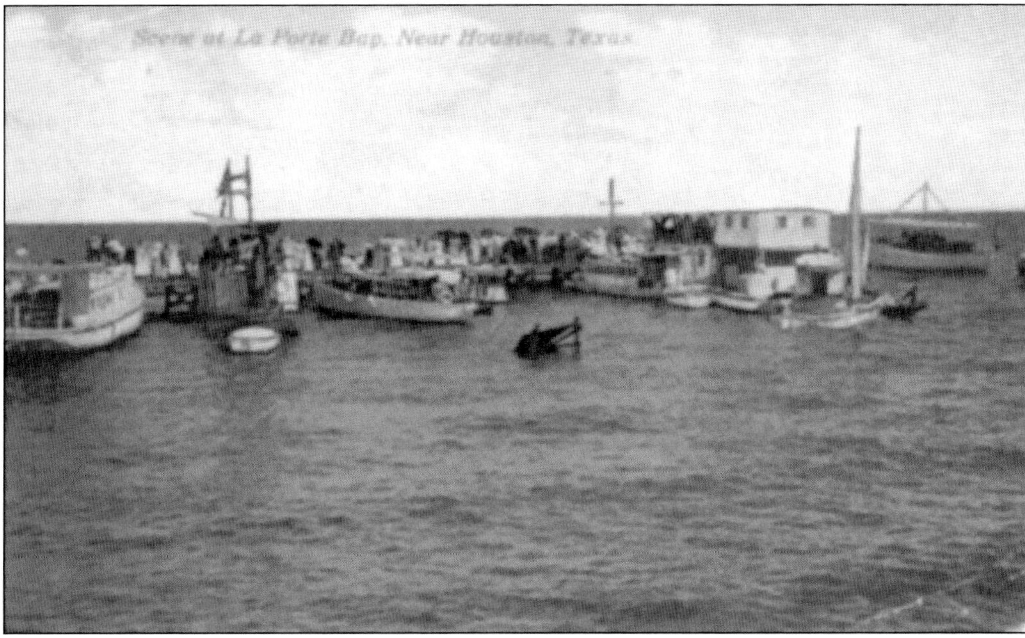

In 1895, sailing enthusiasts lined up at the Sylvan Beach pier for a regatta. People from Houston brought their boats down Buffalo Bayou to join in the fun. This was one of the first regattas held at Sylvan Beach.

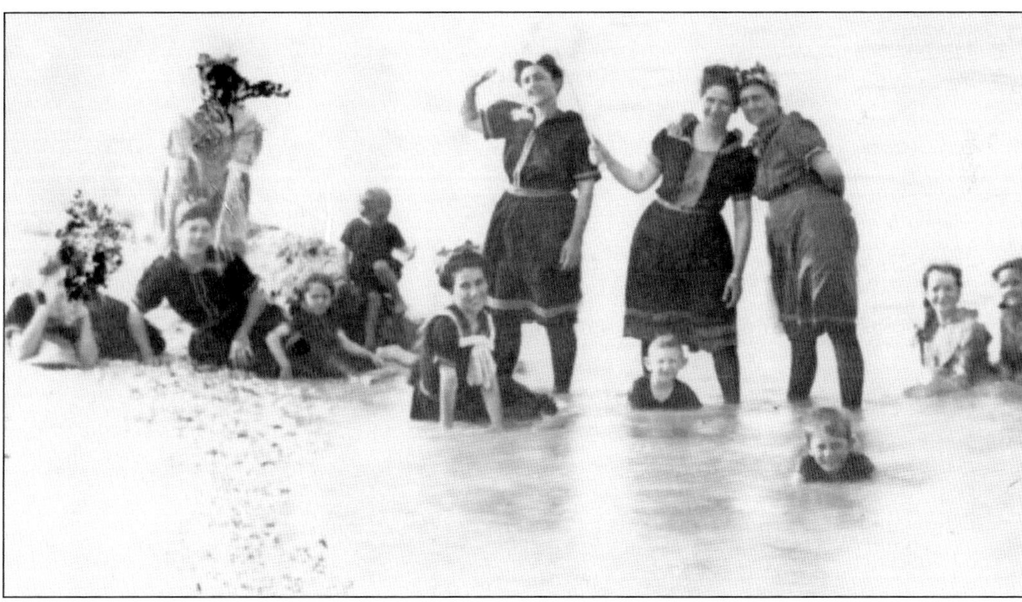

These folks swimming in the bay in the late 1890s are wearing the latest bathing costumes (as swimsuits were called then). It is believed that bathing-beauty contests were held in the Sylvan Beach area before 1924, but that was the first recorded instance found by the authors. In the 1890s, bathing suits looked more like present-day hazmat suits than current swimsuits.

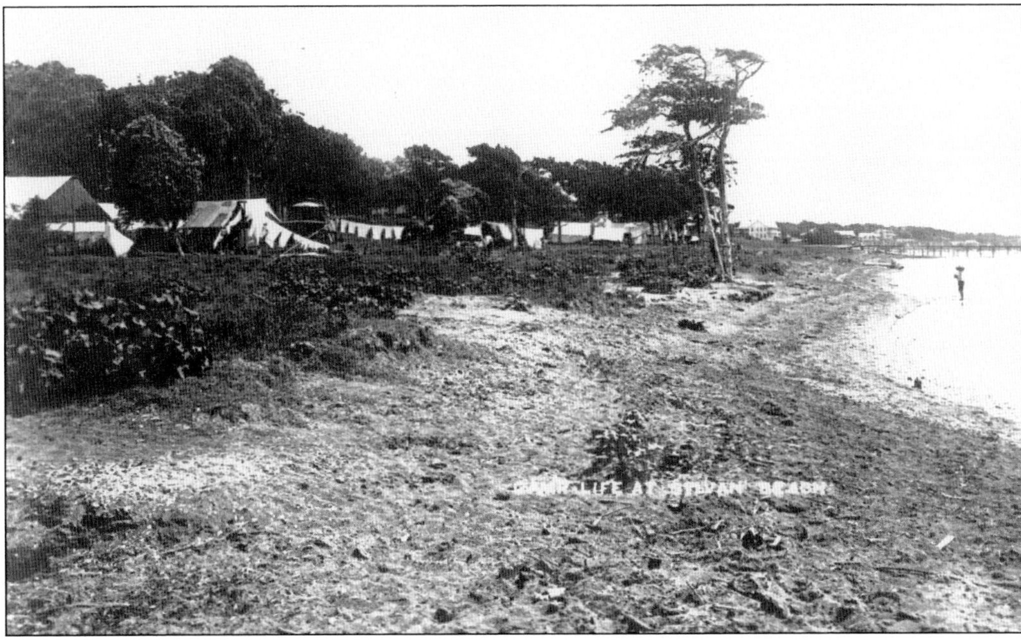

Camping was popular in Sylvan Beach's early days. People could cheaply rent a tent and enjoy the bay. Initially, the beach was sand, and the bay had a sandy bottom (which can still be seen at low tide). A sand beach was recently constructed on shore for sunbathing at Sylvan Beach.

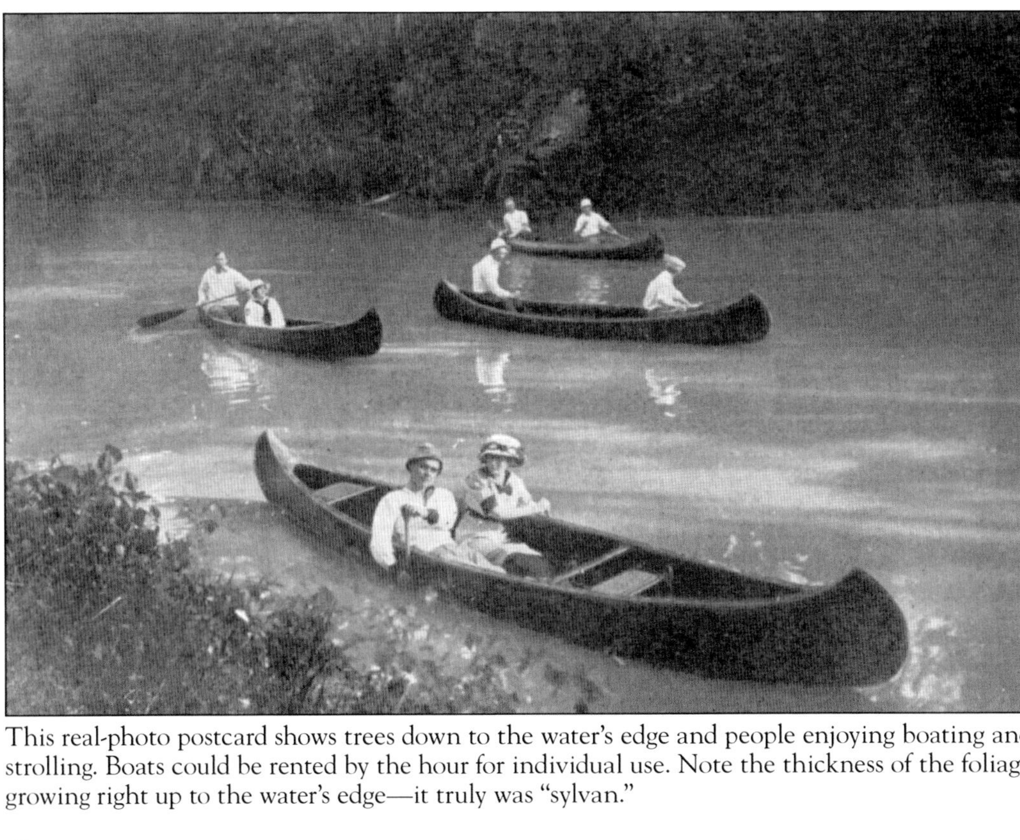

This real-photo postcard shows trees down to the water's edge and people enjoying boating and strolling. Boats could be rented by the hour for individual use. Note the thickness of the foliage growing right up to the water's edge—it truly was "sylvan."

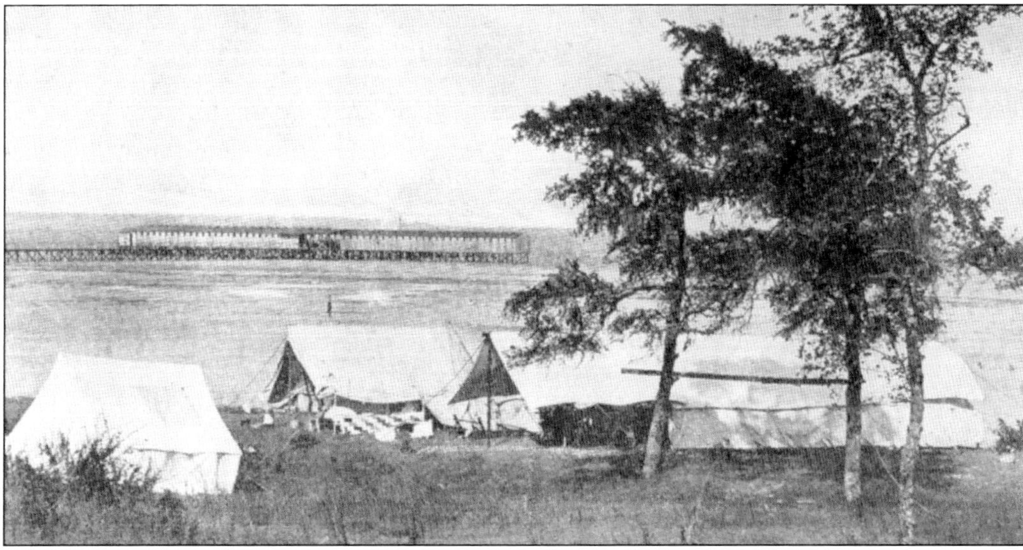

The Baptist Young People's Union had its first meeting at Sylvan Beach in 1902. The group came back for several years, at least through 1906. The restored pier and bathhouse are visible in the background.

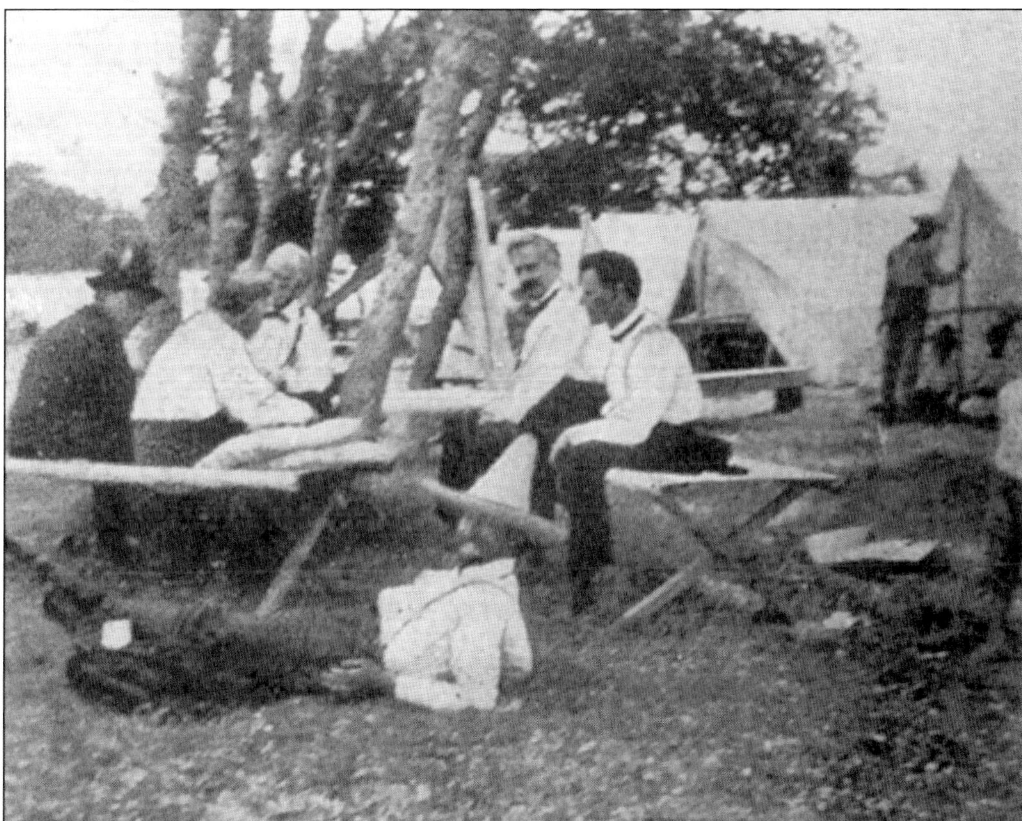

Here, men of the Baptist church enjoy the great outdoors. The men came to chaperone the youth, and special trains brought them all to Sylvan Beach.

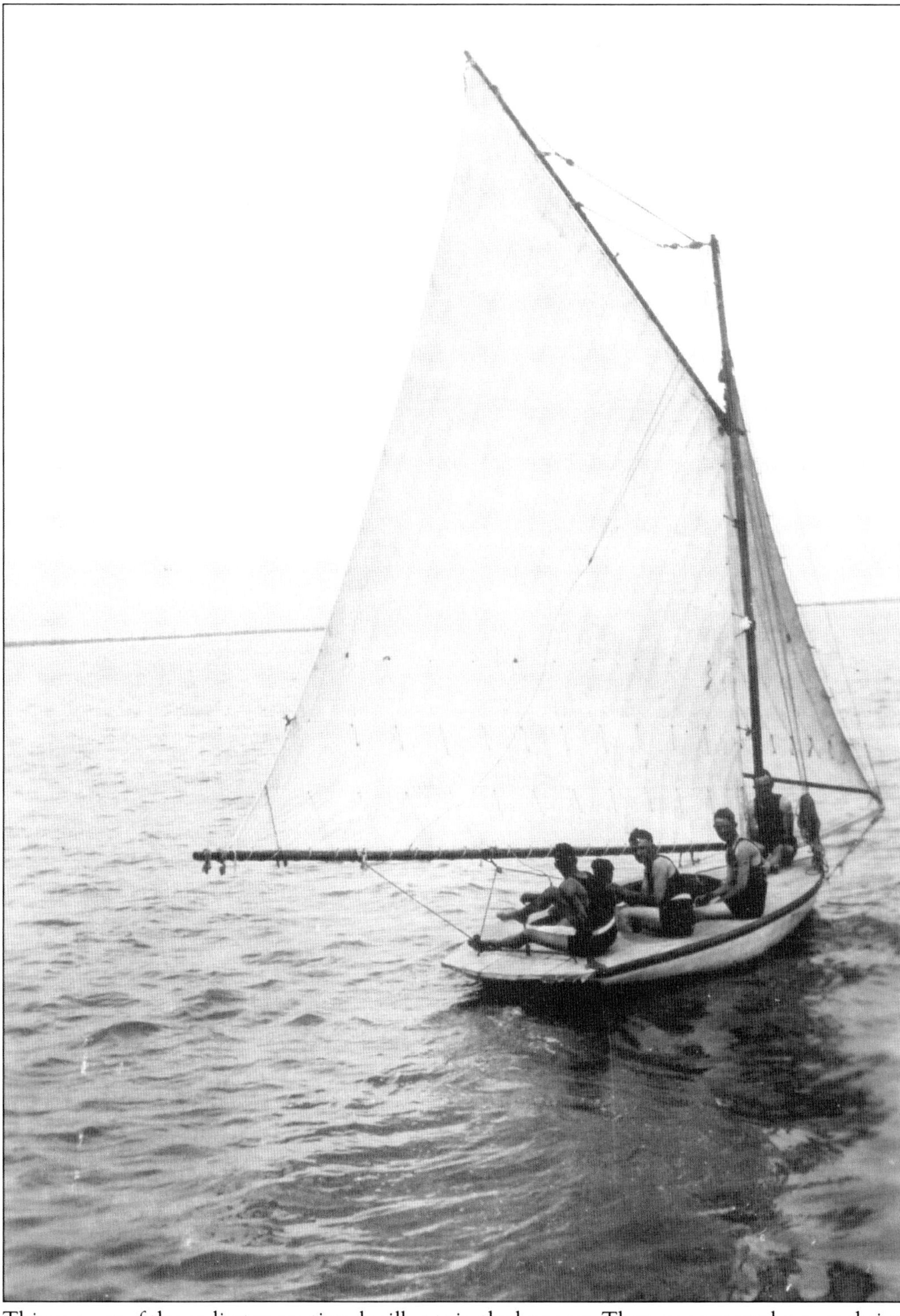

This was one of the earliest recreational sailboats in the bay area. These young people are yachting on the bay around 1920.

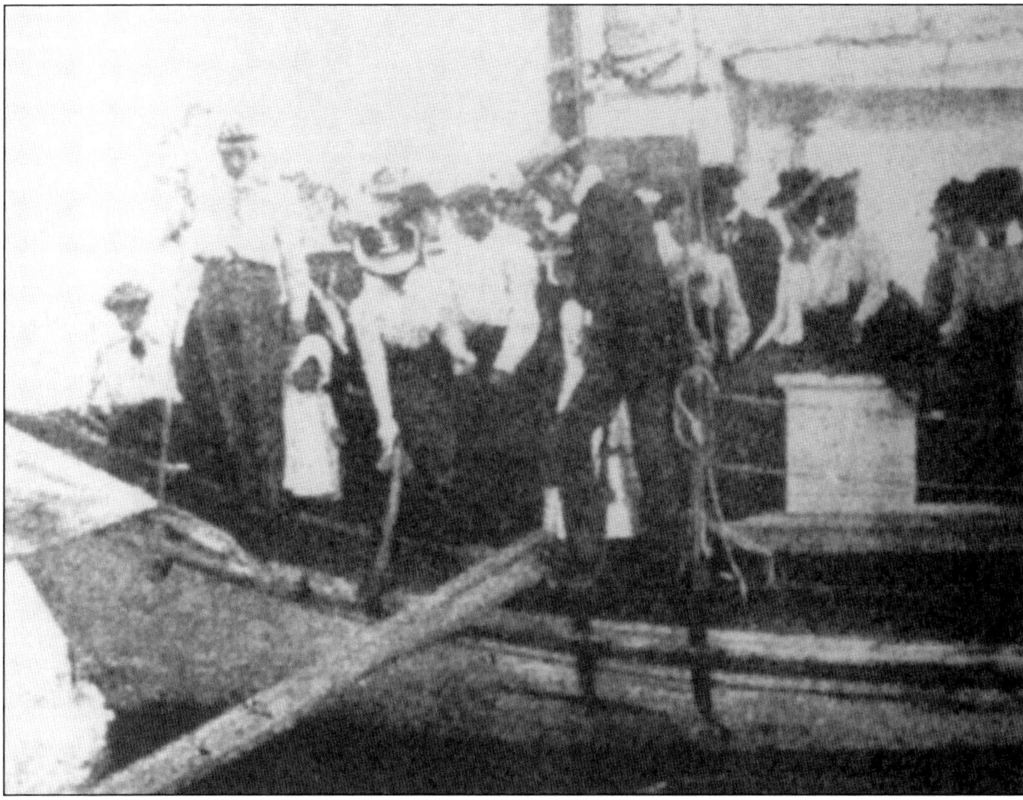

Around 1905, an excursion boat like this one took Sylvan Beach visitors out on the bay. For one-hour rides, the price was 25¢ for adults and 15¢ for children. Many locals used their boats for this purpose.

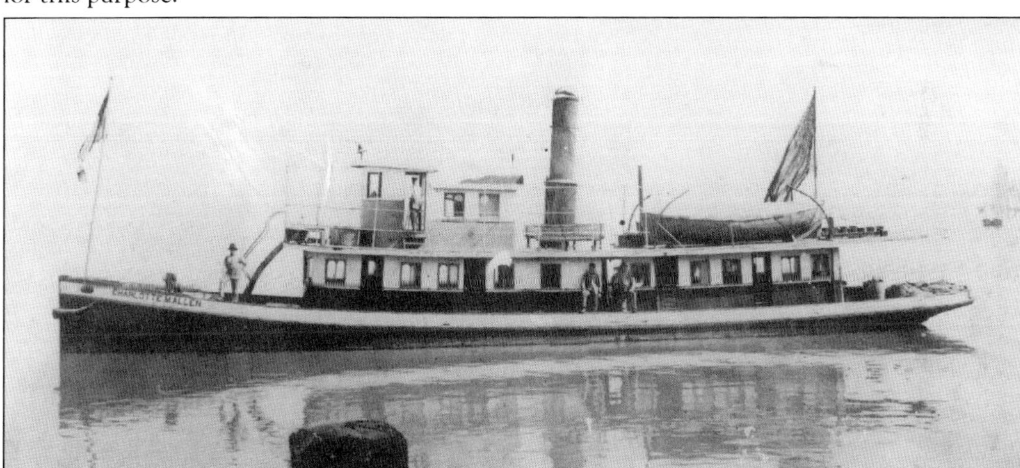

All kinds of boats went into service to bring visitors to the new Sylvan Beach Hotel. Before the hotel's pier was built, the first landing was at Morgan Point's pier. By 1900, the Sylvan Beach Hotel was gone. Around 1903 or 1904, boats could pull up to the Sylvan Beach pier. Sylvan Beach is also the name of the surrounding residential subdivisions, and some of the houses and streets maintain their own piers, including the Garfield Street pier, which has been communally operated by residents since 1927.

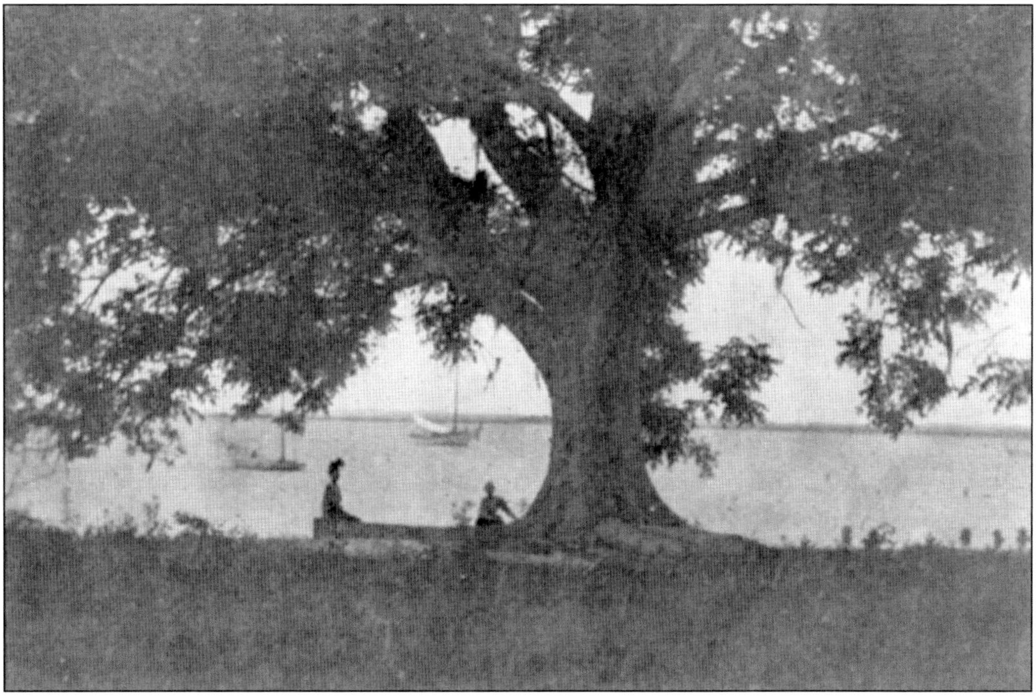

This big tree, pictured here in 1900, was very close to the water's edge. It provided shade for those who just wanted to admire the view and enjoy the breeze. This is a pecan tree, but live oaks and pin oaks were also very common in the Sylvan Beach area.

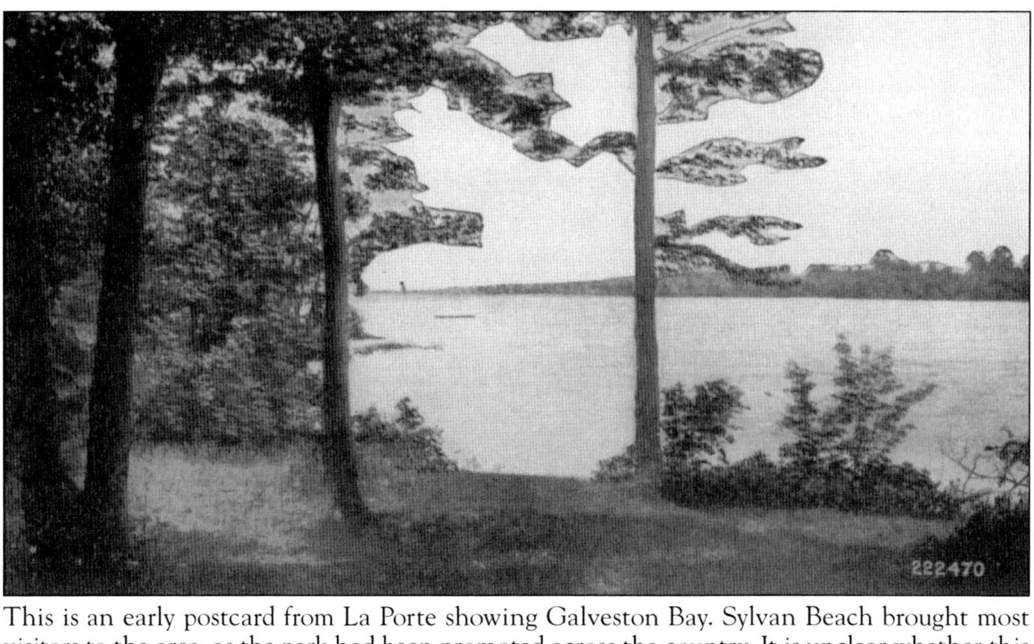

This is an early postcard from La Porte showing Galveston Bay. Sylvan Beach brought most visitors to the area, as the park had been promoted across the country. It is unclear whether this photograph is of Trinity Bay or is in fact an actual photograph from Sylvan Beach.

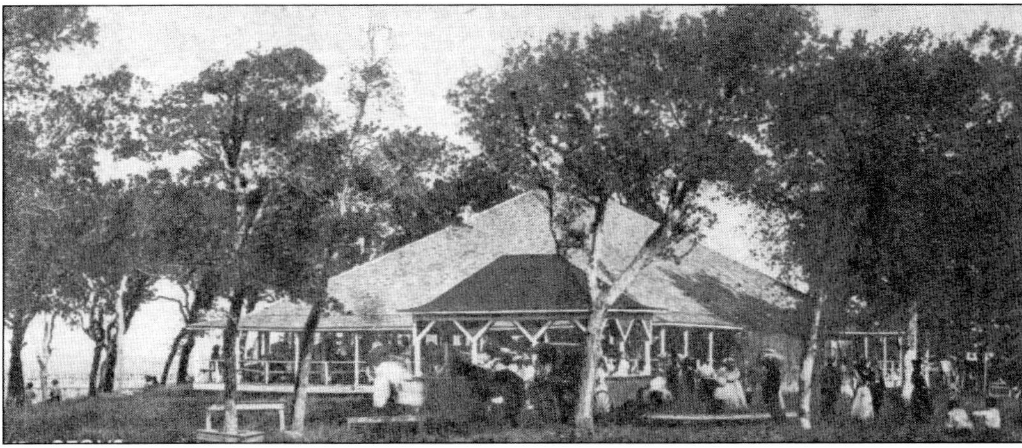

This is one of the early Sylvan Beach pavilions. It is very similar to the first one from 1893, although a bandstand has been added. This structure was probably built in 1901 or 1902, sometime after the 1900 hurricane that devastated the area.

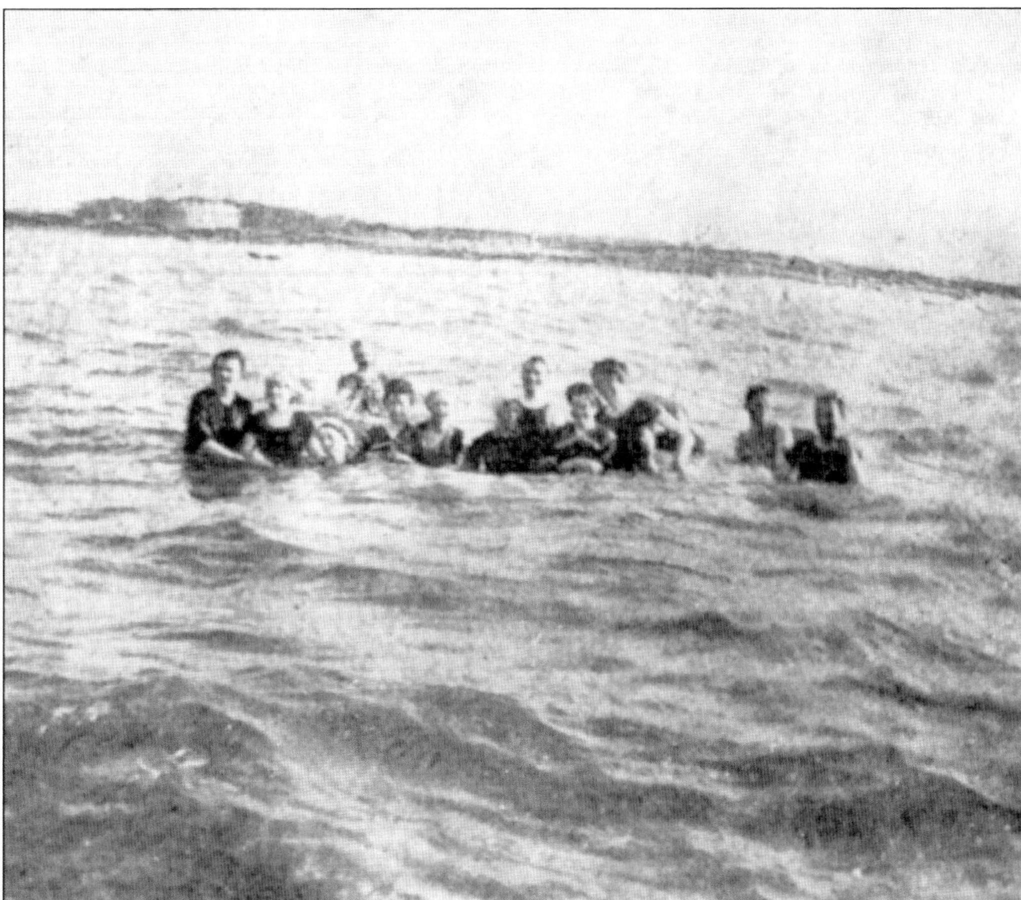

Swimming was one of the area's main attractions for adults and children alike. Most of the bay is naturally only about five to ten feet deep. A much deeper channel has been dredged farther out for the Port of Houston traffic coming through the Houston Ship Channel.

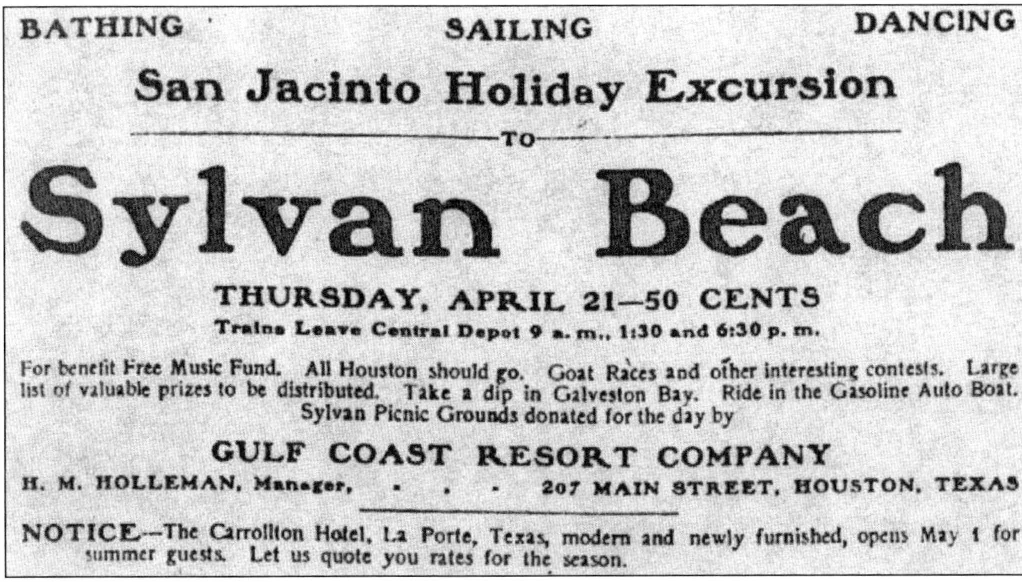
BATHING SAILING DANCING

San Jacinto Holiday Excursion

—TO—

Sylvan Beach

THURSDAY, APRIL 21—50 CENTS

Trains Leave Central Depot 9 a. m., 1:30 and 6:30 p. m.

For benefit Free Music Fund. All Houston should go. Goat Races and other interesting contests. Large list of valuable prizes to be distributed. Take a dip in Galveston Bay. Ride in the Gasoline Auto Boat. Sylvan Picnic Grounds donated for the day by

GULF COAST RESORT COMPANY

H. M. HOLLEMAN, Manager, . . . 207 MAIN STREET, HOUSTON, TEXAS

NOTICE—The Carrollton Hotel, La Porte, Texas, modern and newly furnished, opens May 1 for summer guests. Let us quote you rates for the season.

In 1906, Seabrook, Texas, was to host the San Jacinto holiday excursion but could not raise the necessary funds, so the event moved to Sylvan Beach, where a Ferris wheel and other rides were installed. This was the moment when Sylvan Beach became a real amusement park compared to Coney Island by author and newspaper columnist E.B. Foxworth.

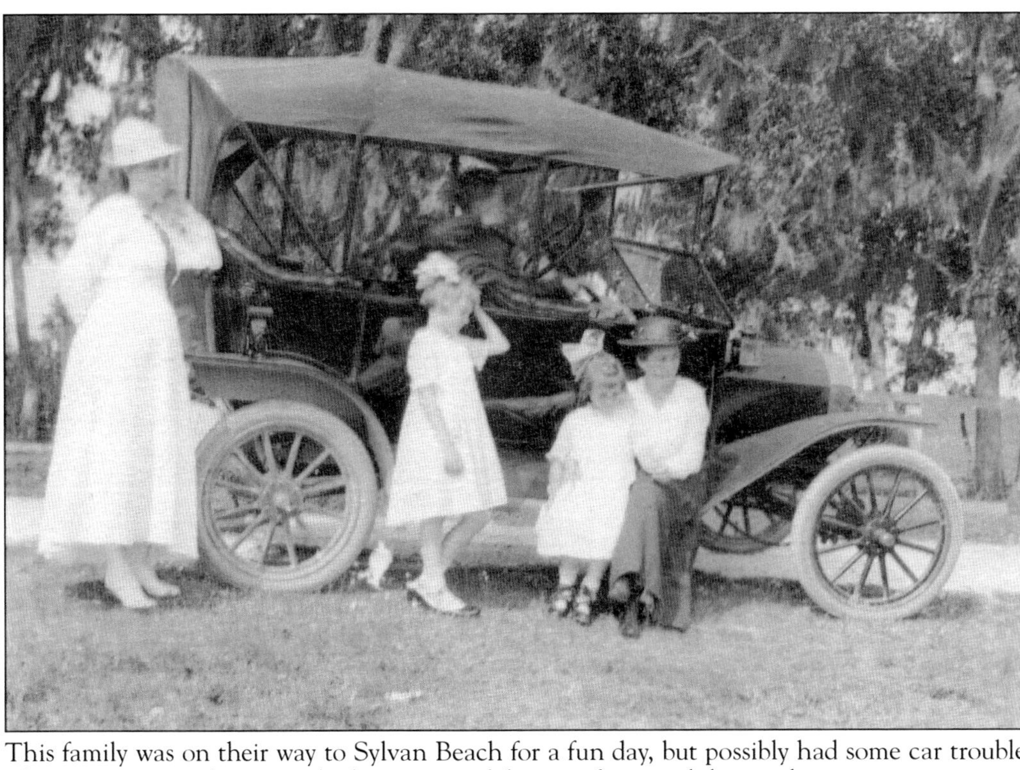

This family was on their way to Sylvan Beach for a fun day, but possibly had some car trouble. This picture was taken near the beginning of the era of automobile travel.

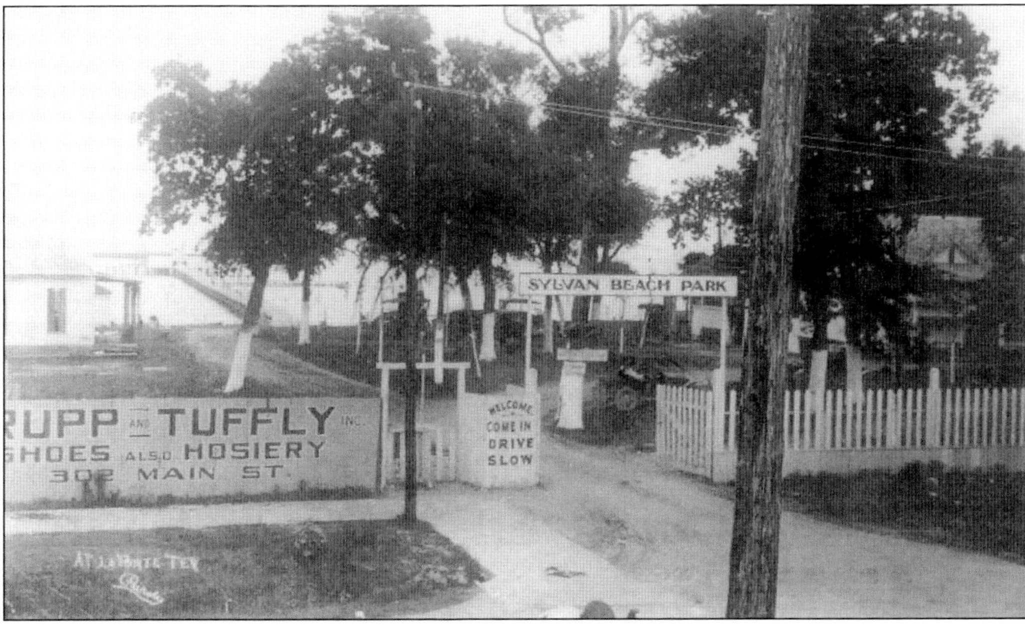

This was the c. 1908 entrance to Sylvan Beach. It was fenced to keep livestock out of the park, as the area surrounding the park was still very pastoral. Note the pier at the end of the road.

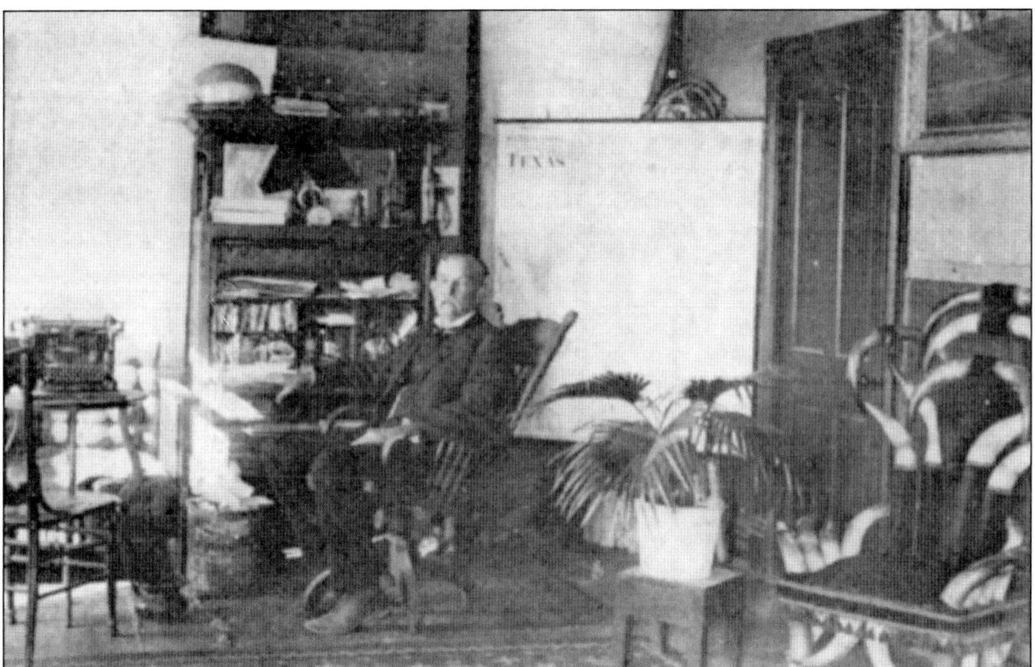

John Caplan's company took possession of Sylvan Beach Park in 1907 after the founders defaulted on their loan. It operated as a city park until the city founders lost a lawsuit against their creditors. Caplan was one of La Porte's original developers (the Nebraska Syndicate) and stayed in La Porte after the others moved on. He and J.H. York built the Ballentine Hotel, and Caplan donated the land on which La Porte's first school was built.

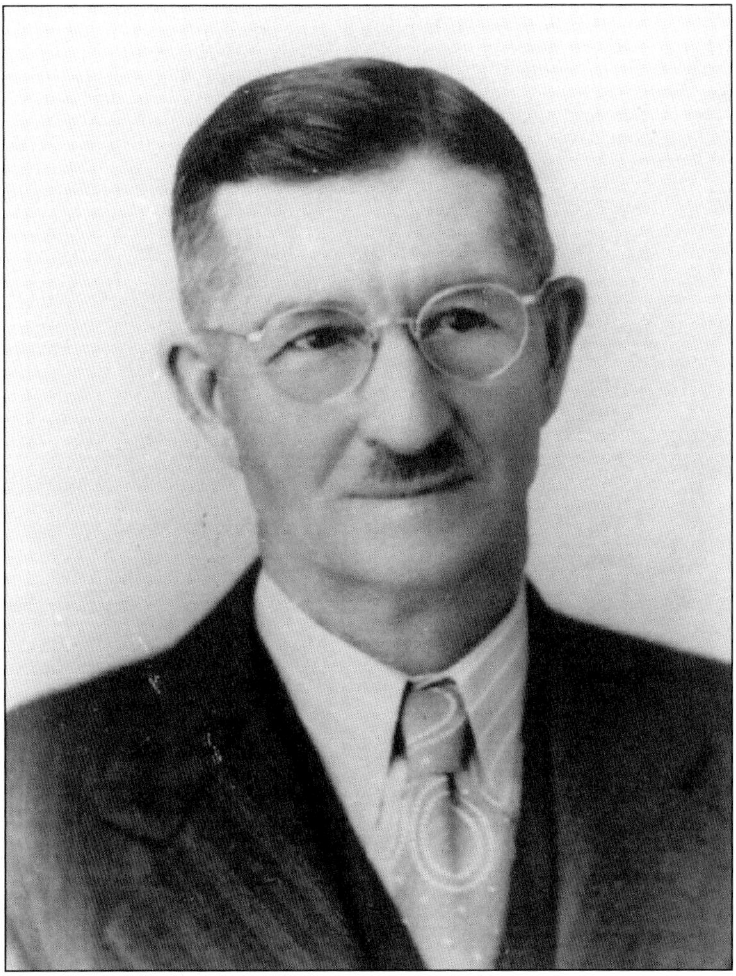

G.D. Samuels, along with his group, became the first owners of Sylvan Beach Park. From 1909 to 1915, Samuels built cabins, brought in rides, and made Sylvan Beach a family park. Samuels bought Sylvan Beach in 1909 from Galveston mortgage firm Adoue and Lobit, then sold it after a 1915 storm damaged the park. Samuels then went back to Houston and opened a nightclub, the End of Main, which was popular for many years.

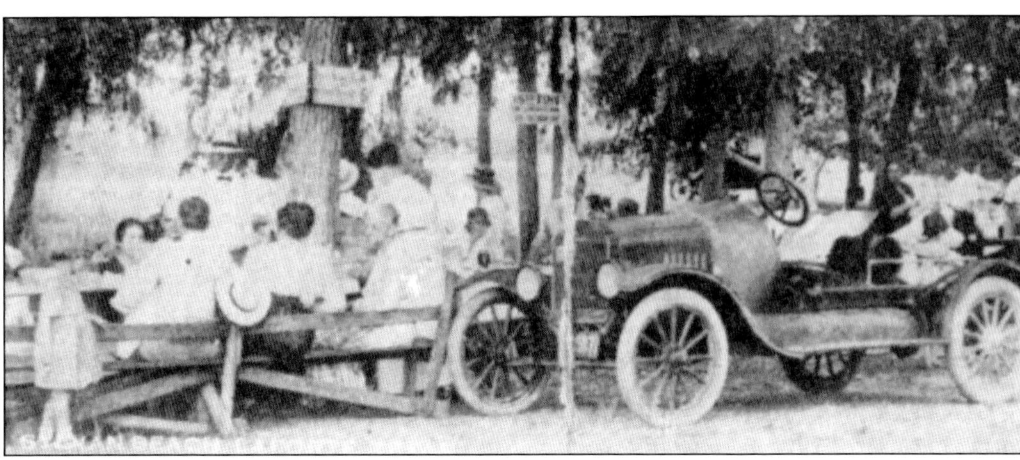

In the earliest part of the 20th century, families came to Sylvan Beach by the hundreds. They could enjoy the park, although a sign shown in this image warned that there was a "$5 dollar fine for littering." By the 1920s, families were motoring down to Sylvan Beach by the thousands.

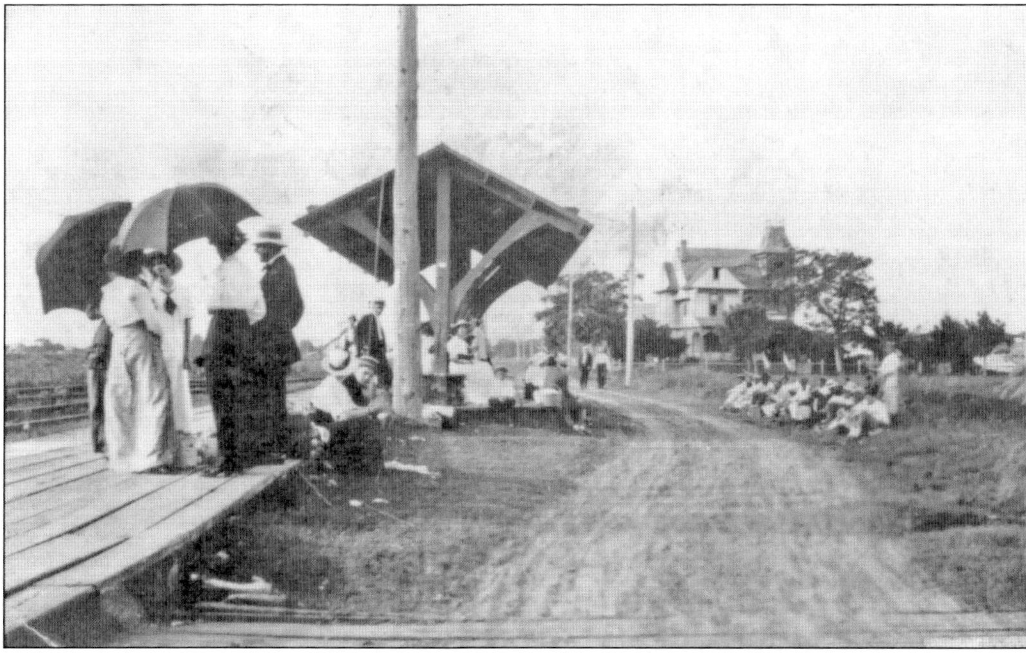

This, the first shelter at the Sylvan Beach depot, was probably built around 1901. These folks are waiting for a ride back to Houston. The Sylvan Beach Hotel is visible in the background, but by 1902, the building had been sold to St. Mary's Seminary. Rail service did not come to Sylvan Beach until at least 1905.

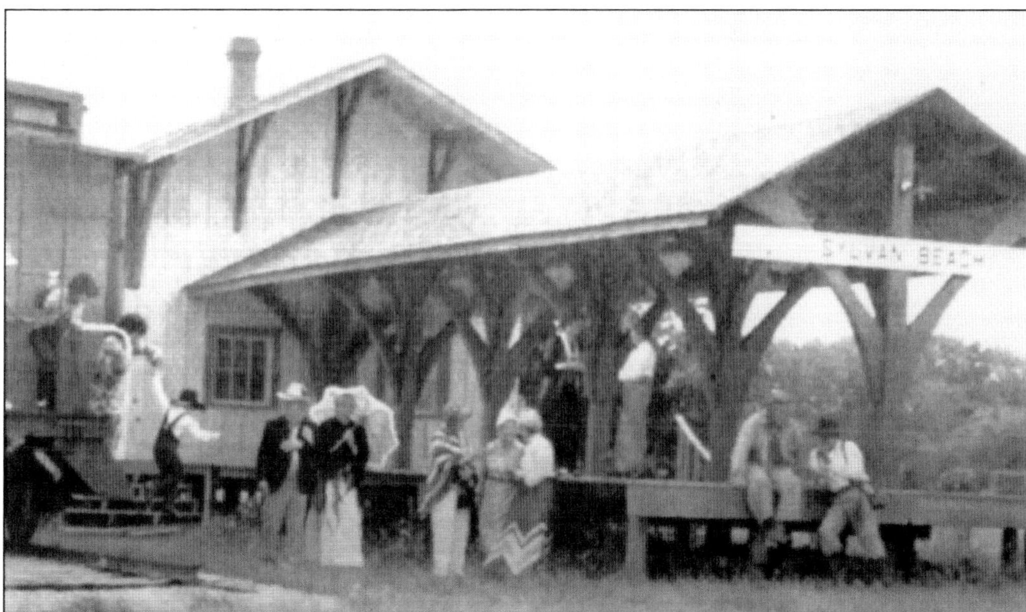

This train depot was moved from downtown La Porte to Sylvan Beach. Thousands came on the weekends and at night to dance at the Sylvan Beach Hotel and, later, the pavilion. Trains began running to Sylvan Beach around 1905. At first, the depot was just a shed to protect riders from the elements. The big depot from La Porte was moved to Sylvan Beach in 1914 or 1915, just before the big 1915 storm (which the depot survived).

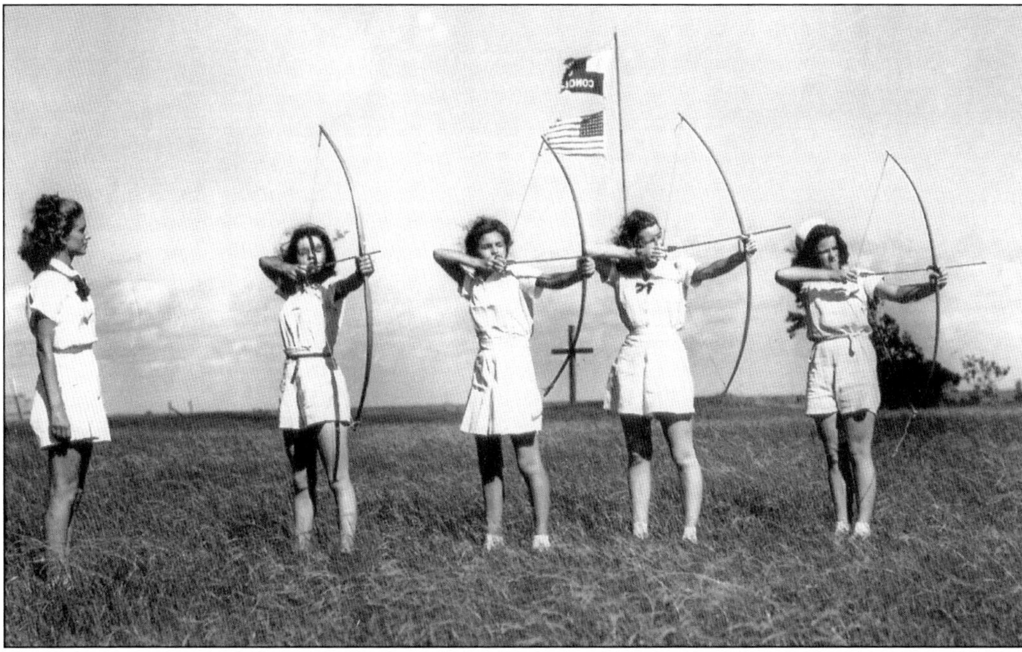

These are photographs of Camp Allen. In the image below, campers relax in front of the flagpole, where an important part of each day was the lowering of the colors. The flag was lowered in a ceremony in the late afternoon before sunset. This was accompanied by a short program and prayers at a site overlooking the water. Archery (above) was among the activities offered. Water sports, such as swimming and boating, were especially popular. The entire two-week program cost $15. Railroad fare to Sylvan Beach was $1.35. The camp remained in its original location until 1928, when a larger facility was needed; Rosa Allen provided this after the purchase of property on Trinity Bay near Baytown. (Both, courtesy of Francita Stuart Koelsch Ulmer.)

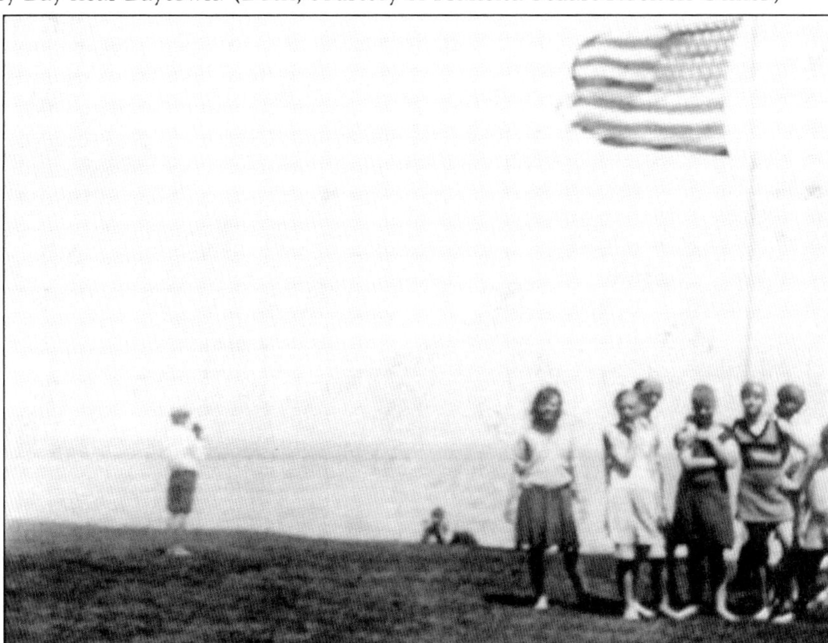

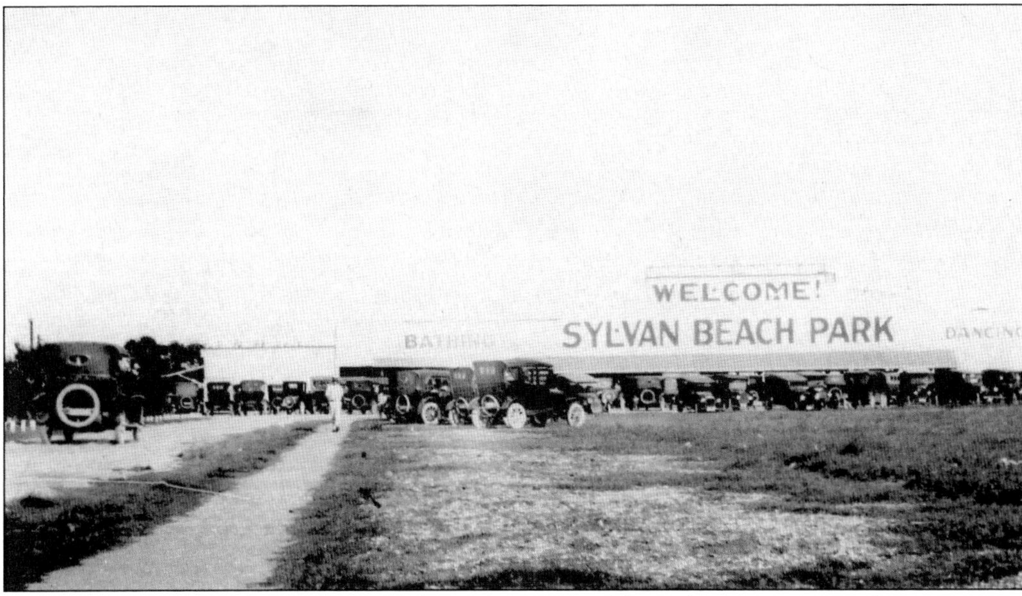

The entrances to Sylvan Beach were always in a state of flux, changing after each storm or new owner. Visitors paid a small fee to enter.

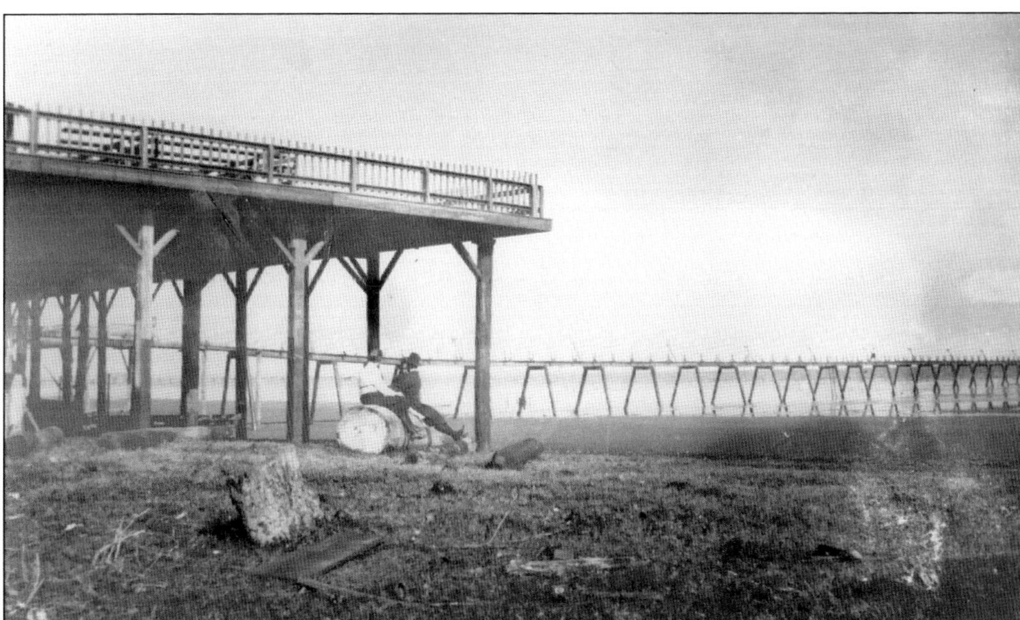

These folks are getting a different view of the pavilion, dock, pier, and water. Note how the pavilion and the pier were built on stilts to accommodate fluctuations in the depths of the bay and the strength of the tide.

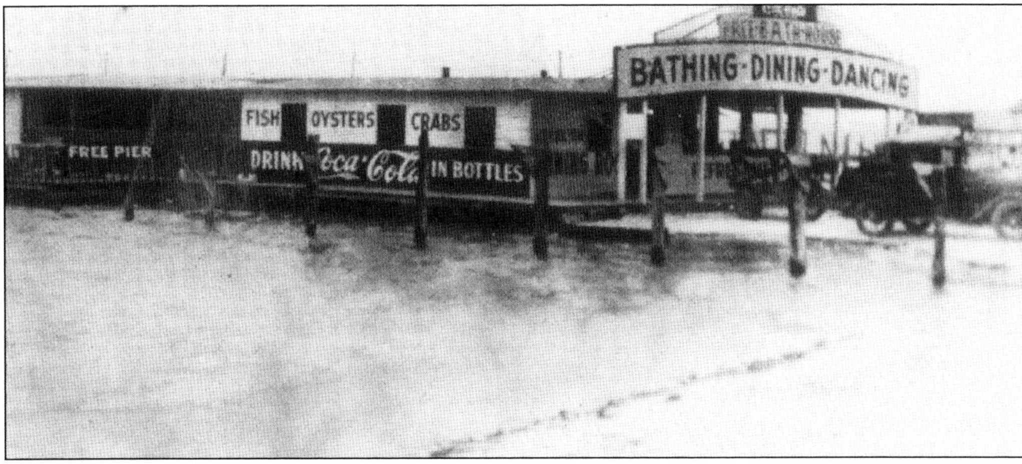

This early restaurant at Sylvan Beach was built out over the water and was very popular. The sign on the side of the building reads, "Drink Coca-Cola in bottles." Galveston Bay yields a rich harvest of seafood, and seafood was featured on this restaurant's menu.

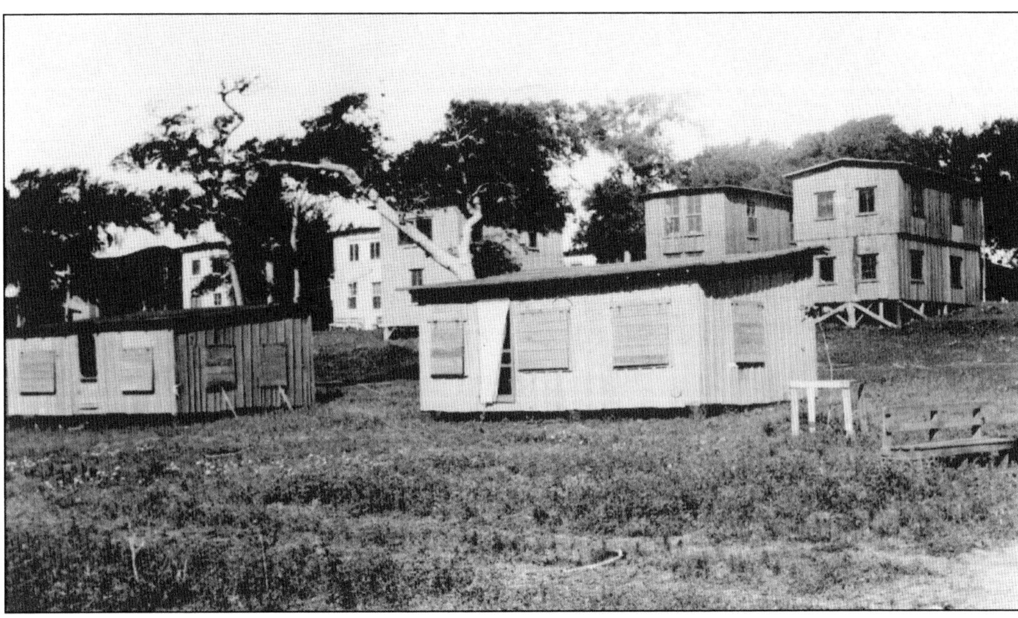

These are some of the cottages built in the park. Ed Eiseman, who owned the park after G.D. Samuels sold it, had more built, creating over 100 rentable spaces. Quaint or rustic names, like "Seldom Inn," adorned some of the cabins. Women's groups could generally rent cabins for free.

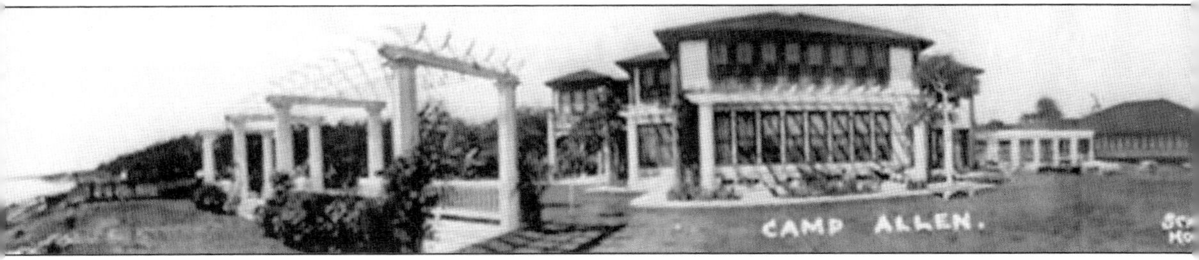

This picture shows the first Camp Allen, founded in 1921 on Galveston Bay near La Porte. It was the inspiration of the Rt. Rev. Clinton S. Quin, bishop coadjutor of the Episcopal Diocese of Texas. Quin wanted to provide a needed recreational facility for the youth of the diocese. Rosa Lum Allen, a prominent Houstonian and member of Christ Church Cathedral, assisted by her grandson, Robert C. Stuart, embraced the idea and offered the use of her spacious summer home. Thirty-six youth from Houston, Austin, Galveston, Dallas, and Tyler attended the first sessions. A second location on Trinity Bay was later purchased by Allen for the camp. The Trinity Bay site was sold to buy the current Camp Allen in Grimes County, where a 1,100-acre camping, educational, recreational, and spiritual facility serves 44,000 adults and 8,000 children each year. (Courtesy of Francita Stuart Koelsch Ulmer.)

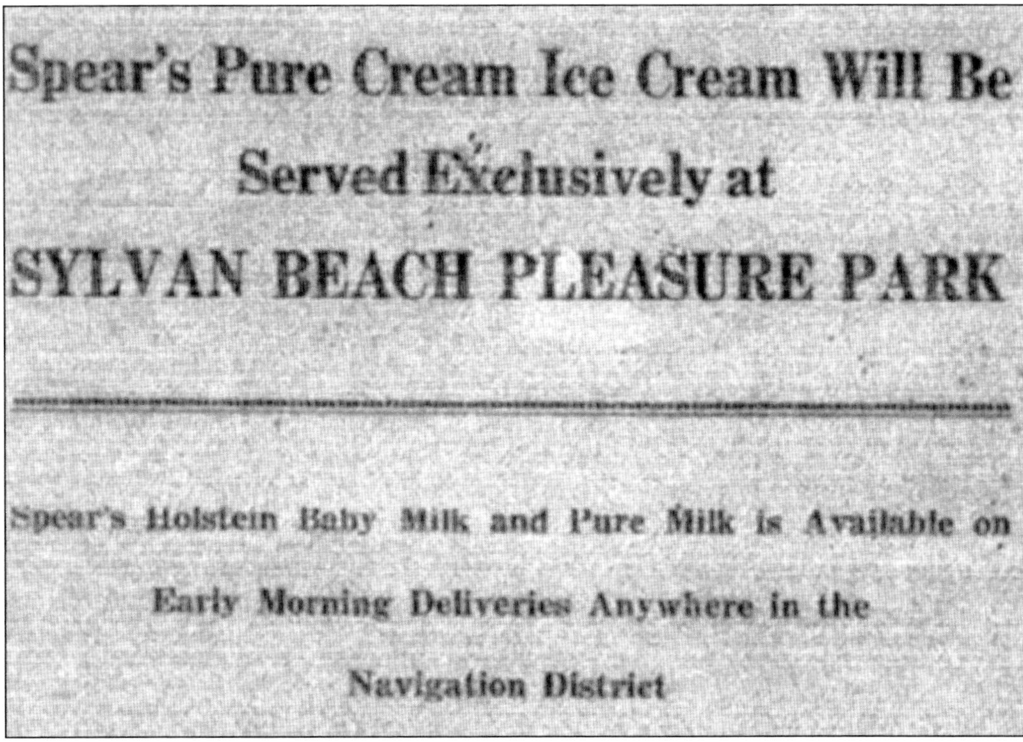

Spear's Pure Cream Ice Cream Will Be Served Exclusively at

SYLVAN BEACH PLEASURE PARK

Spear's Holstein Baby Milk and Pure Milk is Available on Early Morning Deliveries Anywhere in the Navigation District

In 1917, Spear's milk products were a staple—along with those of Phenix Dairy, Klein Ice Cream, Westmoreland, and others—in the Houston bay area. For Spear's, being the exclusive concession for Sylvan Beach was obviously a badge of honor.

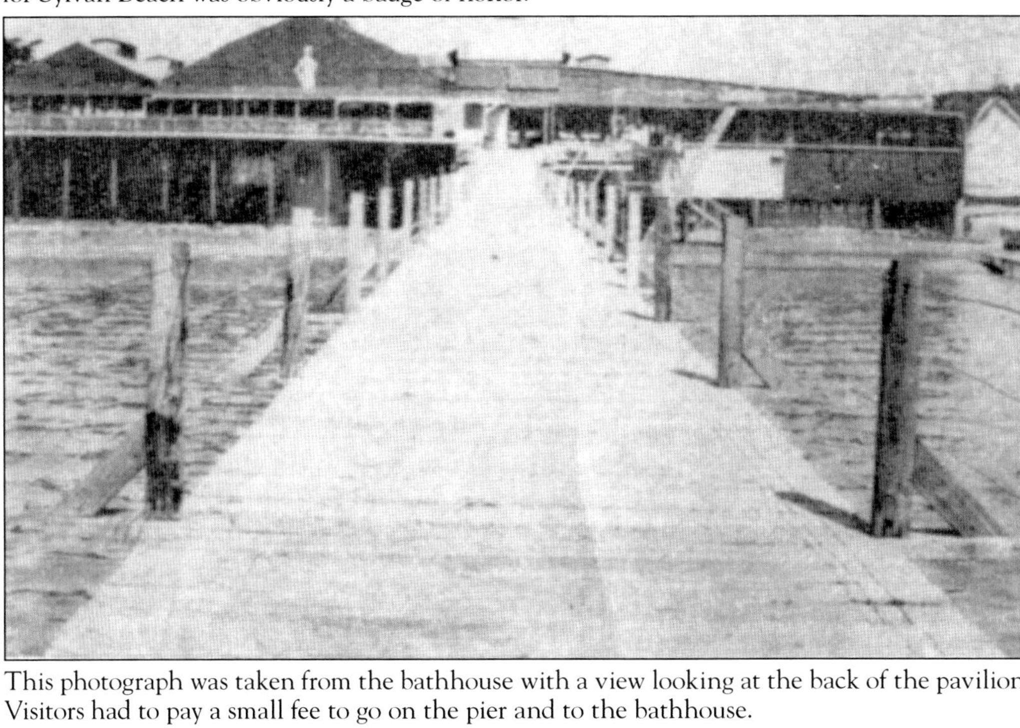

This photograph was taken from the bathhouse with a view looking at the back of the pavilion. Visitors had to pay a small fee to go on the pier and to the bathhouse.

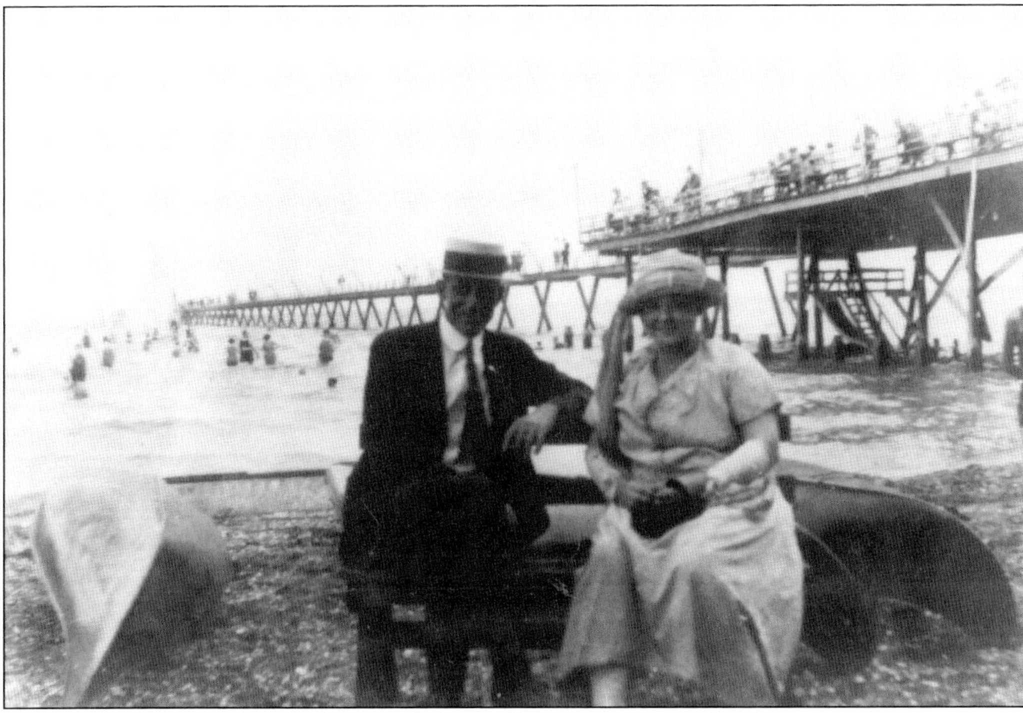

In 1918 and 1919, older folks enjoyed the park—just sitting and relaxing, or enjoying a nice dinner—when World War I was almost over.

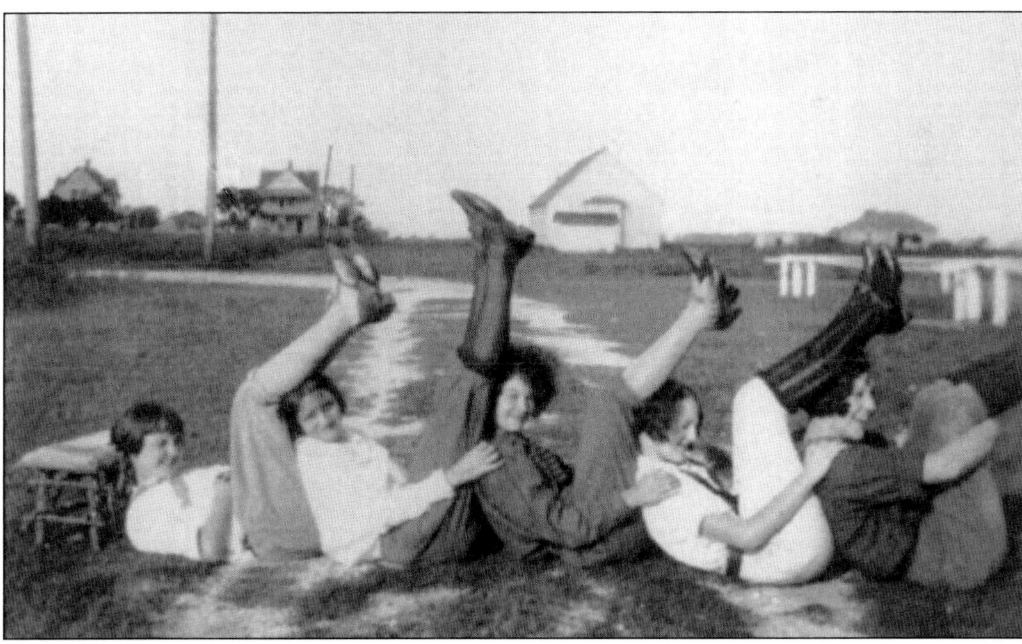

In 1917 and 1918, people were new to having their pictures taken and made many funny poses for the camera.

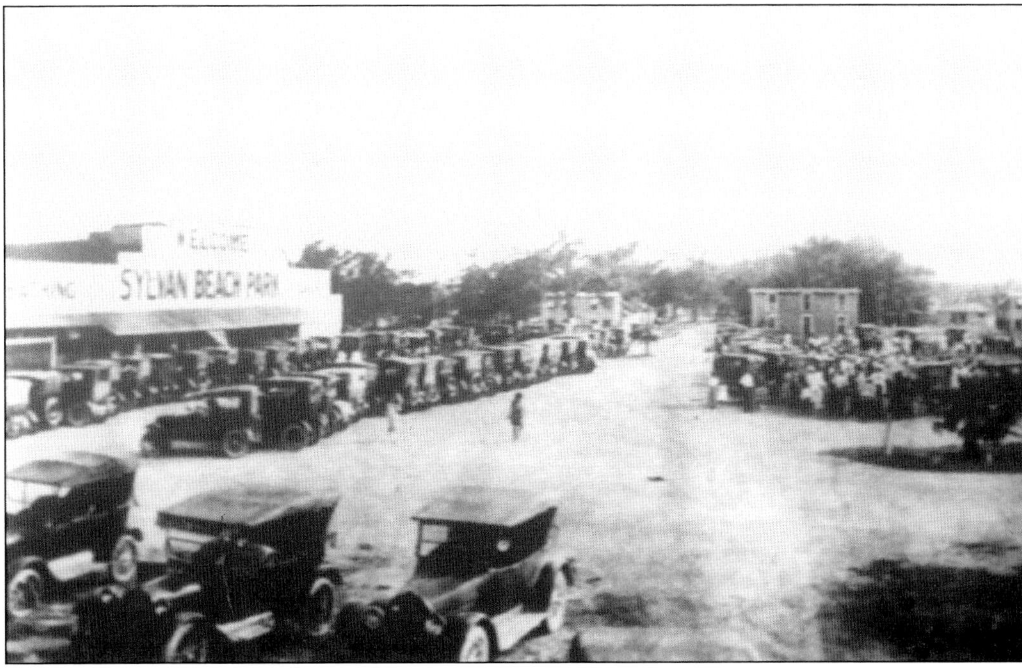

Traffic was heavy at Sylvan Beach. This picture shows many cottages, cars, and people. In the 1910s, the park had more than 100 cottages for rent. The park was in constant change with each new owner, and the Jazz Age of the 1920s was just around the corner.

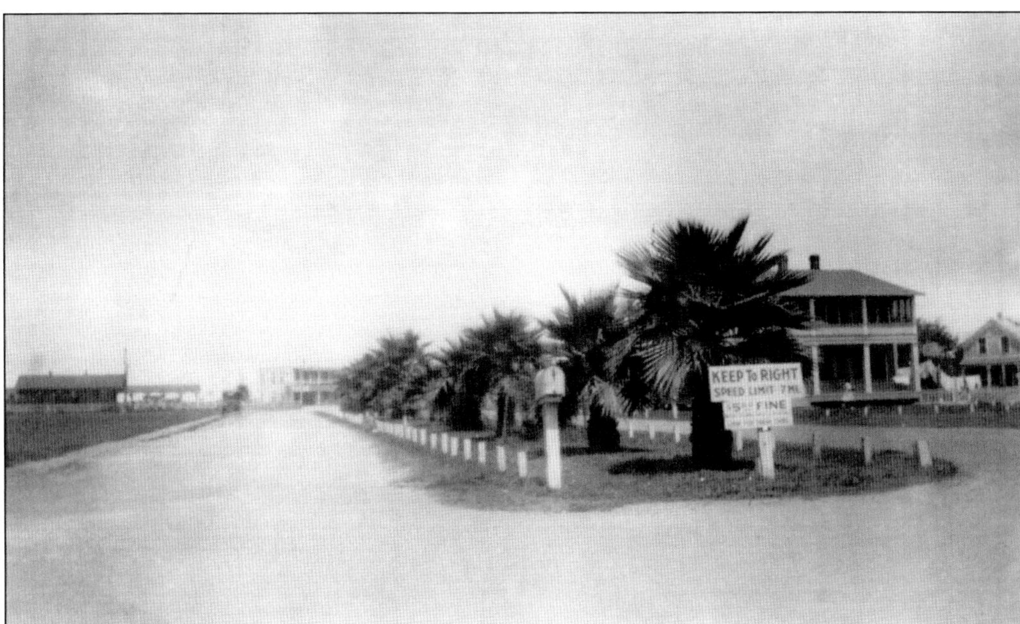

The sign reads, "Speed limit 7 mph—$5 fine." (Four miles per hour is essentially walking speed.) The Sylvan Beach Depot is on the left; the number of people traveling to Sylvan Beach by train began to go down as many bought automobiles.

The smokestack shown in this 1912 photograph was at St. Mary's Seminary, part of which eventually was sold and made a part of Sylvan Beach. Seminarians referred to it as "the Rocket," and it became a symbol of Sylvan Beach.

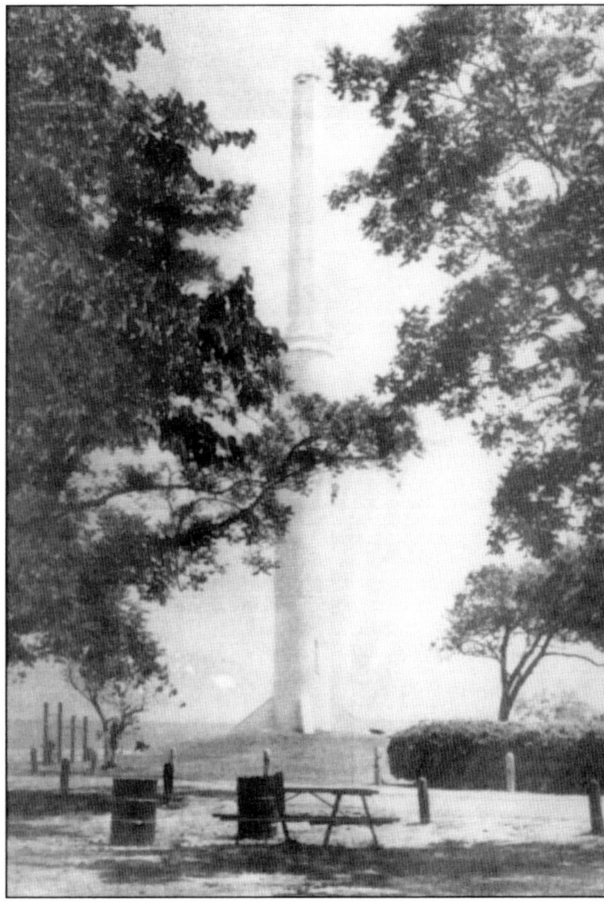

This is Bay Shore Park. It was a competitor located a short distance from Sylvan Beach, but it was only open for a couple of years. It was owned by the Beazley family for a time. Other brief competitors were Surfside Park and Sunset Park (1908 and 1909). The Bay Shore Park Hotel later became Happy Harbor.

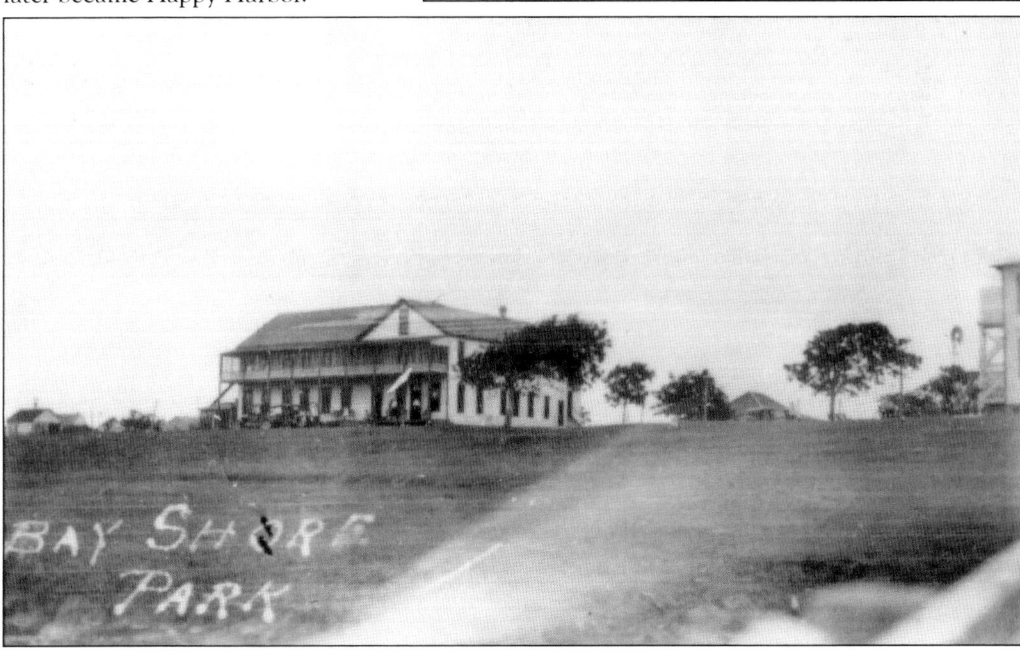

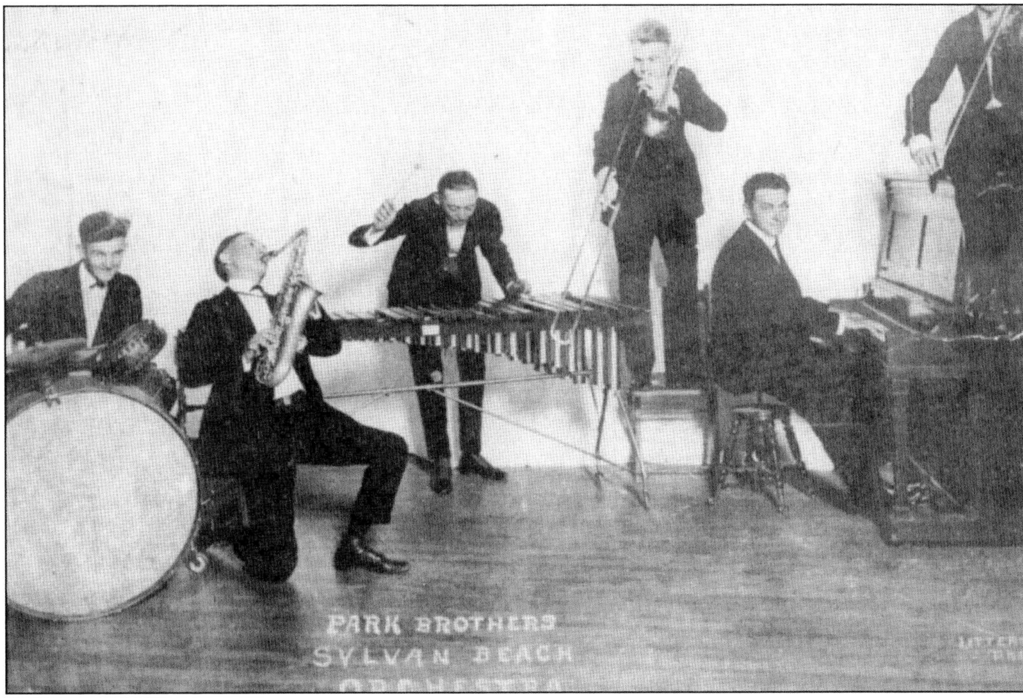

Members of the Park Brothers Orchestra were the "house" musicians at Sylvan Beach during the late 1910s. They traveled the county with park manager Cecil Sisson, touting the resort at Sylvan Beach as having the largest dance floor and best music in the South.

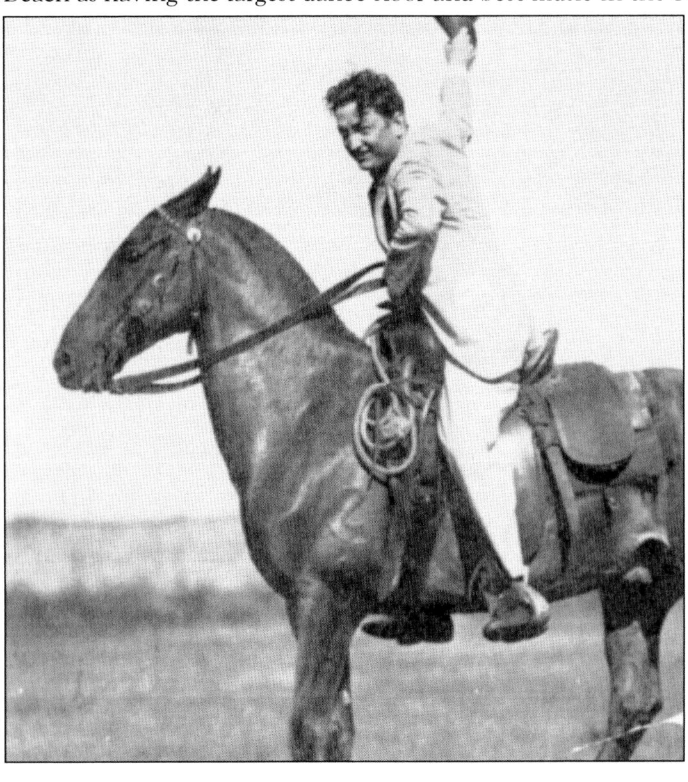

Cecil Sisson was manager of Sylvan Beach Park under Ed Eiseman's ownership. Around 1916, Sisson turned the park into a place a person "had" to visit. He added rides and more cabins to make the park the place to go. It had much more of a carnival atmosphere as Sisson developed it.

Four

The Boom Years

Ed Eiseman purchased Sylvan Beach in 1915 and promptly hired Frank Baker (of La Porte) and Cecil Sisson as his chief lieutenants in the park's operation. A deluxe train, the Sylvan Beach Special, brought customers from Houston to enjoy the reopening of Sylvan Beach in 1916. It was the first excursion train to the park since the 1915 hurricane, and this marked the beginning of the boom years of Sylvan Beach Park.

The floor at the Sylvan Beach Pavilion was relaid and expanded. Rocking chairs surrounded the dance floor; it was still an open-sided pavilion with the bay as a backdrop. Carnival rides and additional concession stands soon followed, along with restaurants, photography galleries, and the first recorded beauty contests at Sylvan Beach. The first Houston Annual Bathing Girl Review occurred in 1924 at Sylvan Beach—less formal bathing beauty reviews had probably occurred in preceding years.

Sylvan Beach was a popular destination and venue for local bands, dances, and the biggest names of the big band era. The Roaring Twenties gave way to the Great Depression, and E.L. Crain purchased Sylvan Beach Park in the 1930s. Crain installed new attractions and orchestrated the building of the famous Art Deco entrance. He installed a dining room that seated 500 people next to the pavilion. Crain's grand opening for the revitalized Sylvan Beach was held on March 2, 1936.

Many older Houstonians remember the years that took Sylvan Beach through one world war and saw the start of another. The "boom years" mirrored the area's oil boom, especially in Goose Creek (Baytown). Myriad companies utilized Sylvan Beach as a venue for picnics and conventions, including Humble, Gulf, and Texas Oil. These years included the Great Depression, the boisterous advent of the automobile revolution, yacht regattas, and Charleston (dance) contests. The Park View Hotel replaced the Sylvan Hotel for visitors who did not want to stay in the park's cottages.

Sylvan Beach was as American and popular as apple pie, and it seemed like nothing could ever dim its quintessentially Texan exuberance, hopefulness, and optimism.

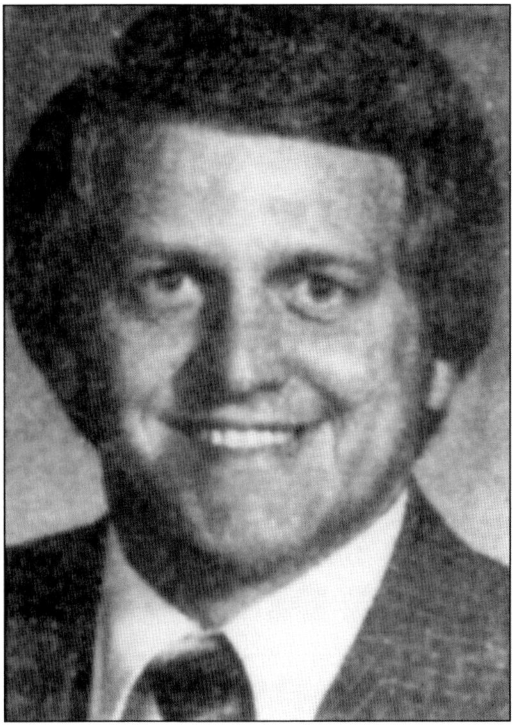

La Porte loves a parade and a circus. The La Porte Day parade was the forerunner of the Sylvan Beach Day parade. The first La Porte Day parade appears to have been held in 1935, the same year Texas folklorist J. Frank Dobie served as commencement speaker at La Porte High School. David Brady, one of many locals who gave their time to make Sylvan Beach Day and parade a success, is pictured at left. Below is a picture of Dobie.

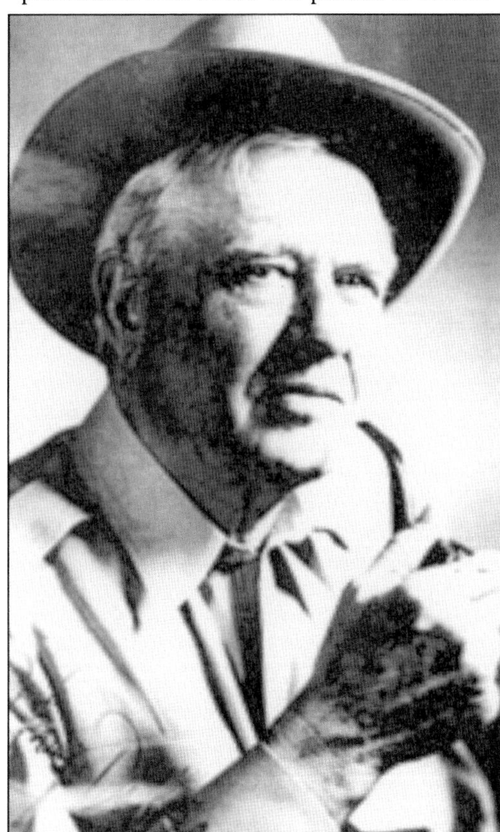

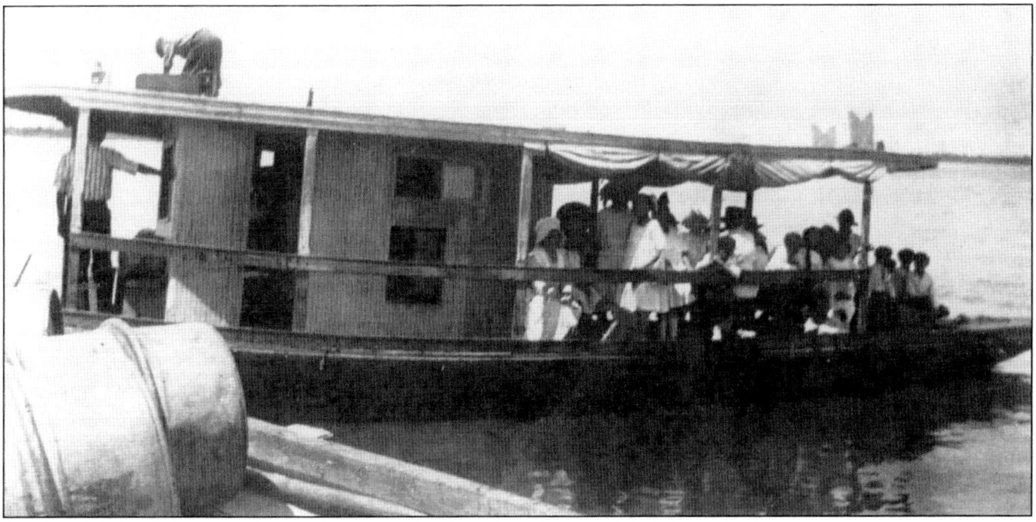

Captain Sutterfield carried people everywhere in his boat, the *Pansy*, especially to and from Sylvan Beach and around La Porte. He had several boats, and he named them all *Pansy*. Before railroads, such boats had been the most reliable way to get to La Porte. Sutterfield continued his "water taxi" service for several years.

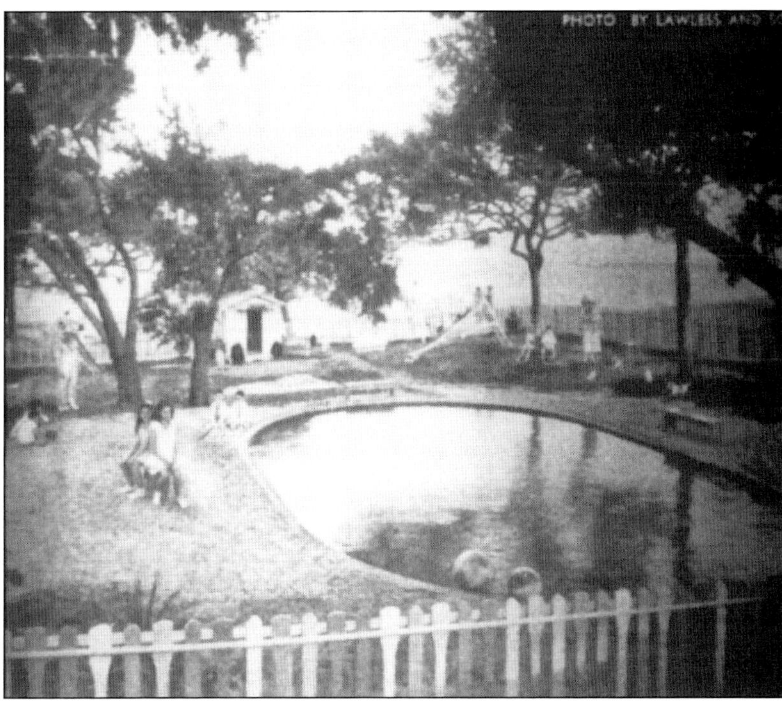

E.L. Crain made a host of improvements to Sylvan Beach, including the construction of the kids' wading pool and recreation area, shown in this c. 1930 photograph. The park provided chaperones for the children while parents did other things.

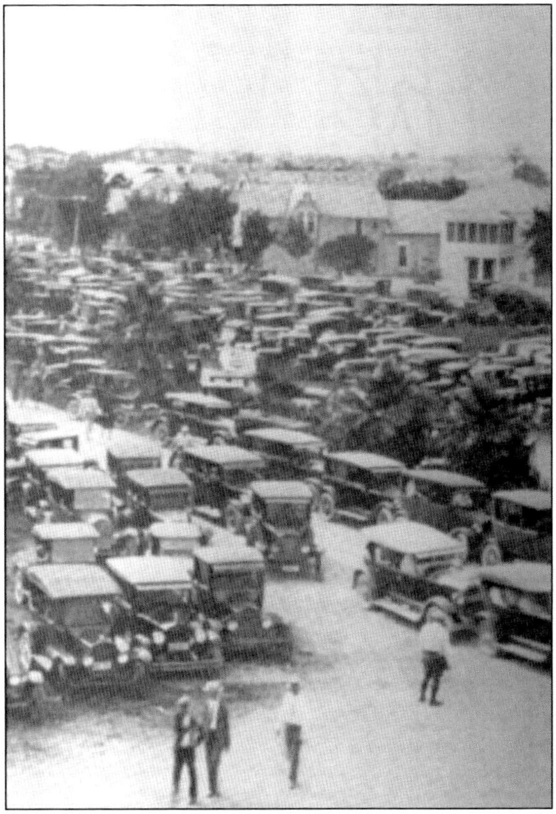

Between 1910 and the late 1920s, it was estimated that as many as 10,000 to 20,000 visitors traveled to Sylvan Beach per weekend, many of them by car.

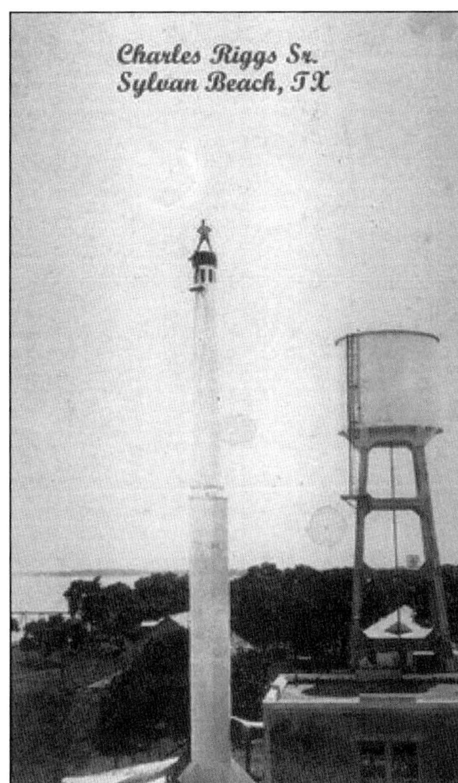

This is another image of the Sylvan Beach smokestack, or "the Rocket," as it came to be known, apparently surmounted by Charles Riggs Sr.

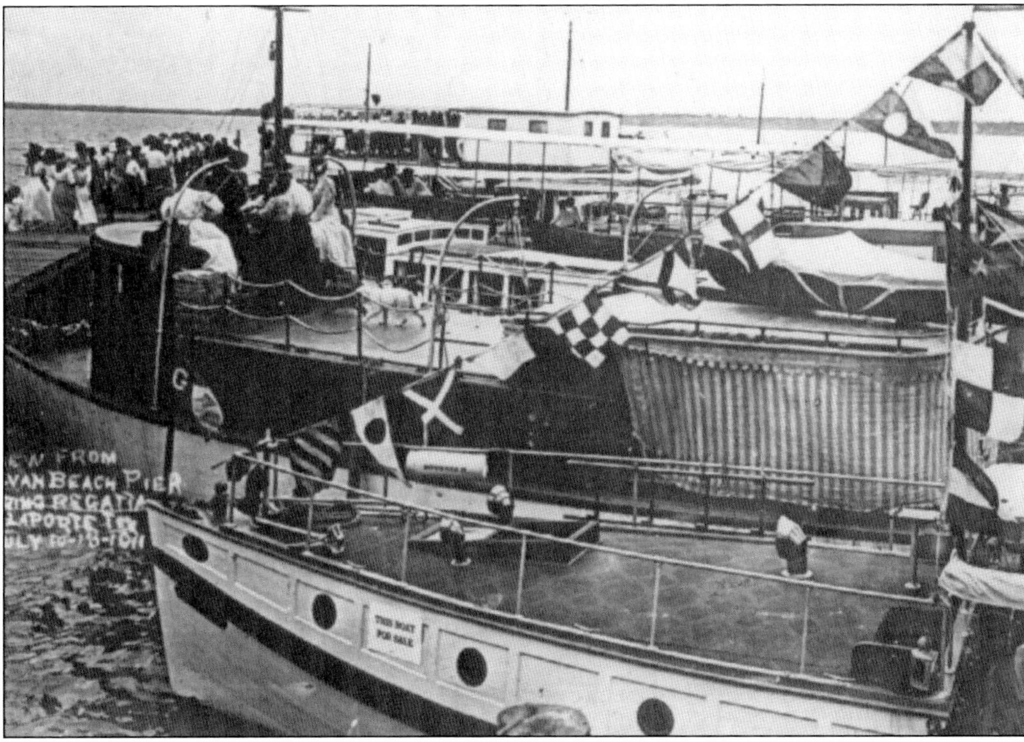

The first recorded regatta at Sylvan Beach was held in 1911 and sponsored by the Houston Launch Club, a predecessor to the Houston Yacht Club. Sylvan Beach has been a popular launch point for sailors ever since.

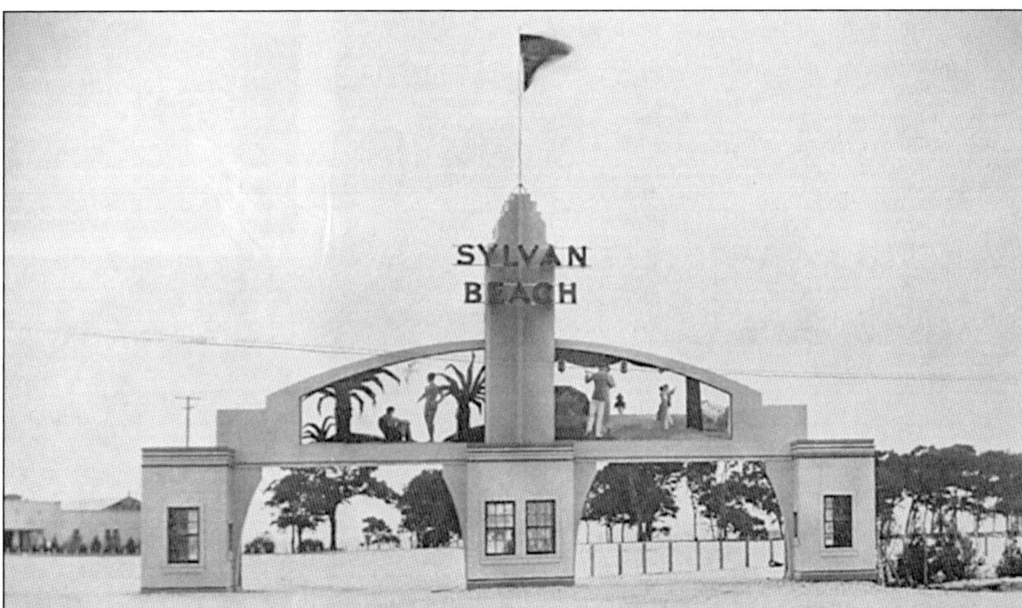

E.L. Crain, the owner of the park after Ed Eiseman, built this inviting entrance when he updated the park in the 1930s. New rides, music, and landscaping enticed people to come. This is the Art Deco entrance for which Sylvan Beach is most famous.

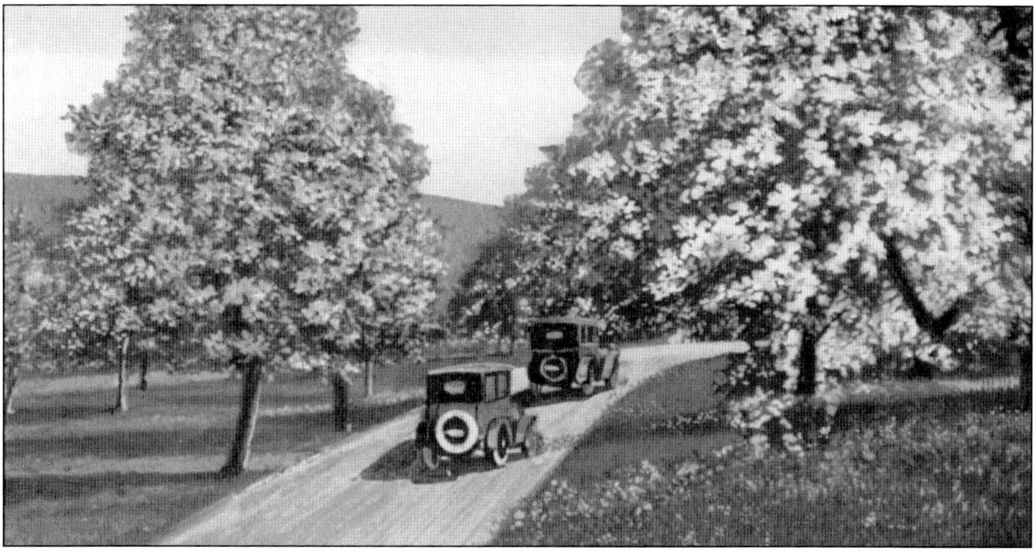

This is a postcard depicting La Porte around 1930. At the time, La Porte and Sylvan Beach were still largely pastoral areas. The postcard is not terribly realistic, but it is considered pretty.

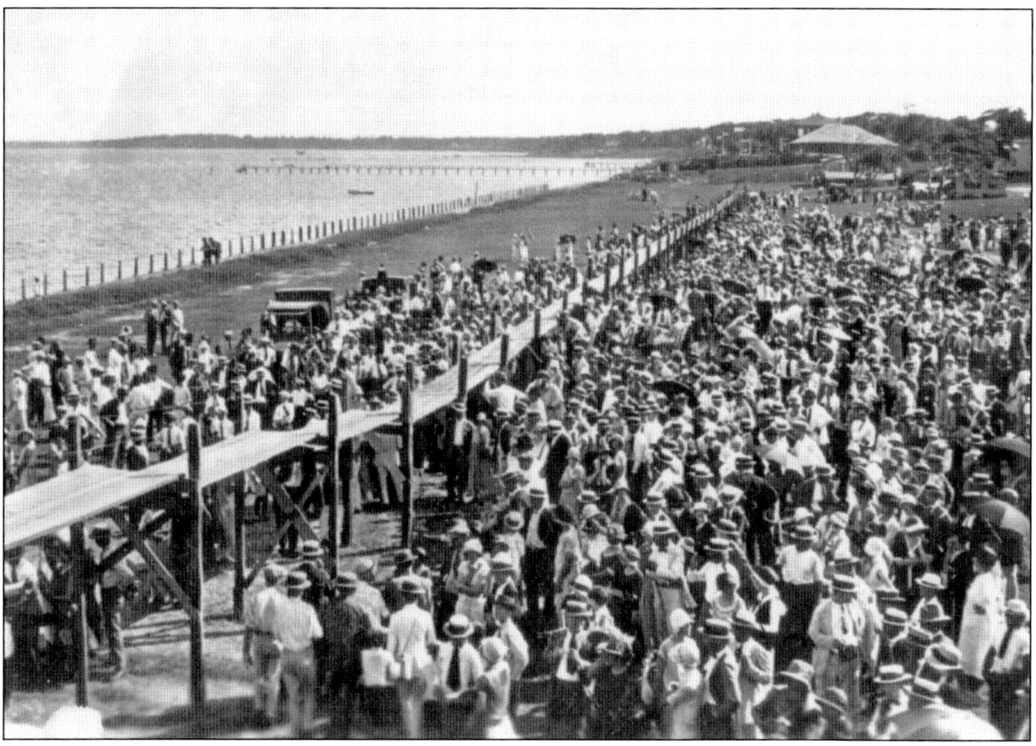

This photograph shows where the bathing beauty contestants would promenade on the elevated boardwalk to the great amusement of the crowd. Swimming and beauty contests were probably the two most perennially popular entertainments at Sylvan Beach over the years.

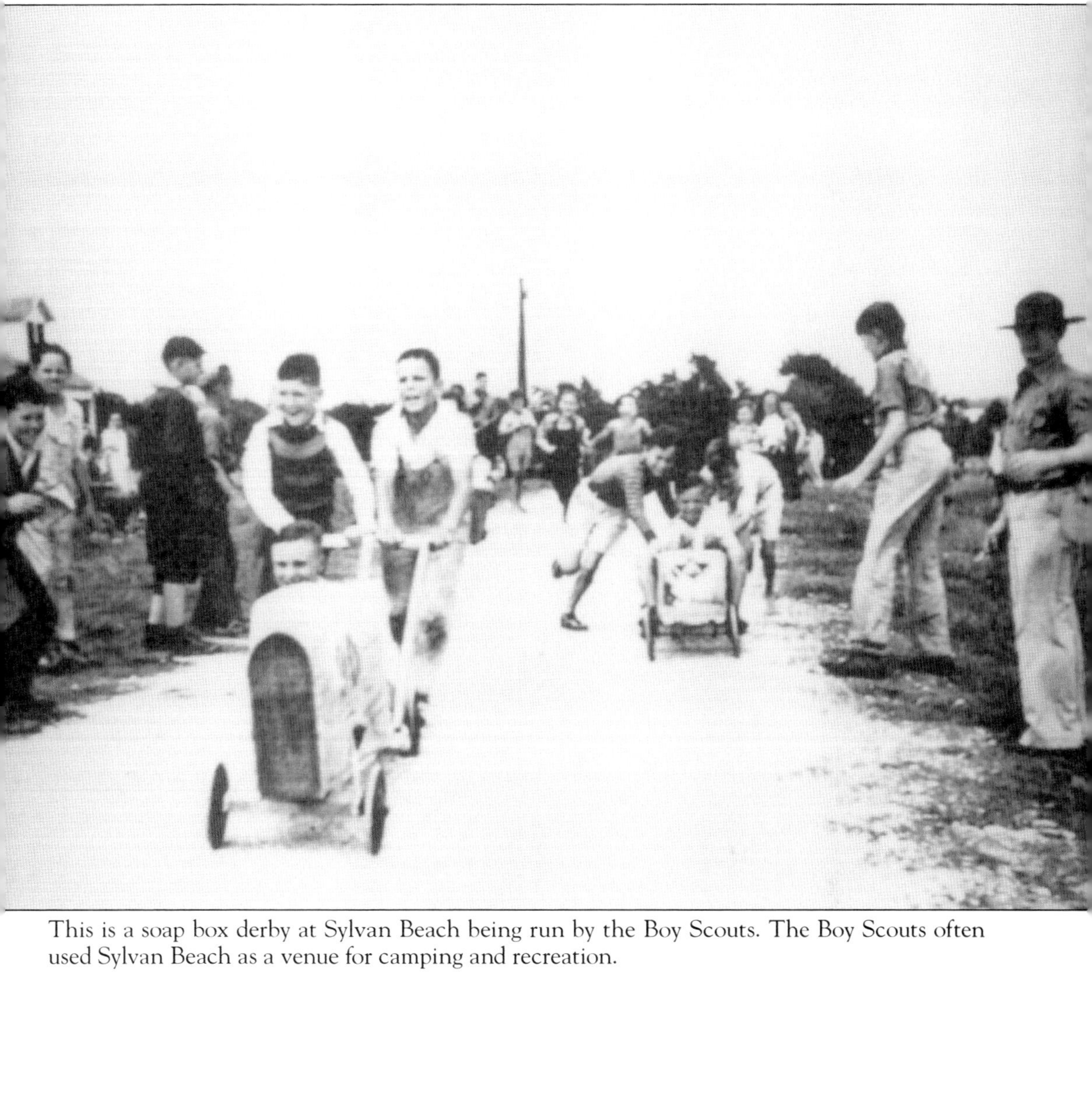

This is a soap box derby at Sylvan Beach being run by the Boy Scouts. The Boy Scouts often used Sylvan Beach as a venue for camping and recreation.

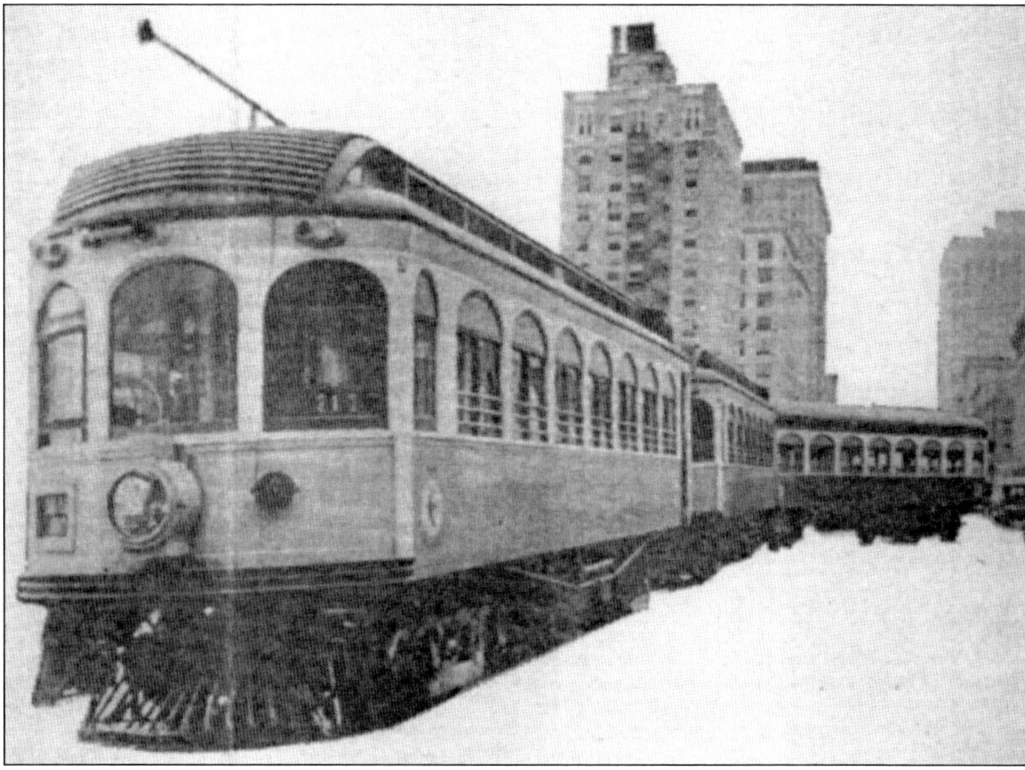

When Ed Eiseman purchased Sylvan Beach in 1915, he persuaded his friend John Scott, president of the Galveston, Houston & Henderson Railroad, to move the depot from downtown La Porte to Sylvan Beach. Over the years, various trains ran from downtown Houston to Sylvan Beach, including the famous "Moonlight Excursion" train, shown here.

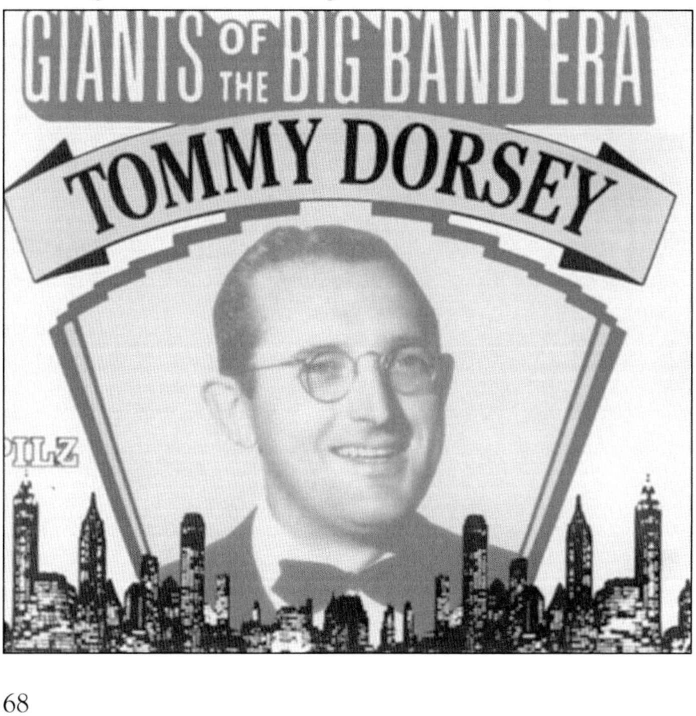

National artists Tommy Dorsey, Rudy Vallee, Artie Shaw, Ewen Hail, Harry James, and Les Brown—and local luminaries like Dan Cannon, John Sullivan, Mark Britt, Ray Price, Fatty Martin, Albino Torres, and "Scat" Davis—all played at Sylvan Beach.

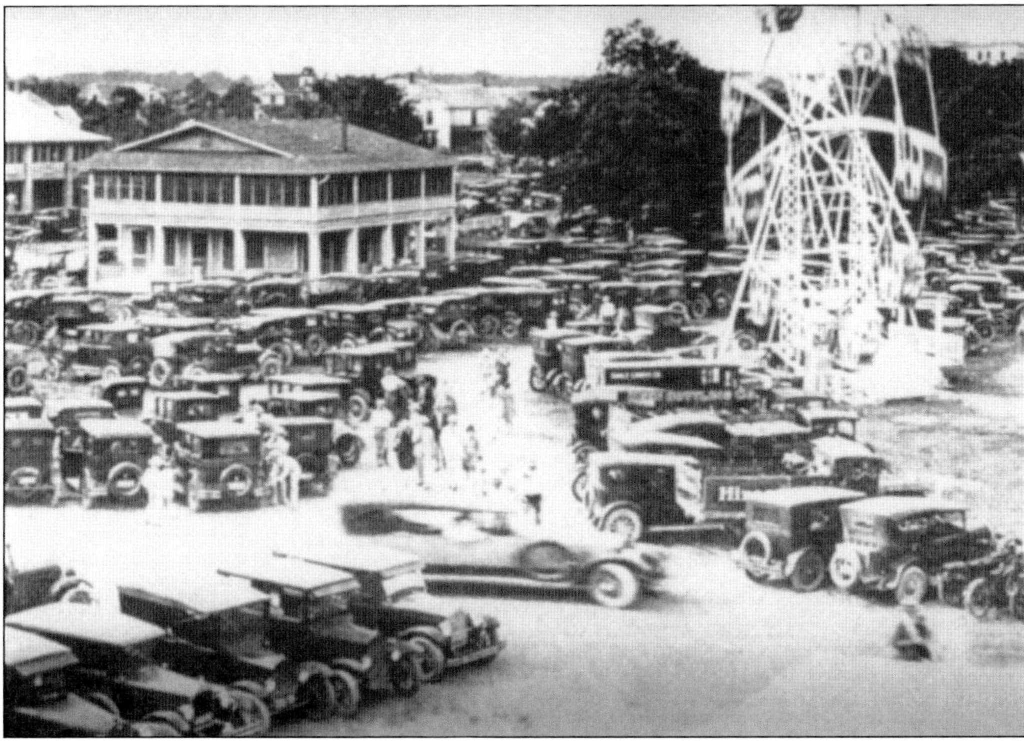

In the 1930s, new owner E.L. Crain brought in a Ferris wheel, a merry-go-round, and other rides and attachments. The 1930s were the years that some older Houstonians and La Portians still remember as the golden age of the park.

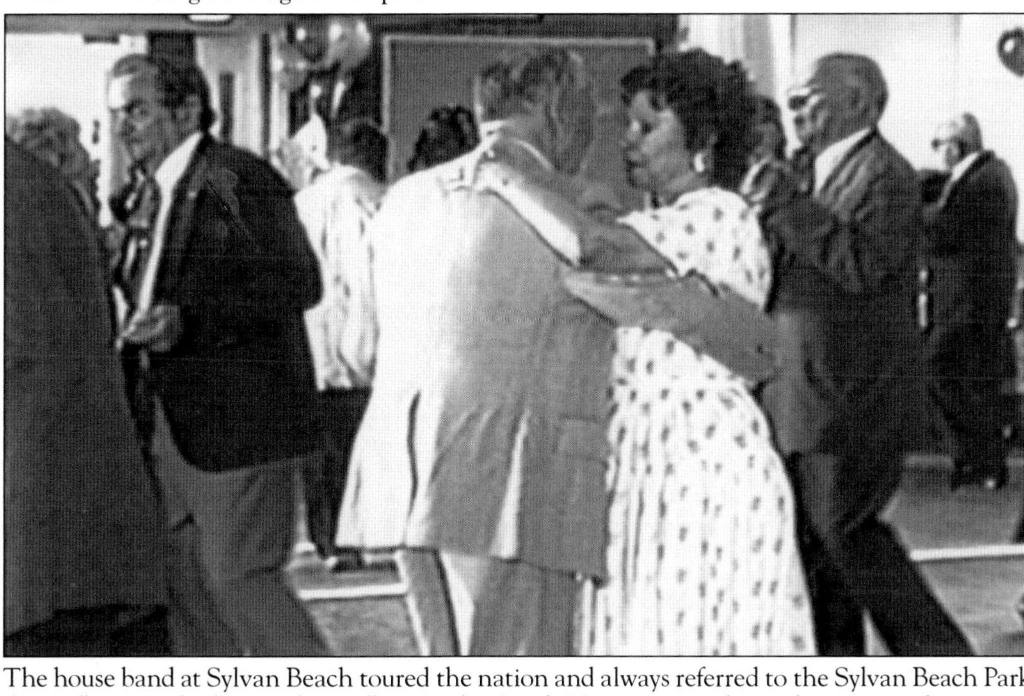

The house band at Sylvan Beach toured the nation and always referred to the Sylvan Beach Park dance floor as "the largest dance floor in the South." It was a popular and romantic place.

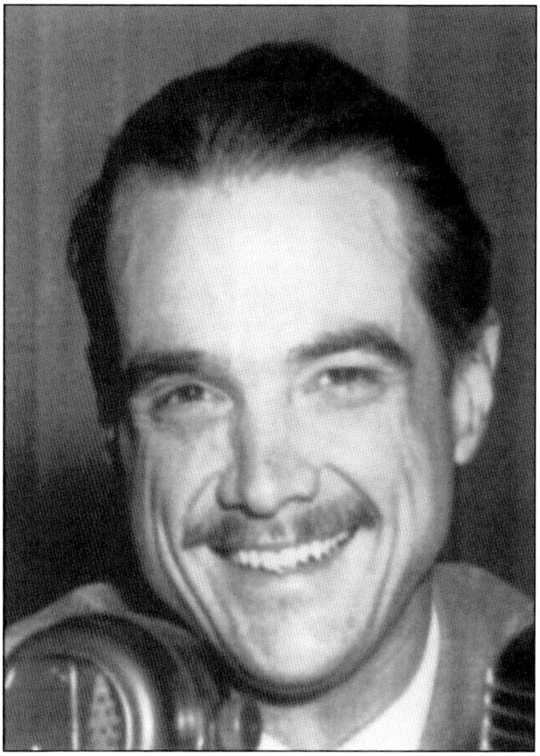

As a young man, Howard Hughes would tie his yacht at the end of Sylvan Beach pier to listen to the music. Occasionally, after a private party on the yacht, his group would disembark and dance at the pavilion after hours when everyone else had gone home.

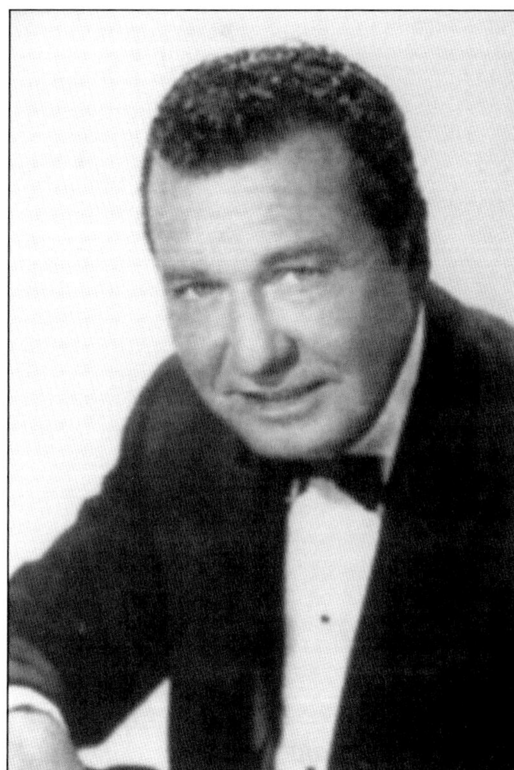

Phil Harris was one of the great bandleaders of the 1930s. He played at Sylvan Beach several times, and when he visited, his wife, actress Alice Faye, would also frequently appear. Harris and Faye returned in the 1970s for a "Remember Sylvan Beach Night" sponsored by a local group.

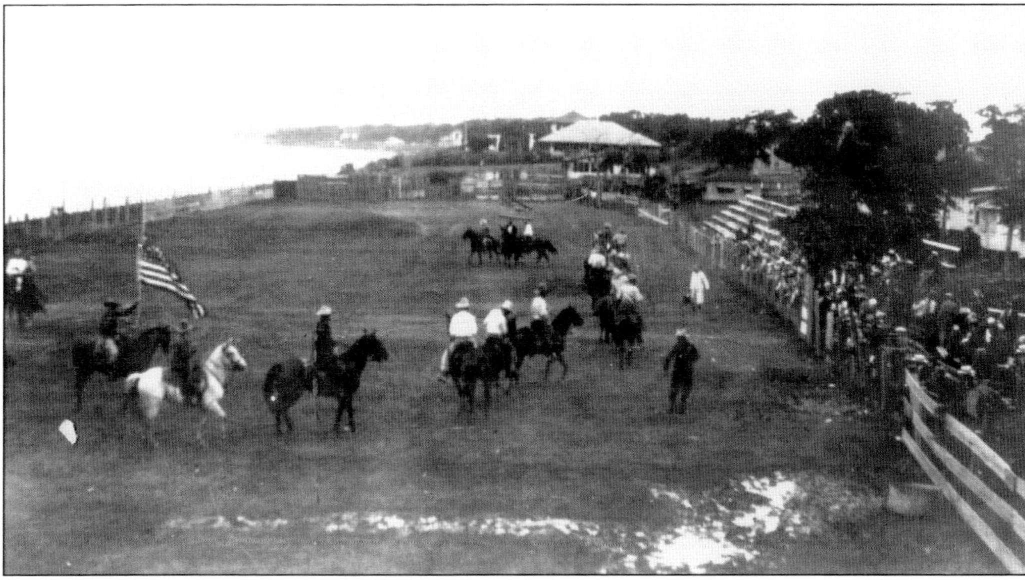

The water rodeo was one of the unique events at Sylvan Beach. It apparently started on land, but some events actually occurred in the water or on platforms over the water.

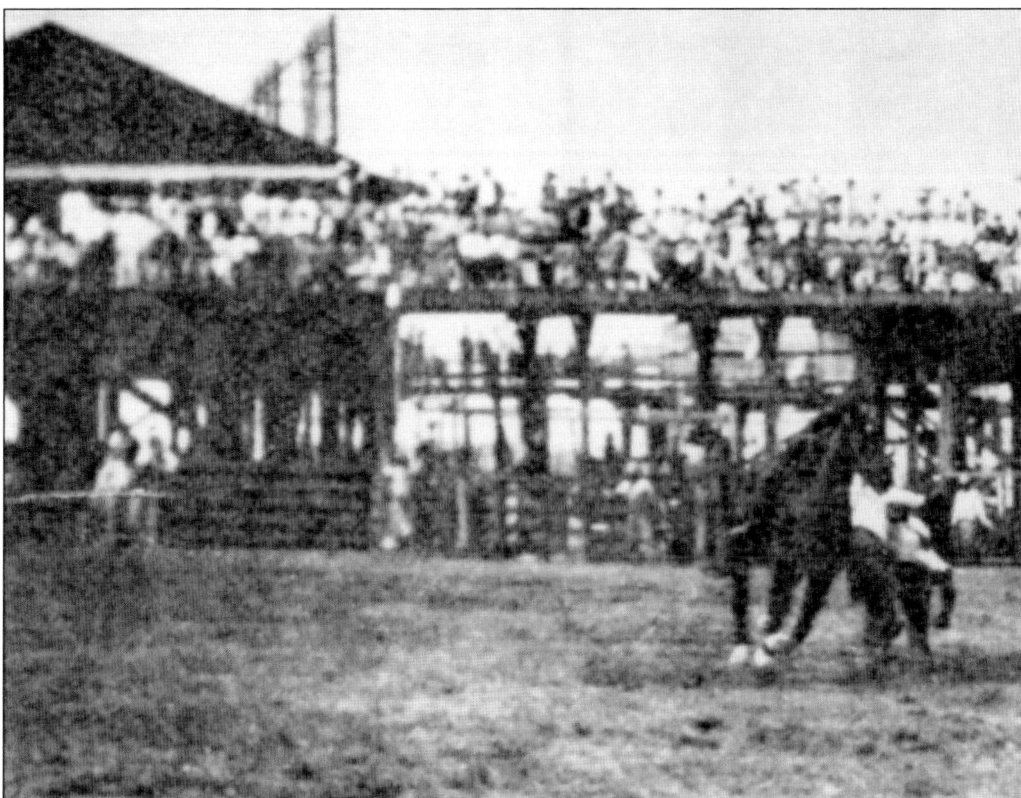

This photograph shows a water rodeo in the 1930s. La Porte and Sylvan Beach truly were where Texas met the sea. Grandstands were built so that visitors would not miss any of the activities.

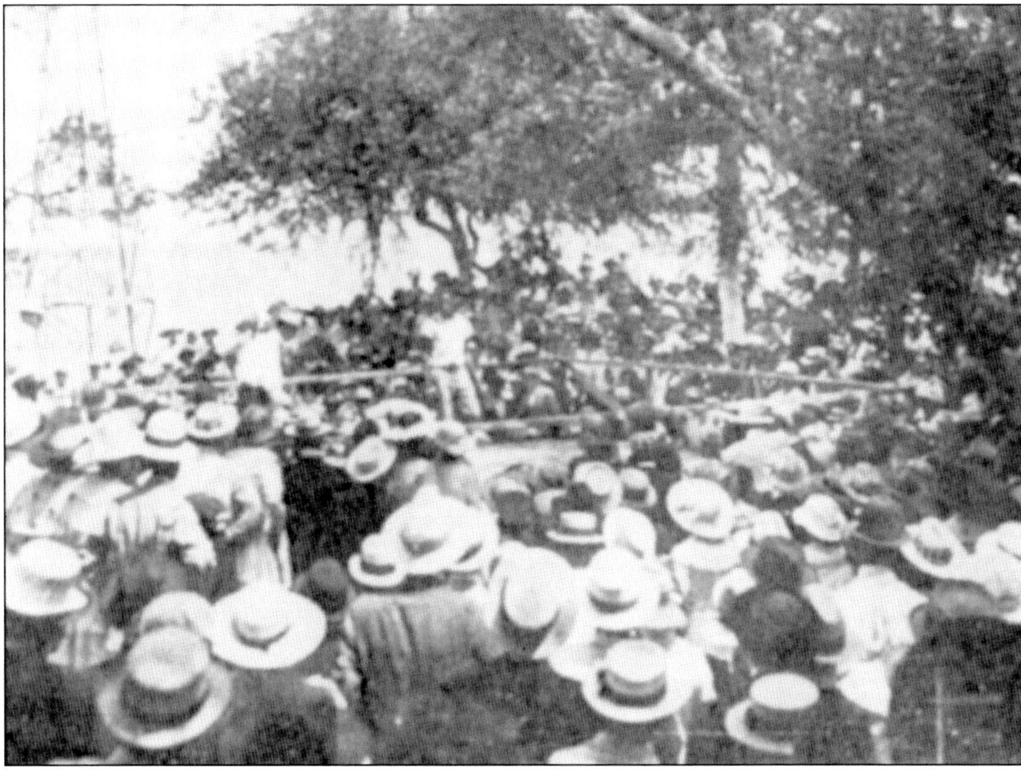

Owner E.L. Crain had to try to keep his investment at Sylvan Beach solvent. He was an accomplished developer and businessman from Houston; some of his developments are still respected residential areas. One of the promotions he tried at Sylvan Beach was live boxing matches.

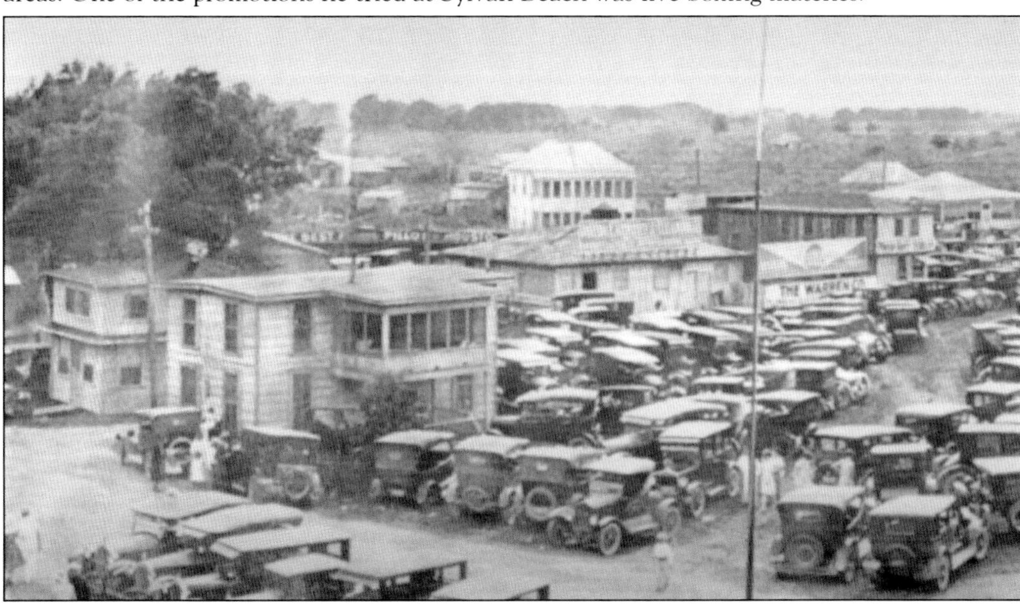

By the 1930s, although La Porte's main downtown development still hugged Main Street, the tourists and attractions at Sylvan Beach had drawn many businesses that provided various services and accommodations just off the Sylvan Beach property.

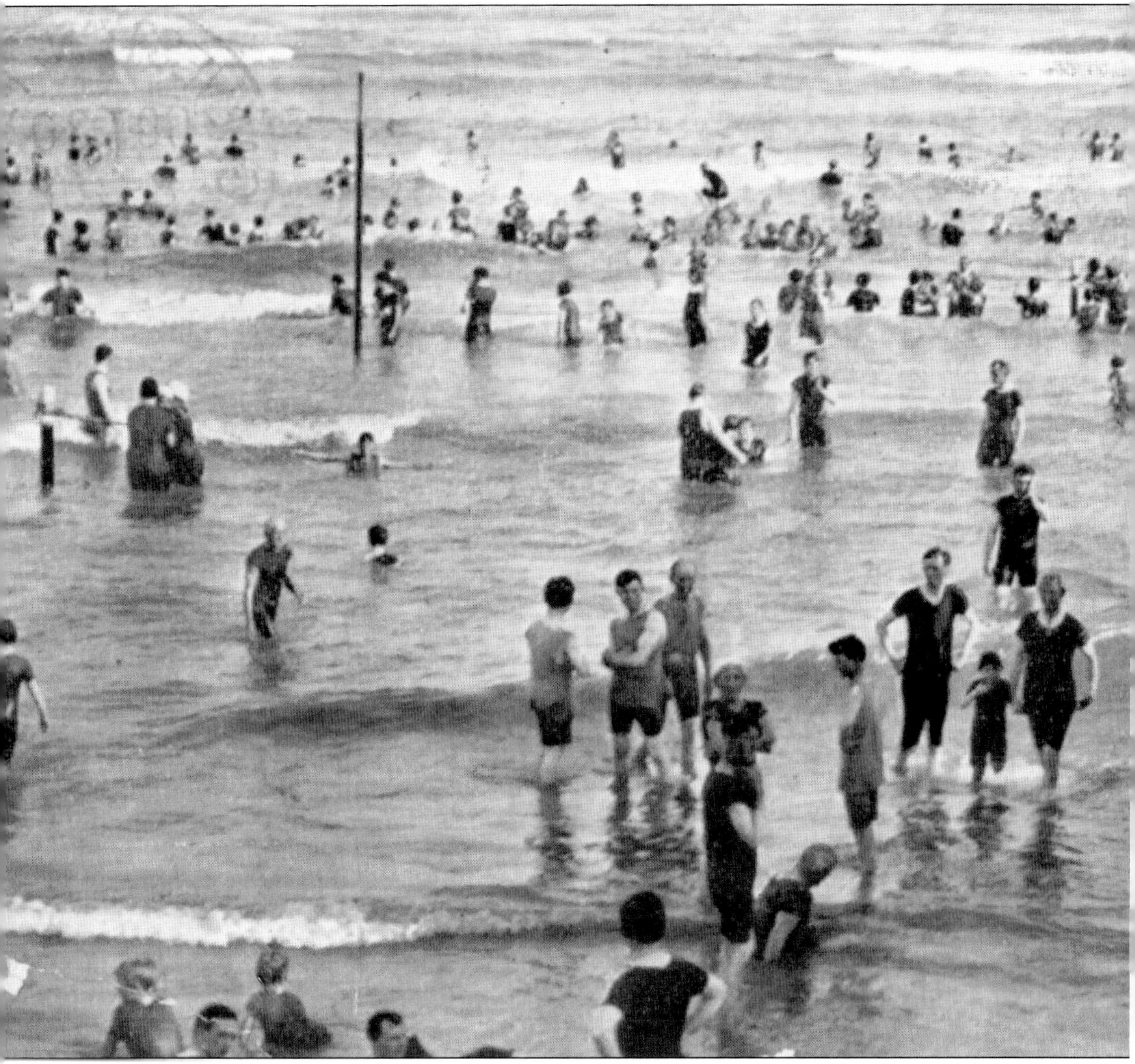

Even with all the attractions and promotions, the cool waters were still the main draw at Sylvan Beach. During the Depression, all businesses were having a hard time making ends meet.

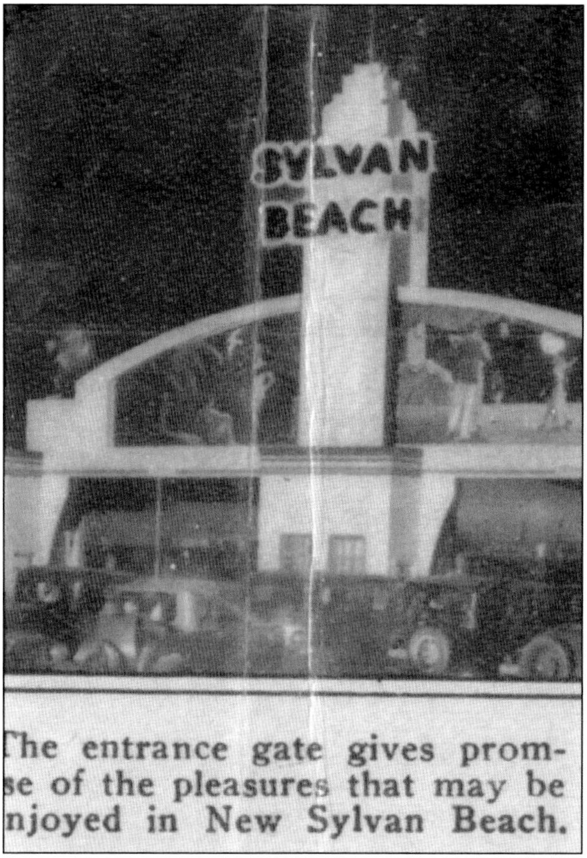

Sylvan Beach was always a family venue and never served alcohol. In the late 1920s and 1930s, throngs continued to drive to Sylvan Beach to enjoy music performed by some of the country's biggest names in entertainment.

Sylvan Beach had its own water tower (pictured below). The many cars shown in this image spelled trouble for the old railroad depot (visible in the background), which now houses the La Porte Bay Area Heritage Society.

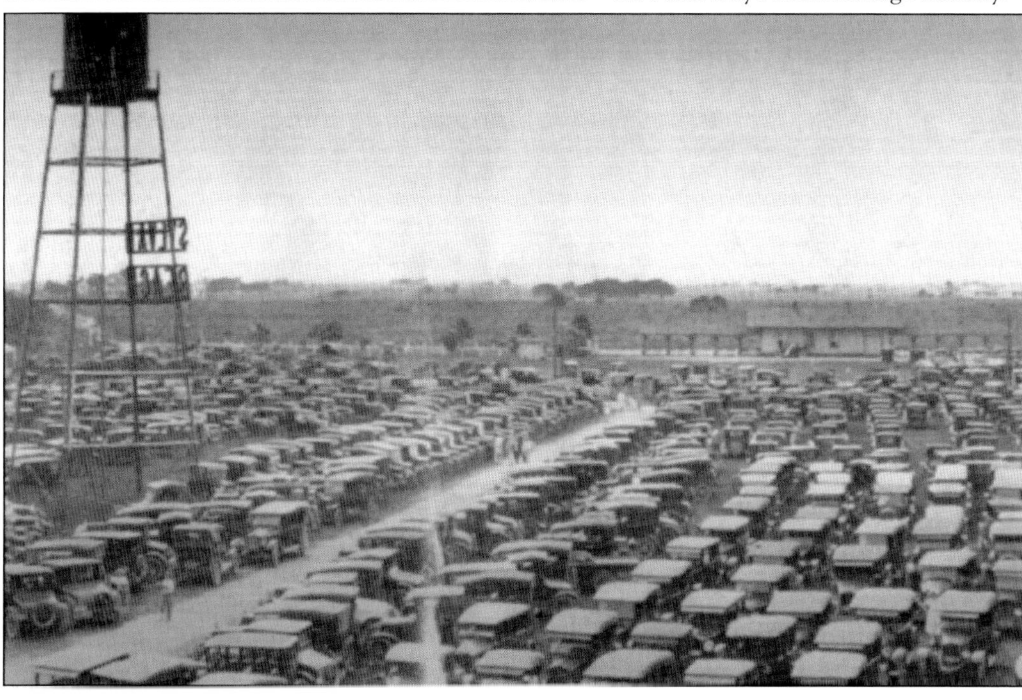

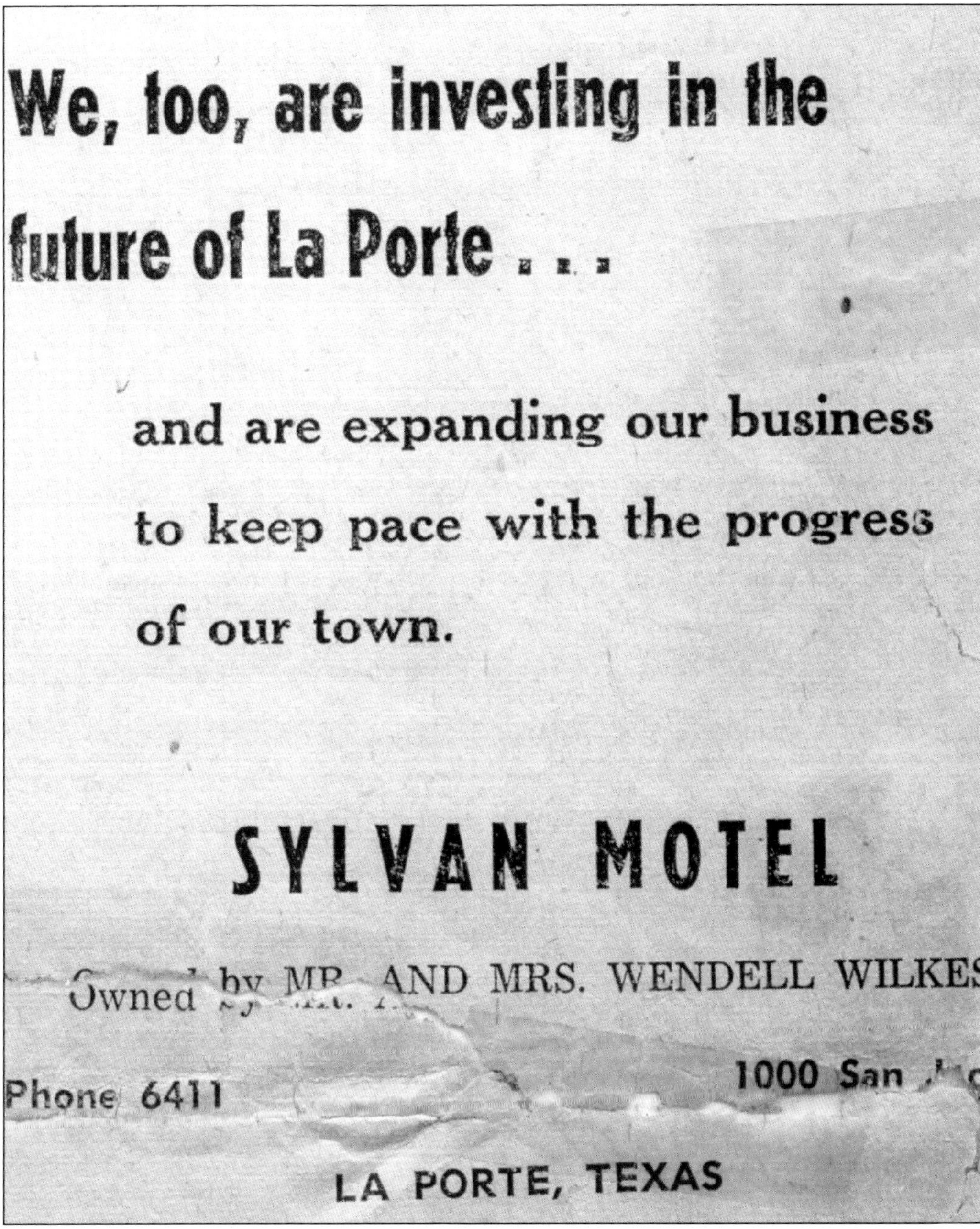

Around 1930, visitors could stay at the Sylvan Motel just a short walk away from Sylvan Beach Park. This is not to be confused with the Sylvan Hotel, which had been sold to St. Mary's Seminary in 1900.

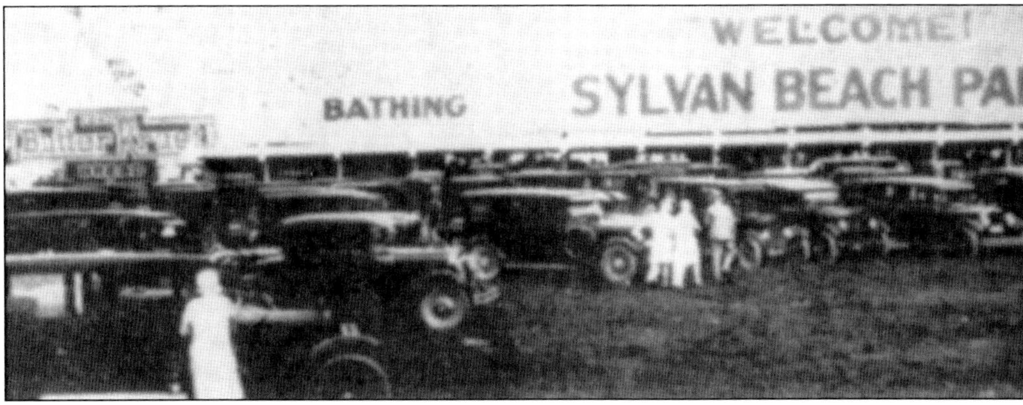

This picture shows people congregating at the entrance to Sylvan Beach Park in 1928. At that time, the automobile had already replaced the train as the primary way to get to the park.

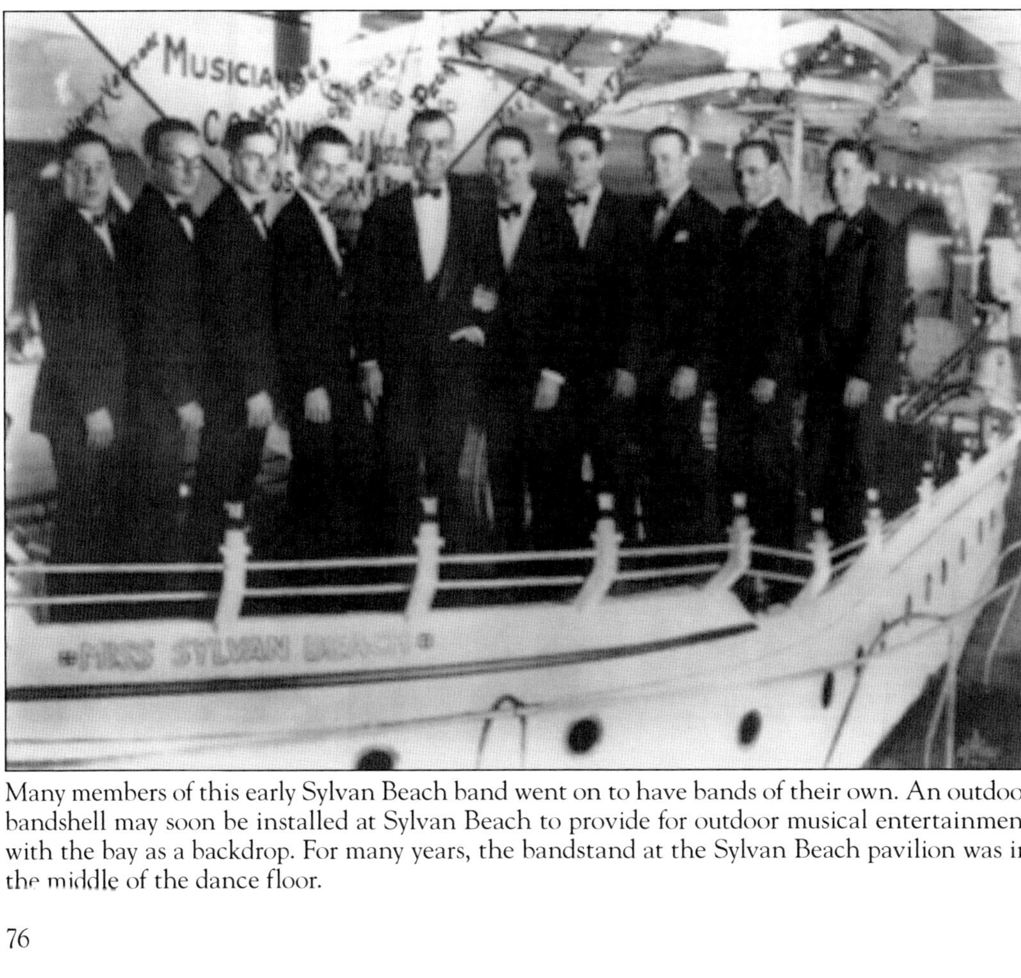

Many members of this early Sylvan Beach band went on to have bands of their own. An outdoor bandshell may soon be installed at Sylvan Beach to provide for outdoor musical entertainment with the bay as a backdrop. For many years, the bandstand at the Sylvan Beach pavilion was in the middle of the dance floor.

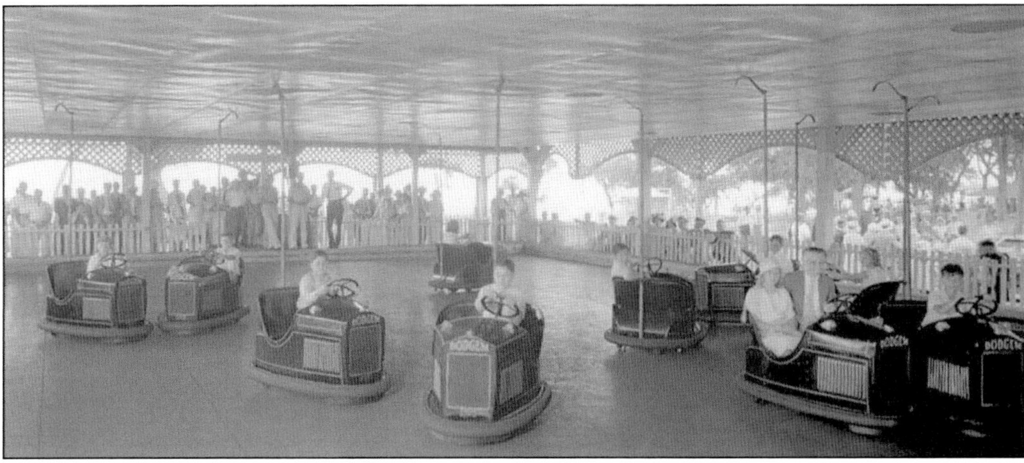

During the 1920s and 1930s, dodgem cars (aka bumper cars) were very popular. Park owner E.L. Crain wanted to include something for children to do off the boardwalk, so he put in numerous carnival-like rides for young people.

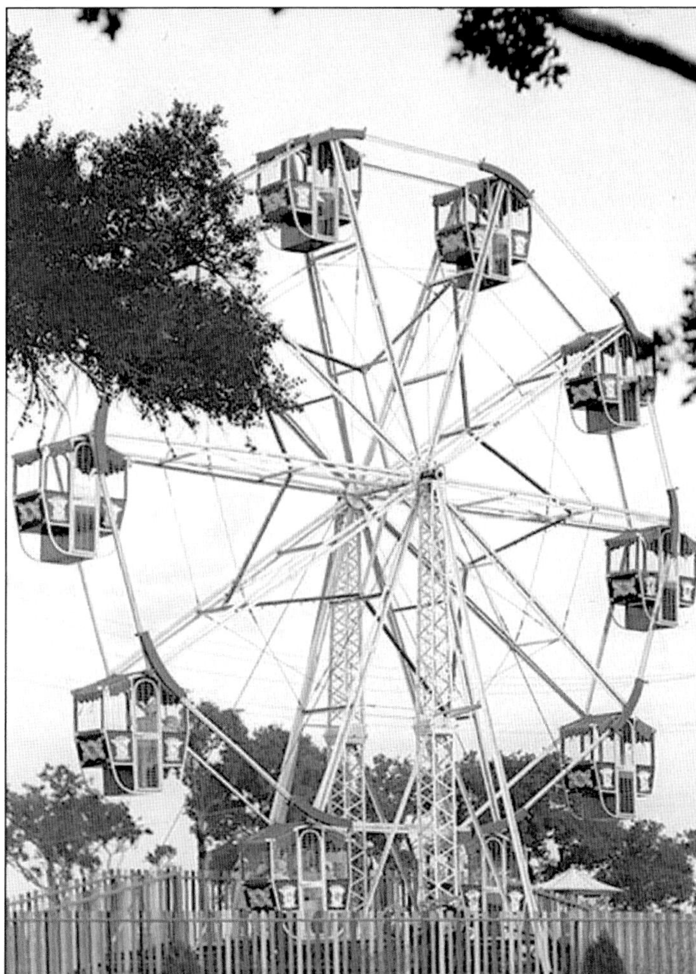

It is easy to see the appeal of a ride on the Ferris wheel on a summer night with the gulf breezes wafting over a rider and his date as they look out over the bay. A bigger Ferris wheel was one of the first amusements brought in by early owner G.D. Samuels, along with other rides. After it was taken down, the park had no rides for a time. Later owner Ed Eiseman added a new Ferris wheel and other rides to make Sylvan Beach a first-class resort. This picture was taken in 1942.

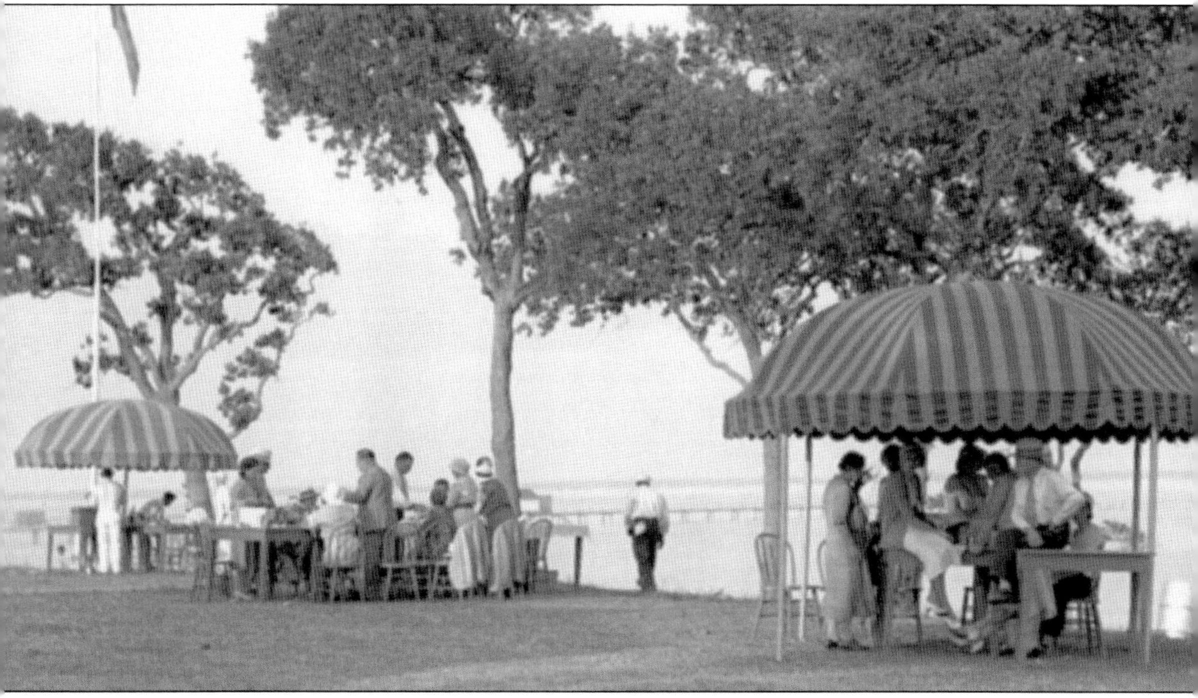

The boardwalk is visible in the background at left. Owner E.L. Crain extended the boardwalk, running it through the park all the way to the property of St. Mary's Seminary. Crain put lights and music outdoors along the boardwalk and throughout the park.

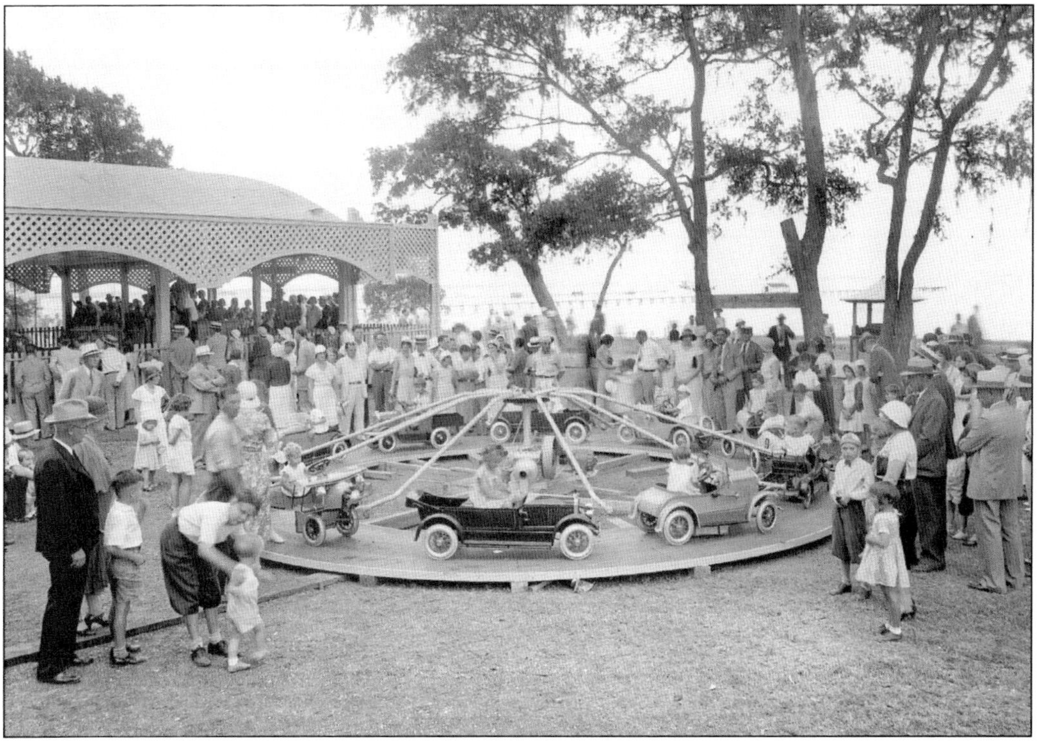

In the 1930s, the automobile had captured the popular imagination. Throughout owner E.L. Crain's tenure, additional roads were constructed to converge on the park, and Crain installed numerous amusement rides featuring cars. Crain also installed bus rides for the kids.

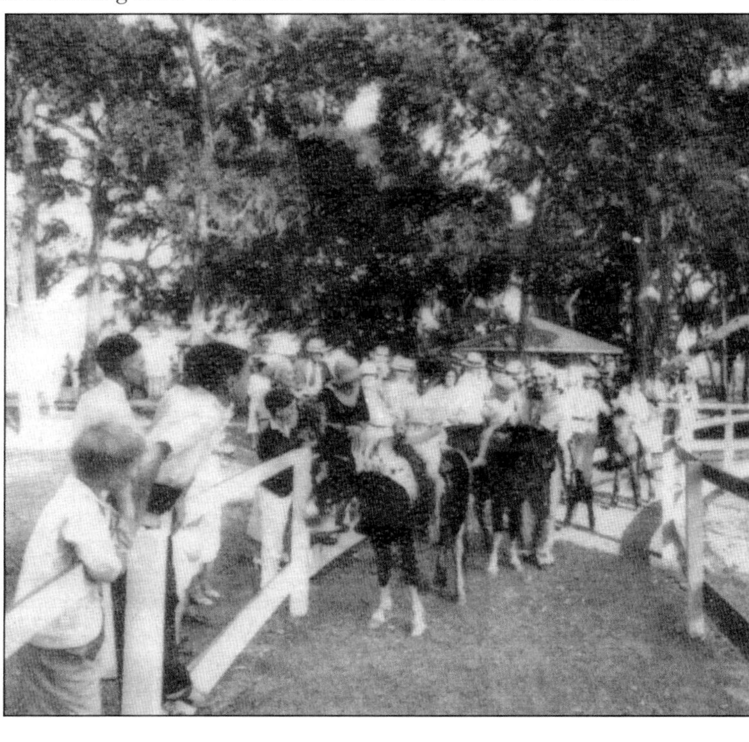

Crain also brought in pony and goat rides. Pony rides had been entertainment for children at Sylvan Beach before. The pony rides—in fact, all of the rides, as well as the concession stands—flanked the wooden boardwalk built by Crain.

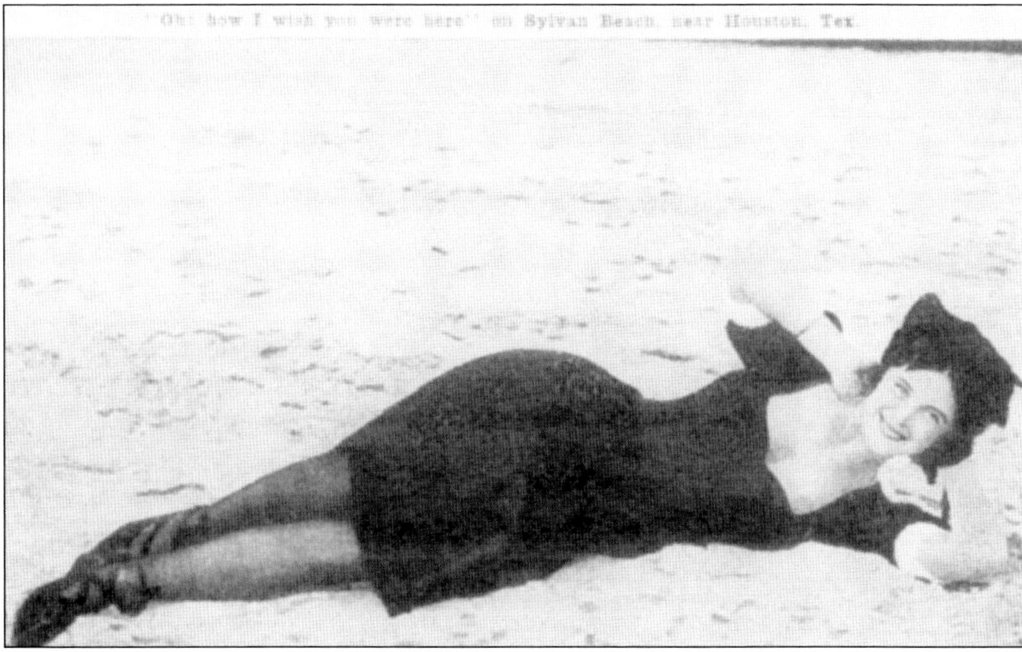

This popular postcard from the 1930s reads: "'Oh, how I wish you were here' on Sylvan Beach, near Houston, Tex." Fellows just had to make sure "here" had the second "e" before mailing this card to their girlfriends.

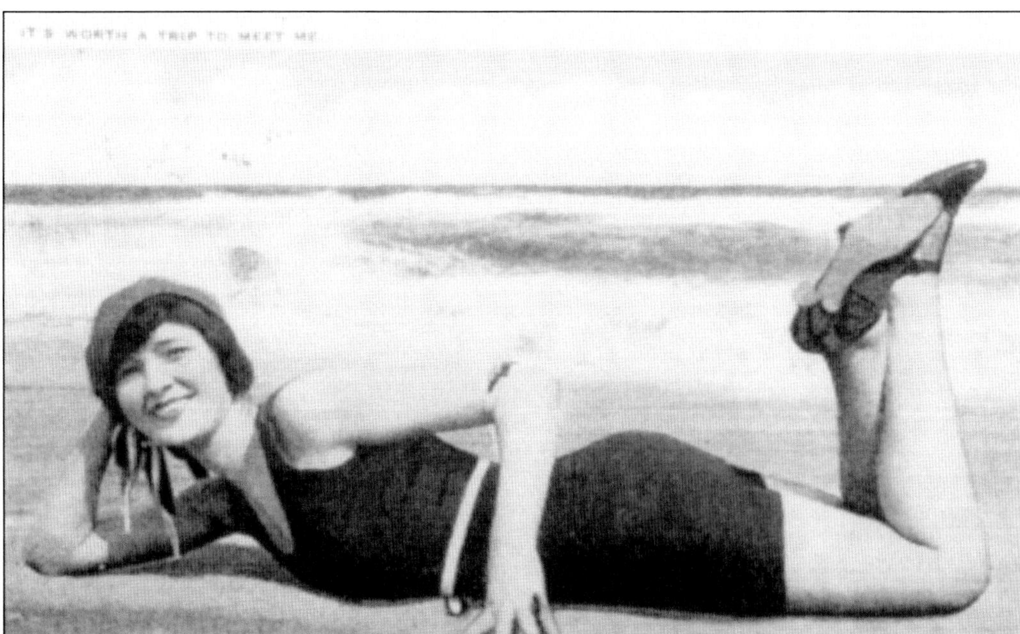

This is another 1930s postcard featuring Sylvan Beach. High heels were not practical footwear on the beach—unless a woman was posing for a postcard. The card reads: "It's worth a trip to meet me."

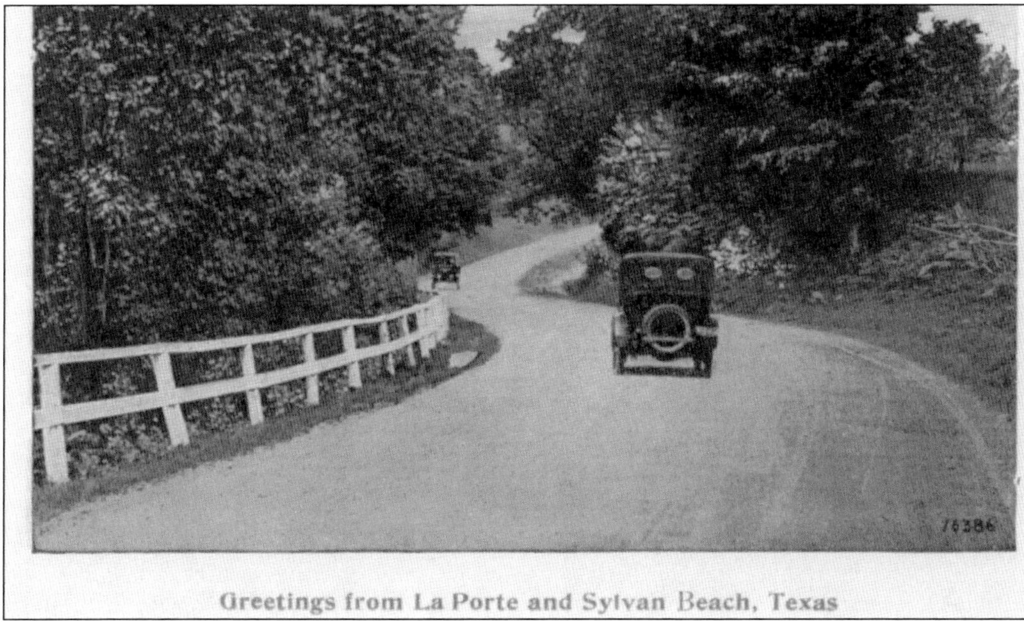

This postcard allegedly depicting Sylvan Beach shows hills that were never in the area. A person cannot always believe what he or she sees on postcards.

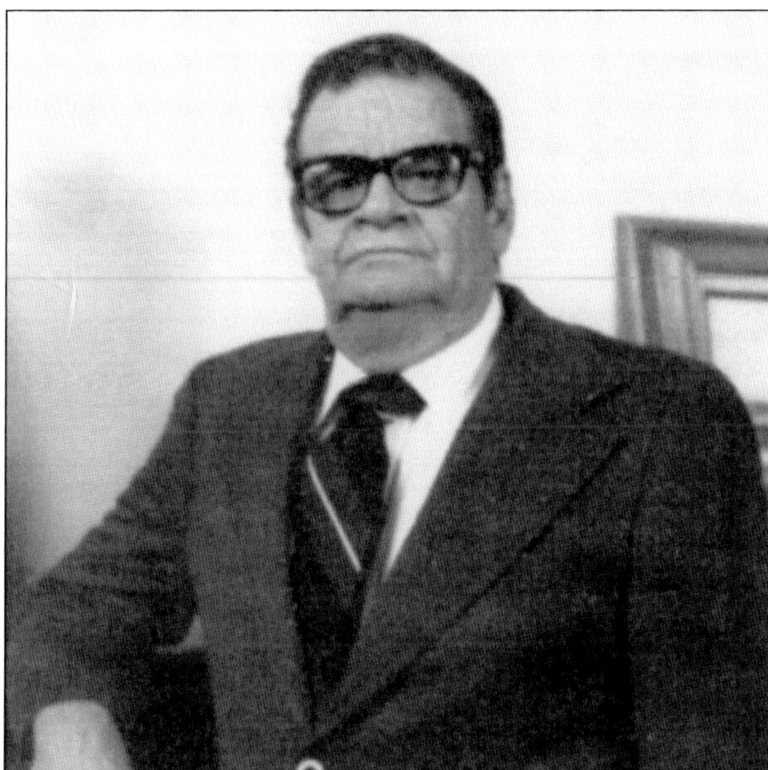

When locals think of Port Theater, they may immediately picture L.R. "Doodles" Rigby; to children in La Porte, he was "Mr. Rigby." He did not just manage the theater but was also involved in city activities. He was city commissioner, mayor pro tem, and filled in as mayor of the city for a short while. His son Louis is now mayor of La Porte.

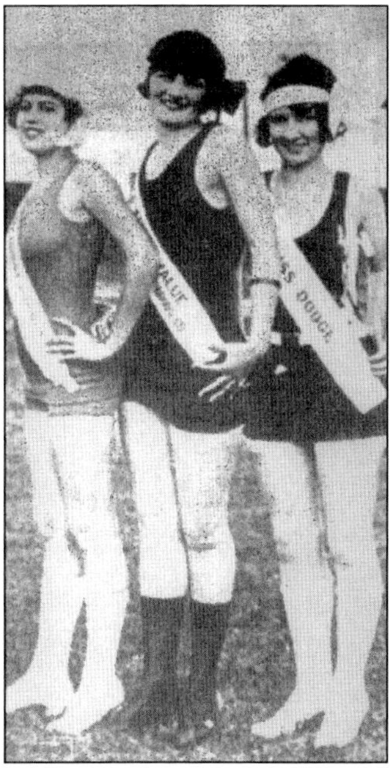

These are three of the young women who joined the ranks of the hundreds that entered the Sylvan Beach bathing beauty contests over the years.

The bathing beauty contests continue to this day. The contest has operated both independently and, at one time, as a franchise of the Miss Texas Pageant. This photograph is from the early 1930s.

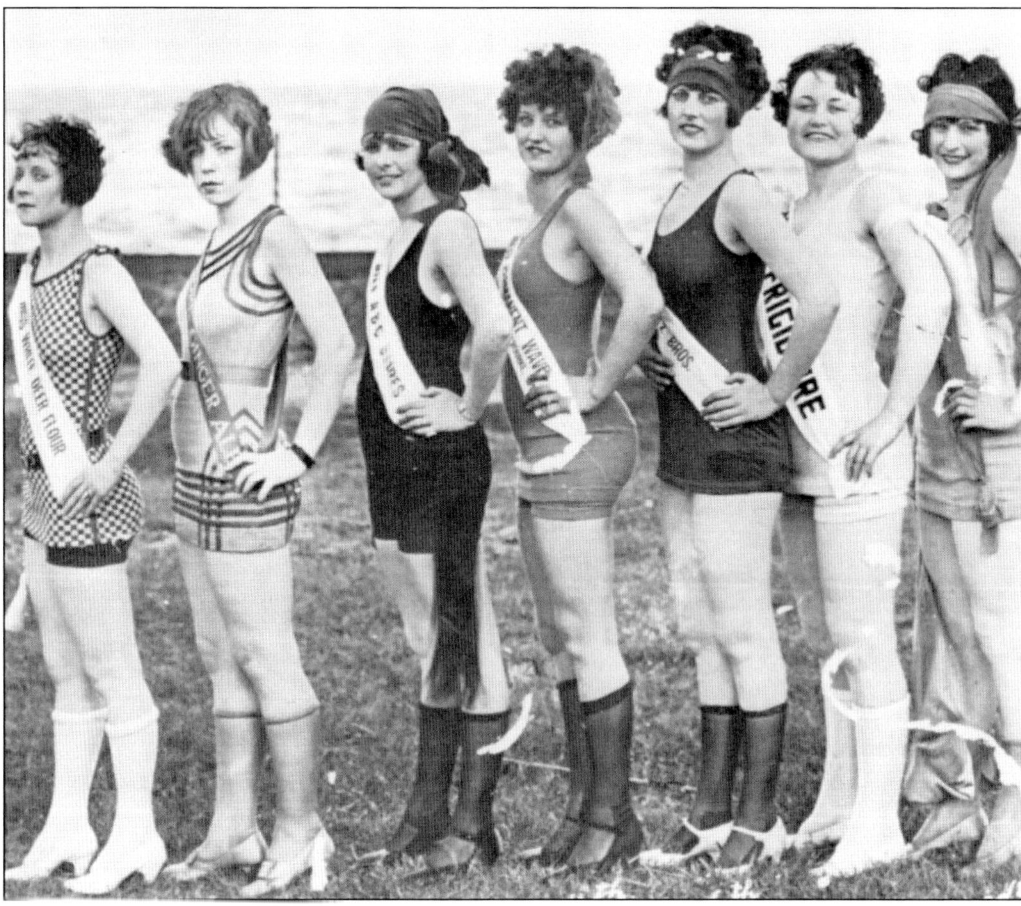

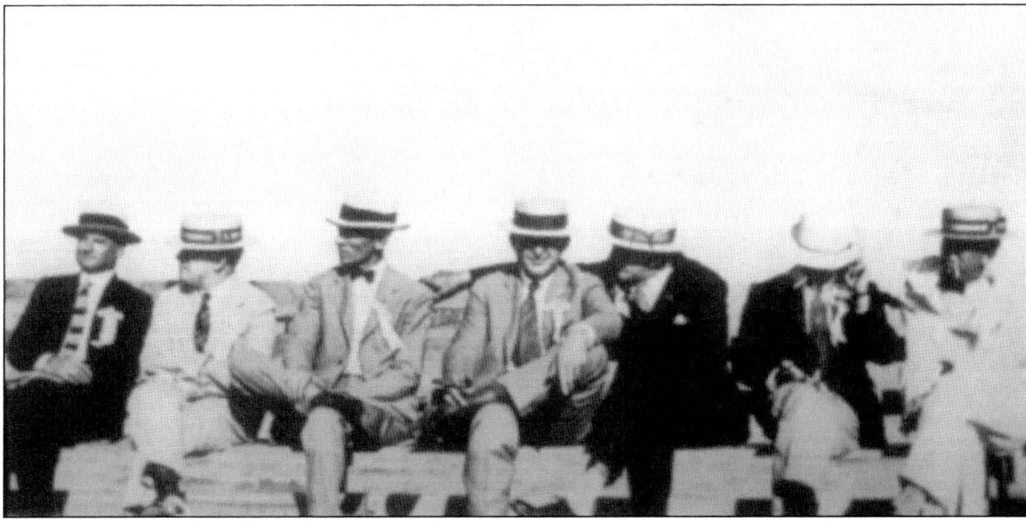

These gentlemen—dignitaries from Harris County, including the mayor of La Porte—were the judges for the first Sylvan Beach bathing beauty pageant in 1924.

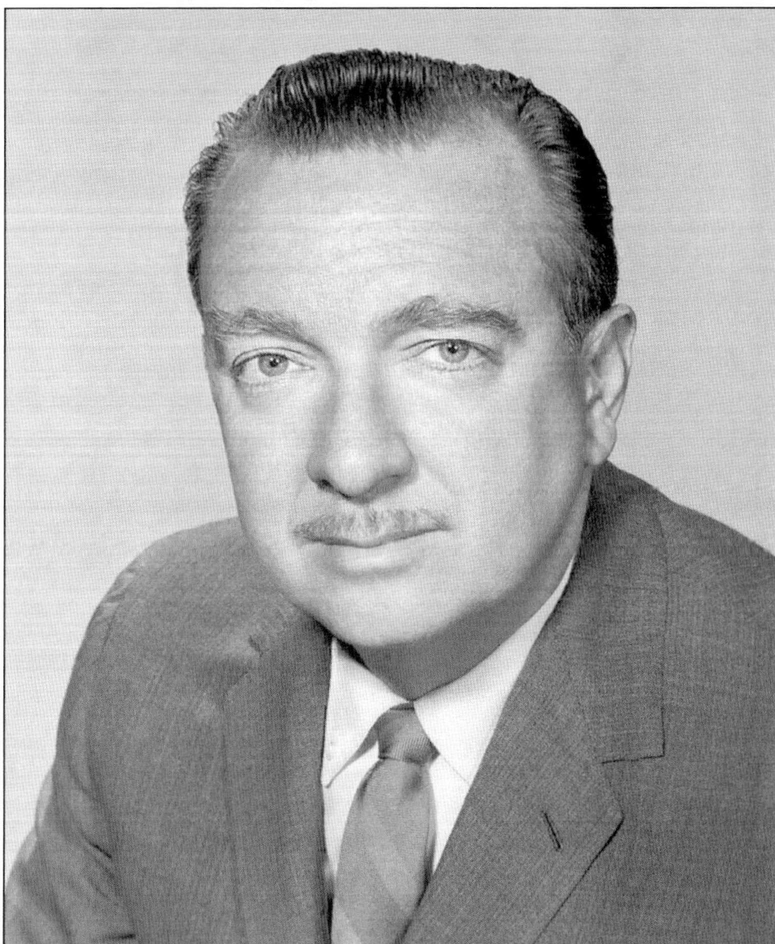

Future newsman Walter Cronkite, who lived in Houston during his teen years, sold hamburgers as a summer job at Sylvan Beach. Future lawyer Richard "Racehorse" Haynes also spent time at Sylvan Beach, and future surgeon Denton Cooley was a frequent visitor.

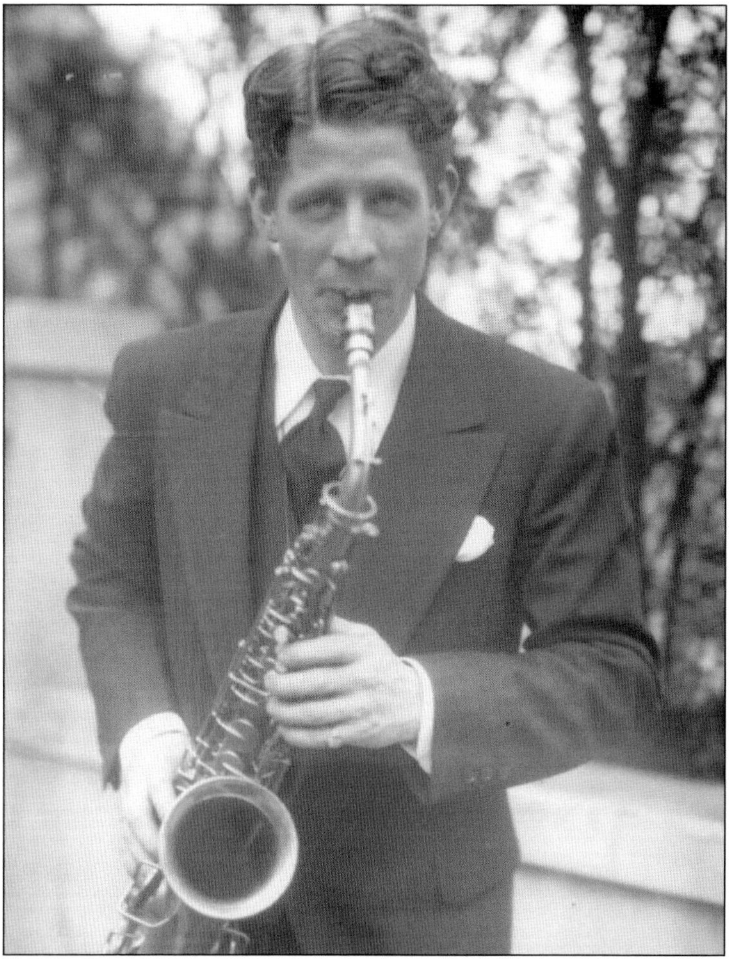

Rudy Vallee and the Connecticut Yankees was one of the first big bands to play at Sylvan Beach. Vallee arrived in a large car with his band and stayed at the hotel. Years later, he said he still remembered Sylvan Beach very fondly.

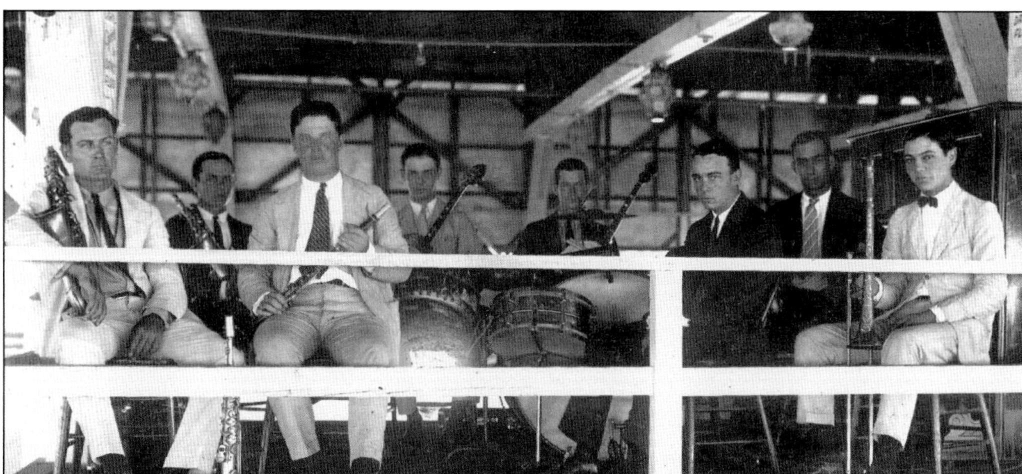

This is Peck's Bad Boys, one of the local bands that played for dancers at Sylvan Beach. The dance pavilion was open, and music from the different bands drifted out over the water. Peck Kelly, the leader of Peck's Bad Boys, frequently played Sylvan Beach.

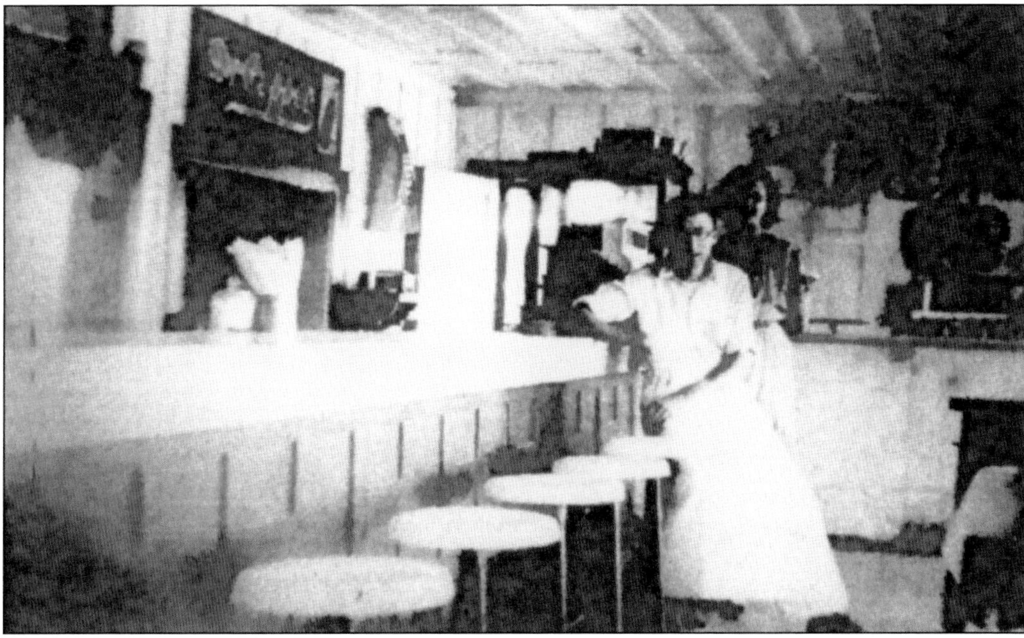

After paying rent for a couple of years, Donald and Lena David purchased the Sharp's Ice Cream Parlor across from the Sylvan Beach gate and converted it to a restaurant, Dave's Sandwich Shop, which Donald operated until his death in 1952. Donald's older brother, Pete, also moved to La Porte and built Pete's Sandwich Shop across from Bo & Maries' Restaurant. Donald and Lena had two sons, Donald Jr. and Raymond, who both still reside in La Porte.

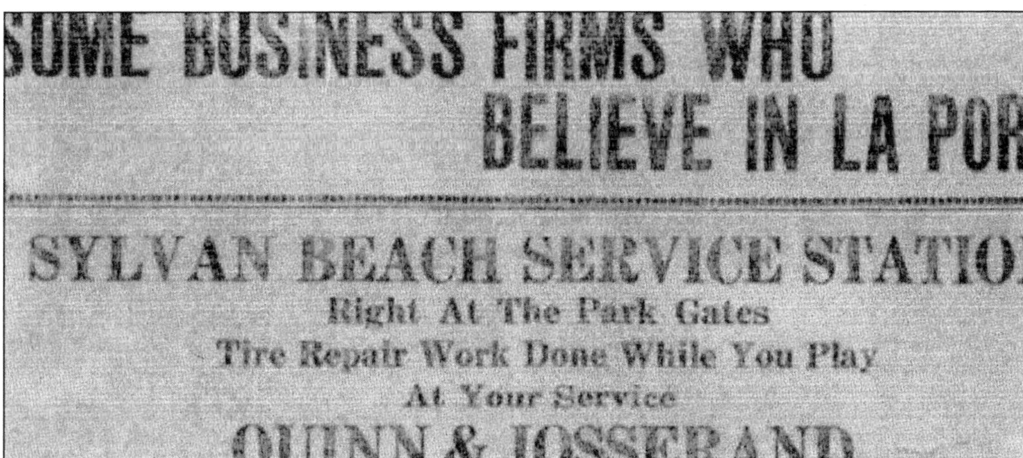

Many businesses were very close to Sylvan Beach Park. Here is an advertisement for one located "right at the park gates" that would get "repair work done while you play."

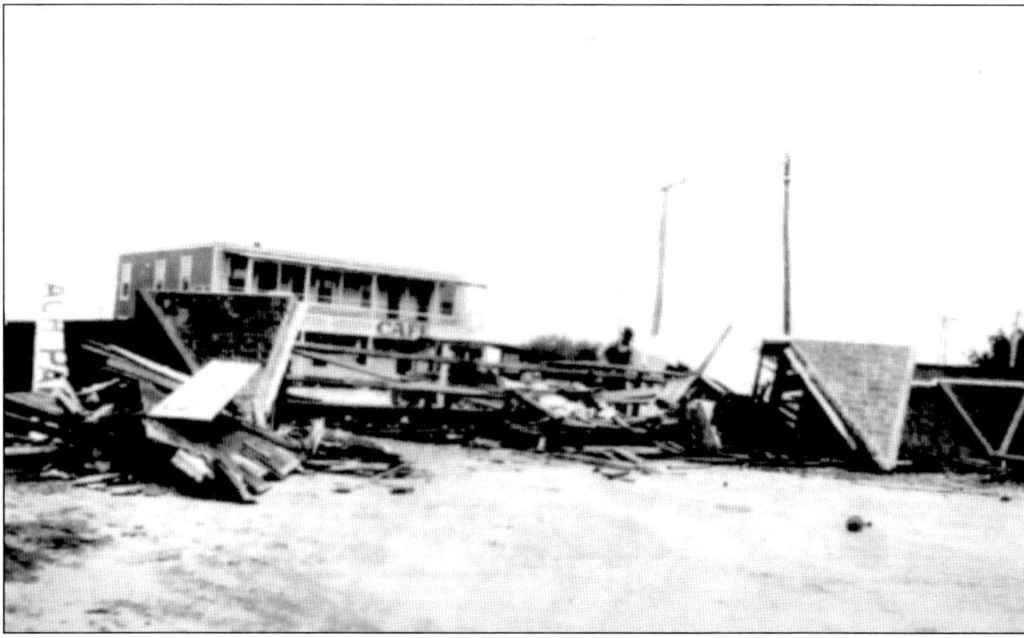

The 1915 storm, one of the worst in La Porte history, destroyed G.D. Samuels' entrance gates and his hope for Sylvan Beach. A discouraged Samuels left Sylvan Beach shortly thereafter. Less than a year later, Houston businessman Ed Eiseman bought the park and had great plans for it.

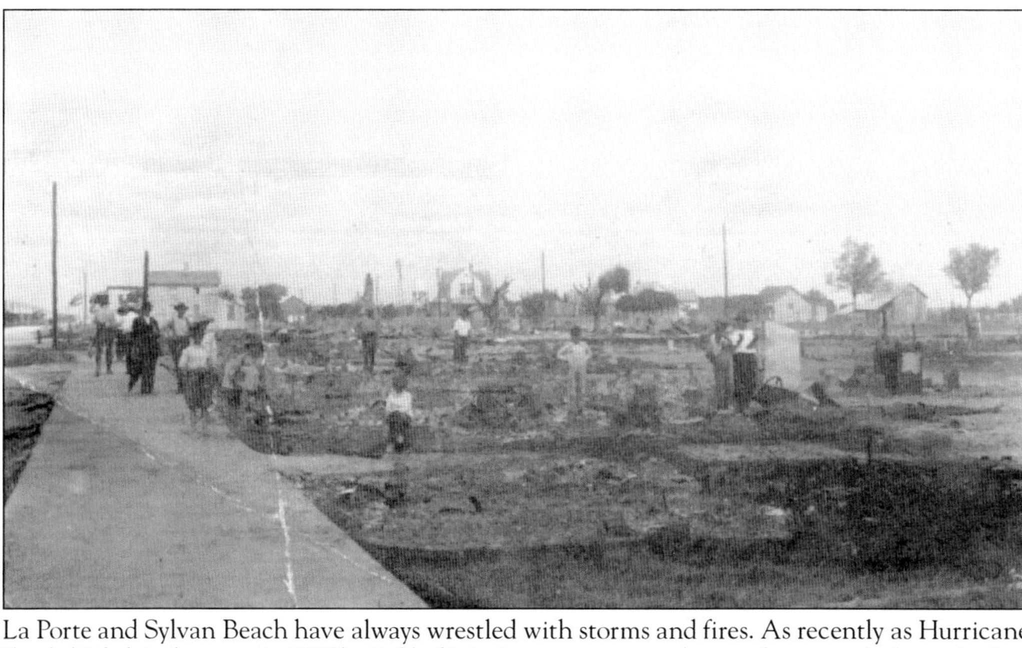

La Porte and Sylvan Beach have always wrestled with storms and fires. As recently as Hurricane Ike (which hit the area in 2008), Gulf of Mexico storm surges have taken vessels from the bay and deposited them on the streets of Sylvan Beach and La Porte.

Five

WATER, WIND, AND FIRE

J.H. York was the first mayor of La Porte. He built a beautiful mansion a couple hundred yards from the current entrance to Sylvan Beach; the house was called Grasmere. On May 14, 1946, after surviving numerous hurricanes, it was struck by lightning and burned to the ground. As discussed in previous chapters, despite massive hurricanes in 1893, 1900, 1941, 1943, 1983, and 2008, plus scores of smaller (but still deadly) storms, Sylvan Beach has always been rebuilt.

Fires like the one that burned the York mansion or the 1915 fire that destroyed much of downtown La Porte also frequently damaged parts of Sylvan Beach, but undeterred men and women kept Sylvan Beach coming back like a phoenix rising from the ashes. Two of the greatest and most intrinsic American virtues define Sylvan Beach and its history: hope and optimism. The same hope and optimism that led to La Porte's founding and the dredging of the Houston Ship Channel have driven the perseverance of the many La Porte and Harris County officials and groups like Friends of the Sylvan Beach Pavilion and the La Porte Bay Area Heritage Society to preserve Sylvan Beach and its beautiful pavilions.

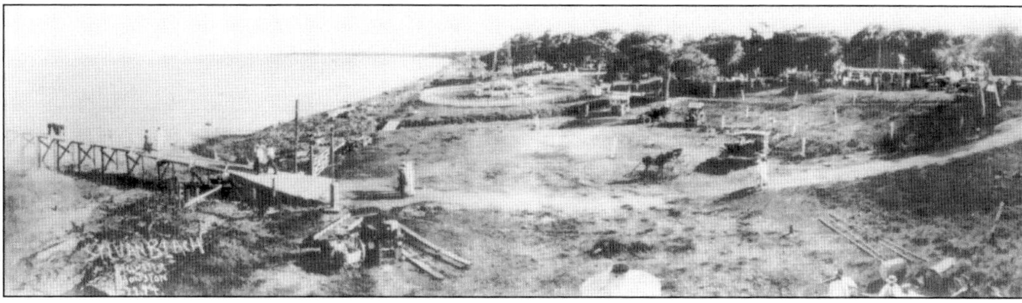

The Grove, or Sylvan Grove, as the park was initially known, was first operated by the founders of the city of La Porte and the syndicate that bought the land for the town. By 1895, a free pier and dancing floor, as well as picnic facilities, adorned the beachfront. People came by horse and buggy, or down Buffalo Bayou, the San Jacinto River, and Trinity Bay to Galveston Bay and the Sylvan Beach Pier by boat or by train via the Southern Pacific Line that became known as the La Porte, Houston & Northern Railroad, which went to Harrisburg, then to Deer Park, then into downtown La Porte, and finally to Sylvan Beach. The national depression that crippled the country and the Great Storm of 1900, as well as title problems, eventually put the city founders in litigation with a Galveston mortgage firm talking over the ownership of the park during the early years of the century. The Galveston mortgage firm Adoue and Lobit obtained the park and then sold it to G.D. Samuels in 1909. He built cottages, rebuilt the pier, and constructed the beautiful entrance gate. Another disastrous hurricane struck in 1915, and the rubble pictured below is all that remained of Samuels' gate. Shortly thereafter, a discouraged Samuels sold the park to Ed Eiseman and his company, the Sylvan Beach Bath and Hotel Company.

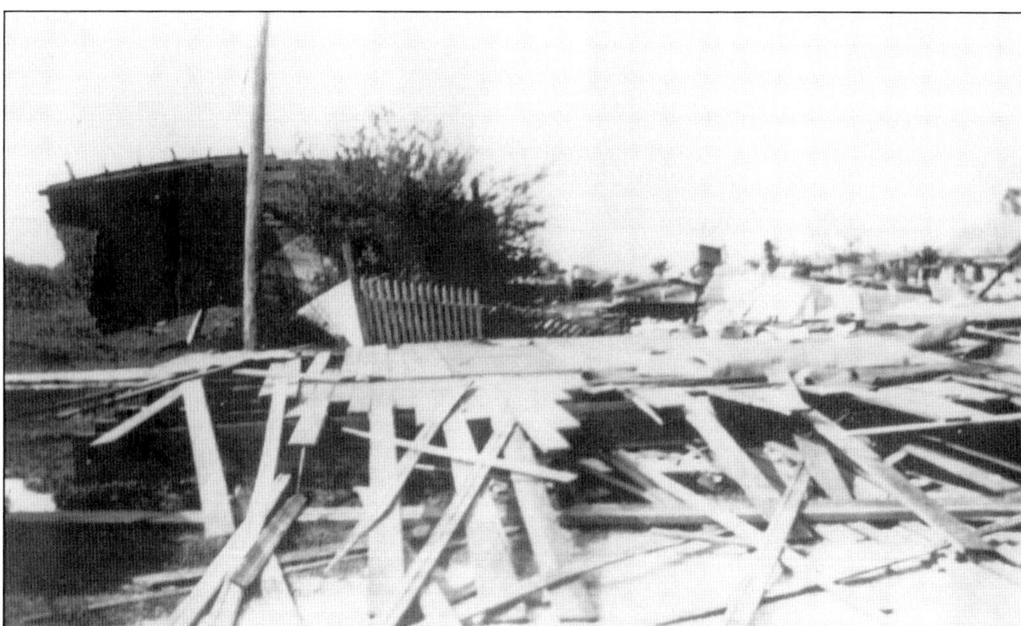

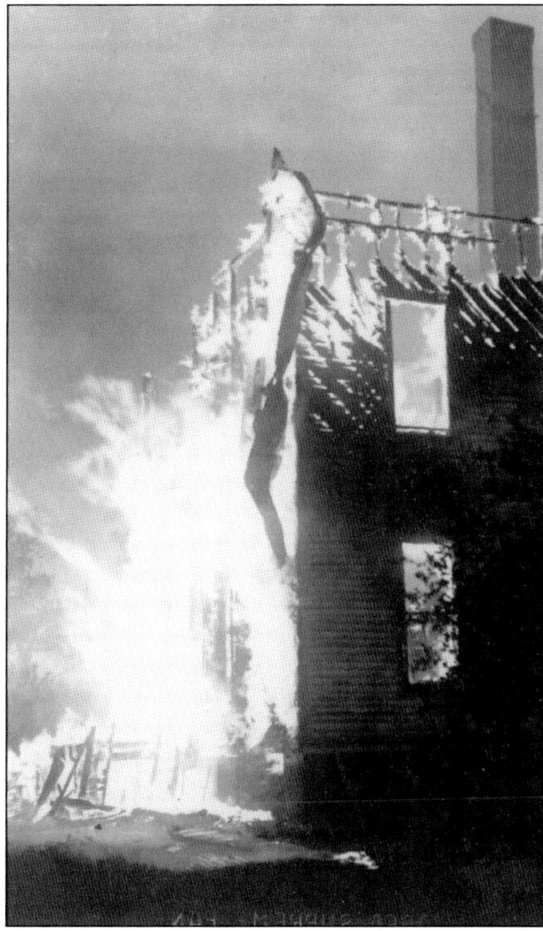

Fire was a constant and repeated danger in early La Porte. The city was severely damaged by fire in 1893 and again in 1898. Madame Besson came from London to the 1893 World's Fair in Chicago, where the city fathers had a booth promoting La Porte. She was so impressed she purchased several properties and commissioned the Besson Building at Second and Main Streets. A beautiful three-story brick structure, it was the pride of La Porte. A back room on the first floor contained a facility for fueling cars with gasoline stored in barrels inside the building. It is believed that the fire that destroyed La Porte in 1915 began in that back room of the Besson Building. The picture at right shows flames engulfing the Besson Building in the 1915 fire. The image below shows the carnage and destruction wrought in downtown La Porte by the same fire.

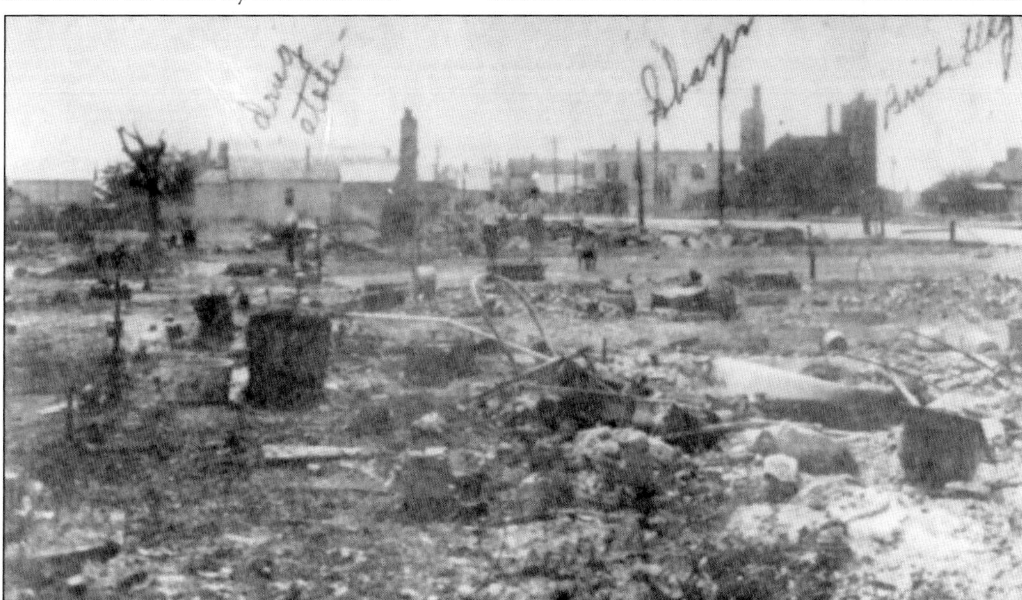

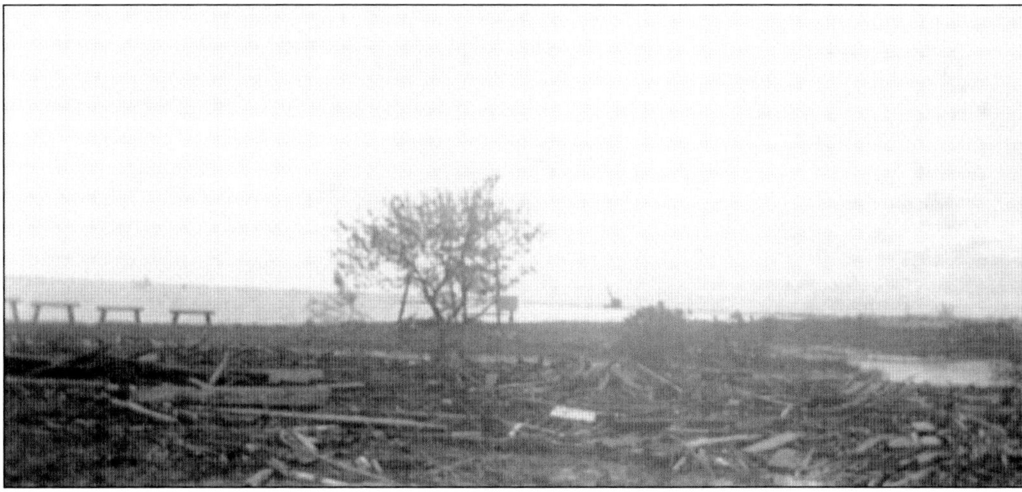

In 1930, Ed Eiseman sold Sylvan Beach Park to E.L. Crain, a prominent Houston builder. Crain promptly spent $100,000 on improvements to the park. He built a 16-foot-wide plank boardwalk that spanned from the dance pavilion to the St. Mary's Seminary property, which abutted Sylvan Beach Park. The boardwalk was 500 feet long; along the sides of it, Crain installed a merry-go-round, a Ferris wheel, goat and pony rides, an airplane swing ride, a children's playground and wading pool, tables and concessions, and a miniature train with rubber wheels. The rebuilt pier was 1,600 feet long, and the pavilion was renovated, remodeled, and enclosed in glass. A grand reopening occurred in 1936. Crain placed John Carter, formerly chief steward of the Houston Country Club, in charge of the pavilion, and Monta Beach was hostess of the dance hall. The great hurricanes of 1941 and 1943 decimated the park. The photograph above shows damage to park structures after the 1941 hurricane, and the photograph below shows how the same hurricane damaged Crain's pier. Shortly after the 1943 hurricane, Crain sold the rides and gave up on operations at Sylvan Beach Park.

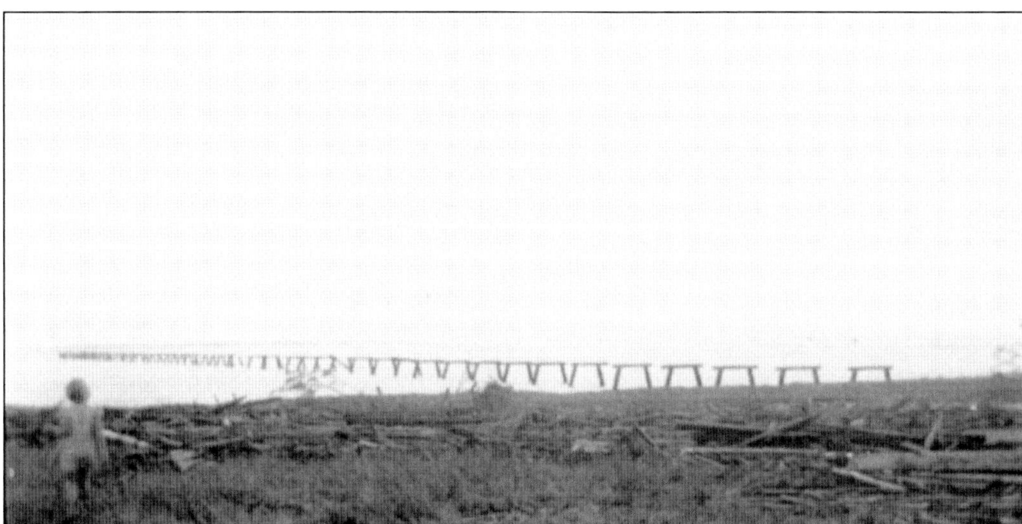

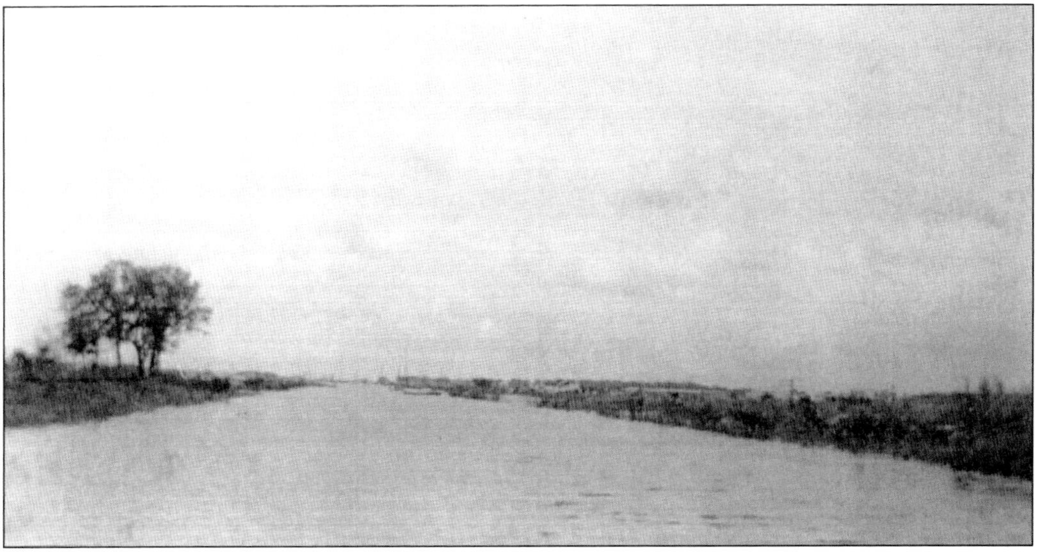

By 1943, the overwhelming majority of visitors to Sylvan Beach Park came by car. The photograph above shows a road providing egress to the park temporarily turned into a river by the 1941 hurricane. The image below shows a truck upended by the 1943 hurricane. Crain had offered to sell the park to the city of La Porte for $300,000, but the city was still recovering from the Great Depression and could not buy it. For a time, Crain leased the park to M.J. Buest of Houston, who booked many of the biggest names of the big band era to play at the park—Rudy Vallee, Bobby Meeker, Tommy Dorsey, Ted Weems, Ted Fio Rito, Phil Harris, Nick Stuart, Ozzie Nelson, and Herbie Kay (whose girlfriend Dorothy Lamour would sometimes show up to dance). But the one-two punch of the 1941 and 1943 hurricanes, in a time of war, led Crain to the decision to not rebuild after the 1943 hurricane, and the land lay largely dormant for the next 10 years.

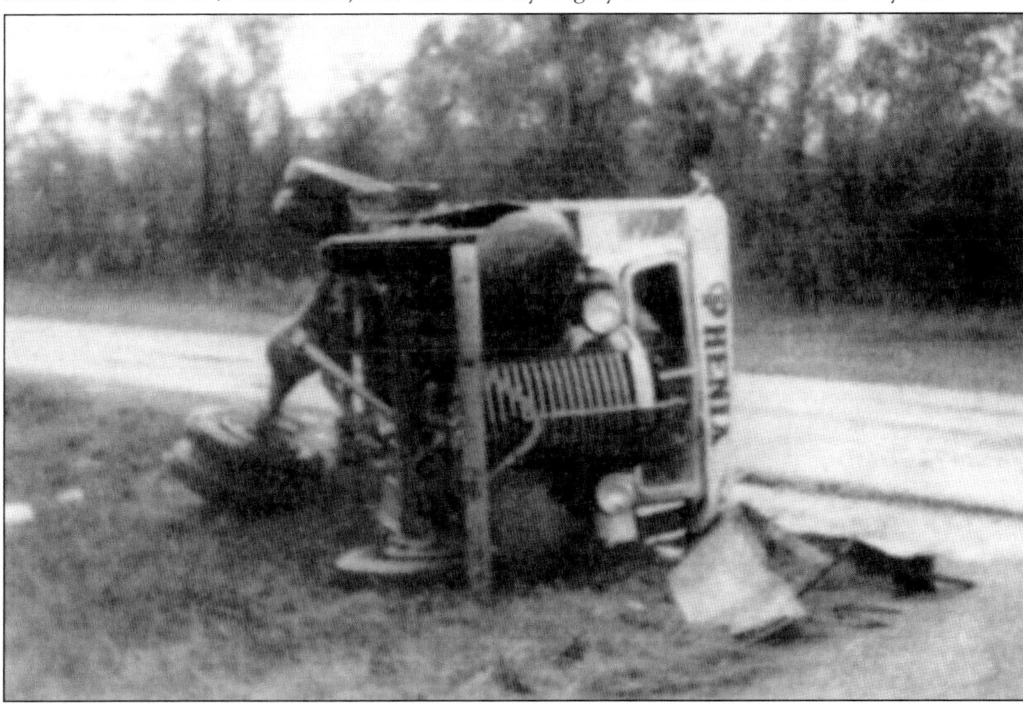

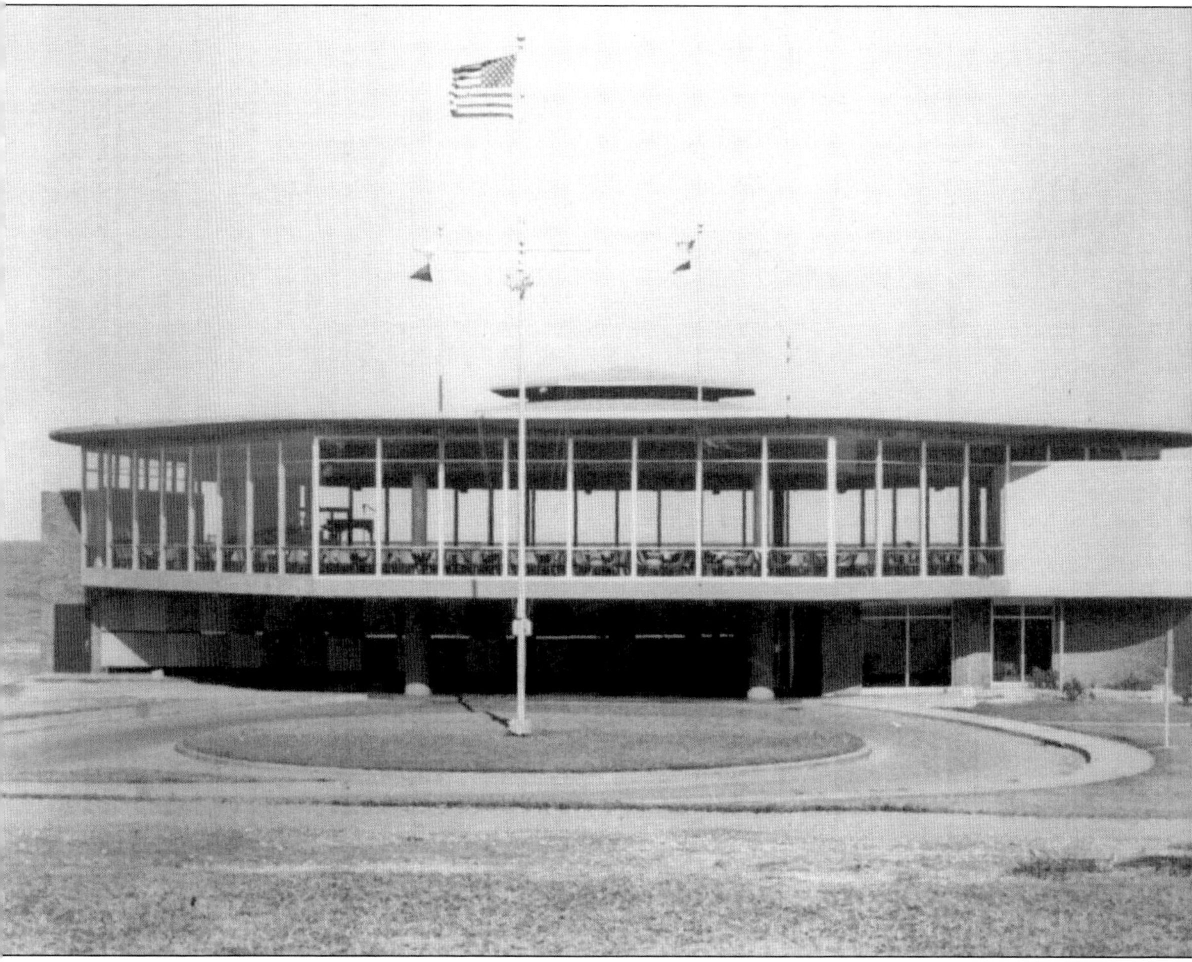

By 1948, the city of La Porte was actively lobbying Harris County to buy Sylvan Beach Park from the estate of E.L. Crain, and around 1950, the county began the purchase of the park. In 1954, Harris County began reconstruction on the Sylvan Beach Pavilion. The pavilion, which was finished in 1956 and still stands, was originally built with a ground-level entrance beneath the ballroom, a first-floor musician's dressing room and a men's restroom, a ramp to the main stairs, and a foyer on the second floor next to the ballroom. The ballroom and outside terrace were built on piers so that the ballroom and terrace offered the illusion of dancing or sitting above the waters of Galveston Bay. As shown in this picture, Hurricane Carla, which hit the area in 1961, made that illusion a reality and left the Sylvan Beach Pavilion literally in Galveston Bay. After that storm, a 13-foot long levee was built (and remains to this day) to protect the structure from storm surges of future hurricanes. The levee has been successful in that regard.

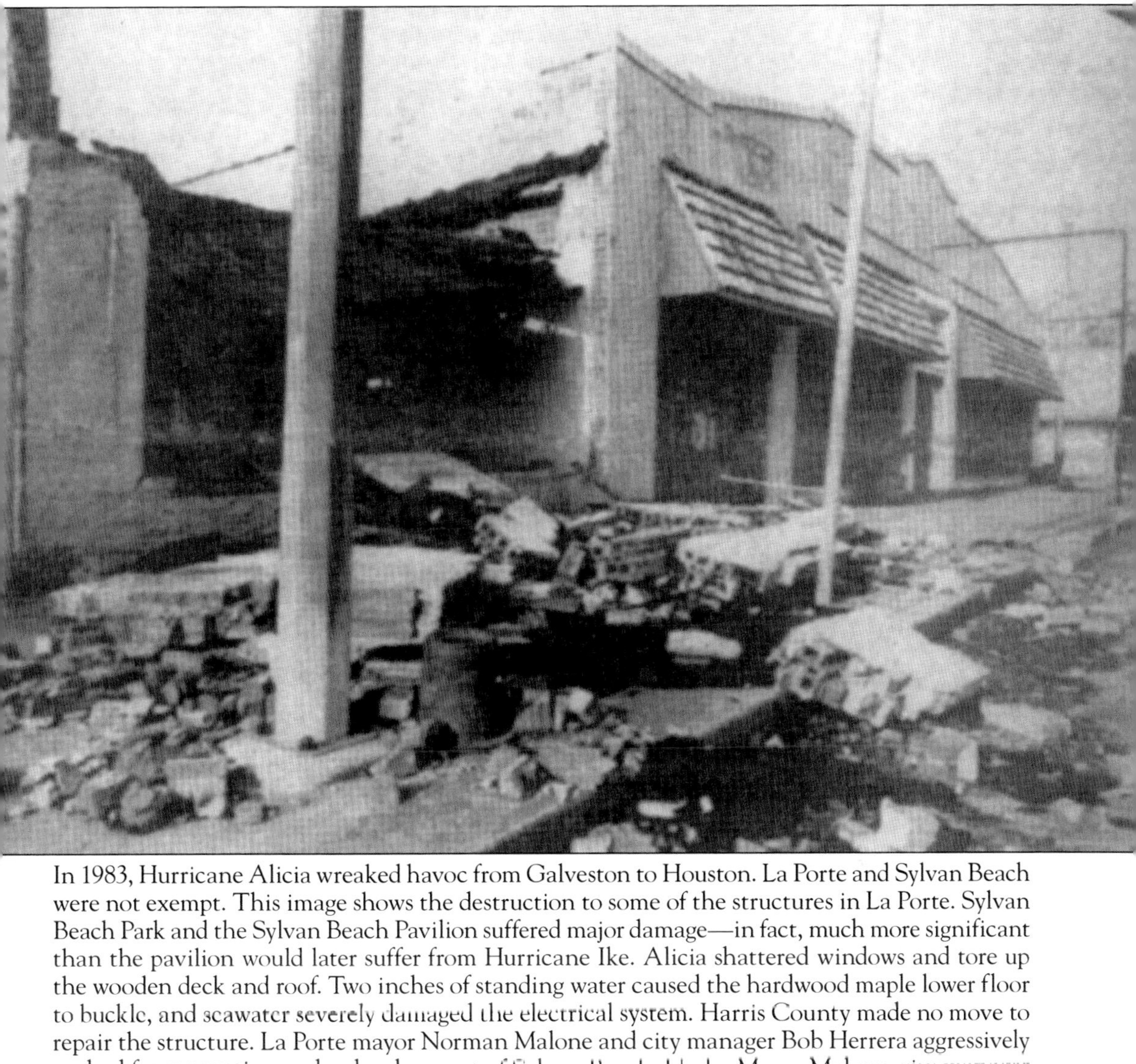

In 1983, Hurricane Alicia wreaked havoc from Galveston to Houston. La Porte and Sylvan Beach were not exempt. This image shows the destruction to some of the structures in La Porte. Sylvan Beach Park and the Sylvan Beach Pavilion suffered major damage—in fact, much more significant than the pavilion would later suffer from Hurricane Ike. Alicia shattered windows and tore up the wooden deck and roof. Two inches of standing water caused the hardwood maple lower floor to buckle, and seawater severely damaged the electrical system. Harris County made no move to repair the structure. La Porte mayor Norman Malone and city manager Bob Herrera aggressively pushed for renovation and redevelopment of Sylvan Beach. Under Mayor Malone, city manager Herrera, parks and recreation director Stan Sherwood, and assistant Olivia Moeller, the damage from Alicia was repaired and the pavilion was renovated. Gov. Mark White attended the ribbon-cutting ceremony after the restoration. After Hurricane Ike in 2008, management of the pavilion was turned over to the able hands of Harris County and Harris County Commissioners Court.

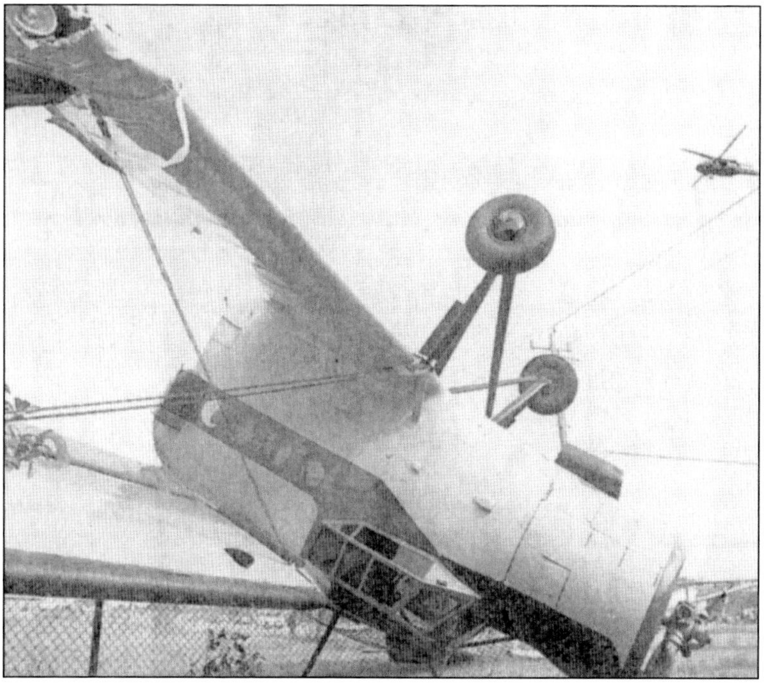

Hurricane Ike was an incredibly powerful storm that ripped Houston apart in 2008. The photographs on this page show some of the carnage it inflicted around La Porte. The image at left shows how Hurricane Ike left an airplane torn in half and upside down at the La Porte Municipal airport at the corner of Spencer Highway and North Farrington Boulevard.

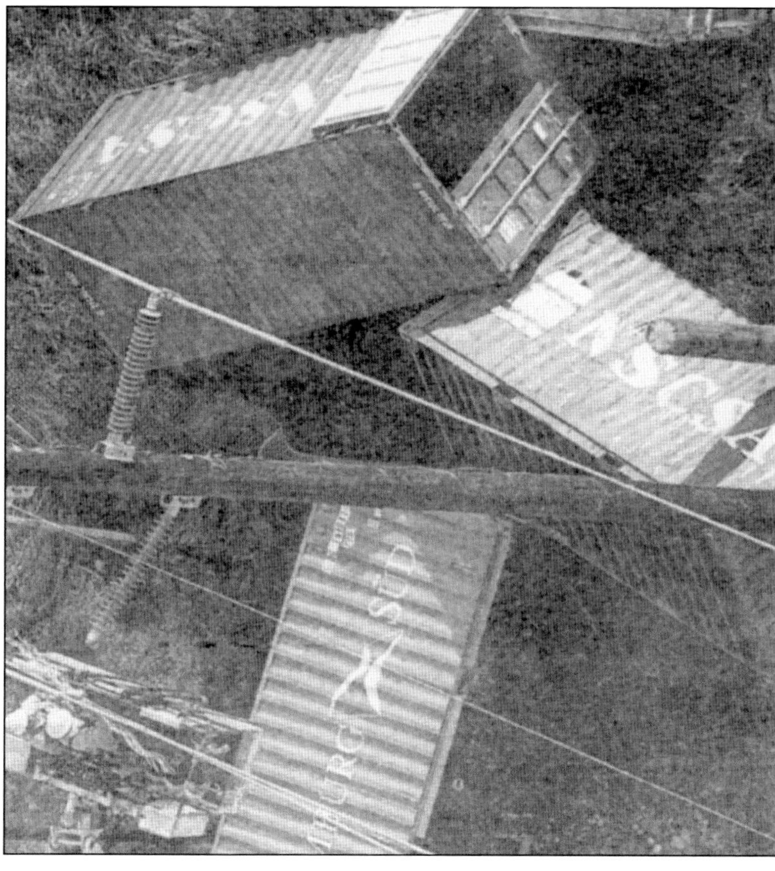

The winds of Hurricane Ike were so powerful that, as shown in this image, they picked up the massive containers from Barbour's Cut, shuffled them around, and threw them to the ground as if they were matchsticks. Despite the strength of the storm, the damage inflicted on the Sylvan Beach Pavilion was largely cosmetic, and the 13-foot levee constructed after Hurricane Carla (and rebuilt after Hurricane Alicia) was largely effective.

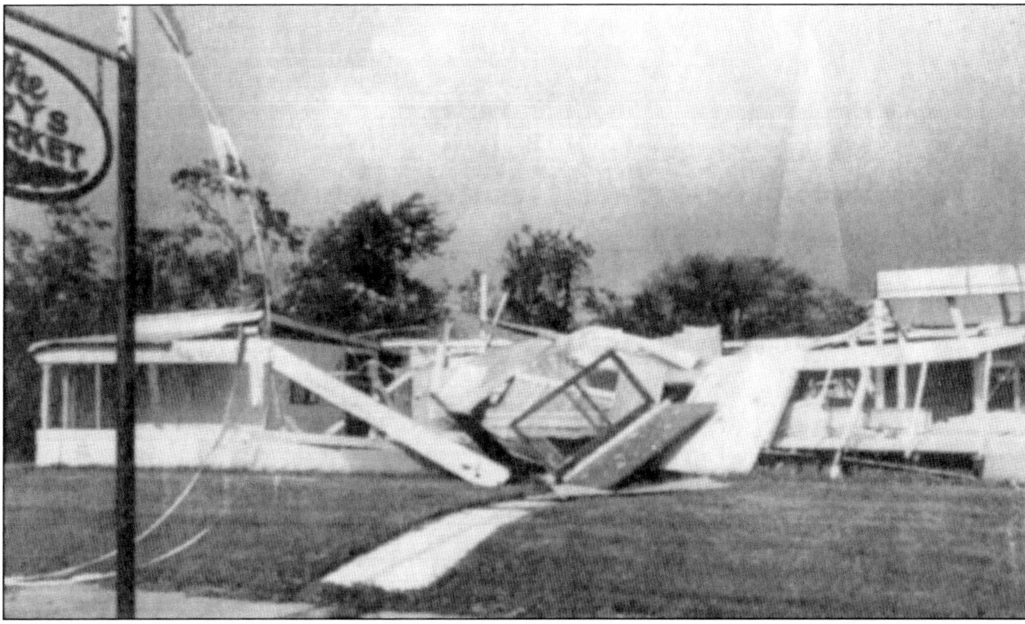

This is a photograph of damage near the front of Sylvan Beach Pavilion following the hurricane in 1941. As noted earlier, owner E.L. Crain did not repair or replace the rides and structures damaged in the wartime hurricanes, and the park lay largely dormant from 1943 until Harris County purchased it and began construction of the new Sylvan Beach Pavilion in 1954.

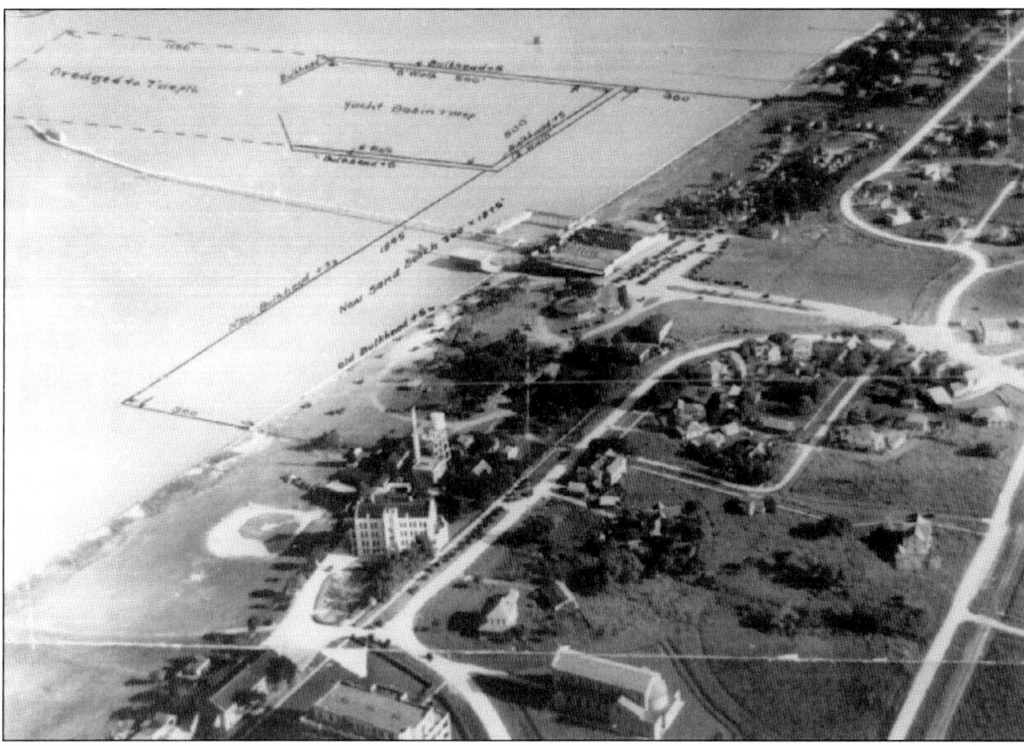

It is unfortunate that the hurricanes disheartened E.L. Crain. This aerial photograph and drawing shows the extensive plans that he had for Sylvan Beach Park both on land and in the bay.

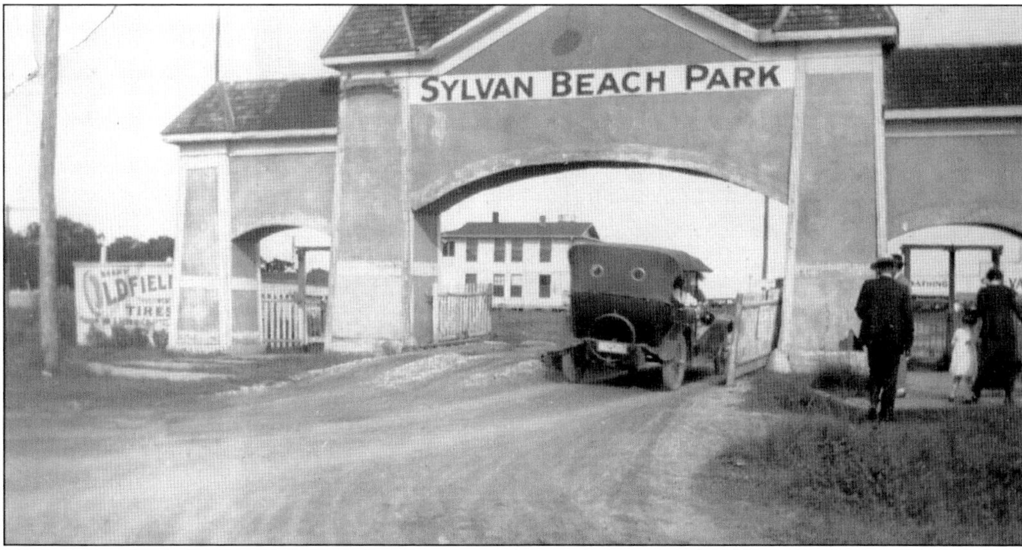

This photograph shows the main entrance gate G.D. Samuels built when he began running Sylvan Beach Park around 1910. A lonely car drives through the gate into the park; at this point in time, most visitors were still arriving by foot, hackney, or train. Sour Lake had already come in, and the Goose Creek oil boom was just around the corner. Samuels would rely heavily on Humble Oil, Texas Oil, and Gulf Oil to bring business to Sylvan Beach Park.

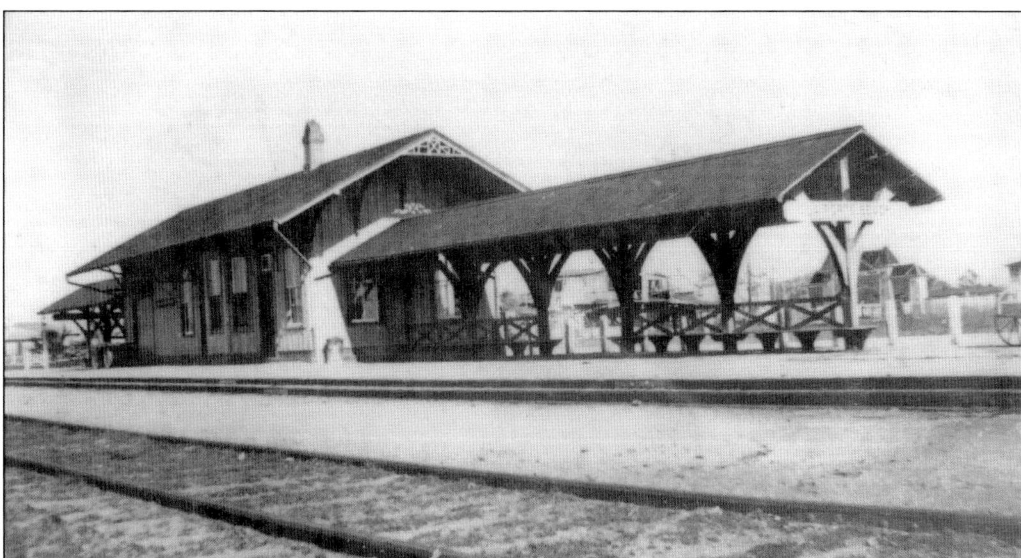

This train station, first constructed in downtown La Porte, had a journey of its own. After construction, the La Porte city fathers—aware of the popularity of the area as a vacation spot—moved the structure to Sylvan Beach in 1915. After train travel ceased, local businessman Charlie Ashton bought the depot and moved it back to an area close to its original location in downtown La Porte. In 1980, it was given to the La Porte Bay Area Heritage Society and moved to its current location at Sylvan Beach, where it now offers visitors a glorious view of the bay.

Six
CARS AND WARS

Automobiles changed the world, along with the oil necessary to fuel them. Certainly, the oil and energy industry changed Houston, and La Porte and Sylvan Beach were not immune to these changes. Spindletop came in 1901, Well No. 3 blew at Sour Lake in 1902, and the Goose Creek oil boom followed in 1916. Humble Oil, Texas Oil Company, and Gulf Oil Company all had major production and refining facilities nearby, and the early part of the century saw many oil company picnics and parties convene at Sylvan Beach.

When Sylvan Beach was laid out with La Porte in 1892, people spoke of going to the Pelly or Goose Creek areas in present-day Baytown for the healing "mineral waters." The next 40 years saw a radical transformation of the land around La Porte as the oil boom and massive growth along the Houston Ship Channel transformed the area.

The impact of the 1943 hurricane on La Porte and Sylvan Beach and the inability to rehabilitate the park after the storm were closely related to the amount of aviation fuel the petroleum refineries along the Houston Ship Channel were providing for the Navy (some say as much as 90 percent). As the ship channel and surrounding communities became more industrialized, one small park was left to remind people of the beauty and the way of life that had once characterized the area.

Similarly, today, when World War II is a distant memory and so few of the heroes who fought that epic contest remain, the Sylvan Beach Pavilion stands; its windows are a prism through which people can gaze and imagine men and women swaying to the songs the big bands played in the years leading up to the war.

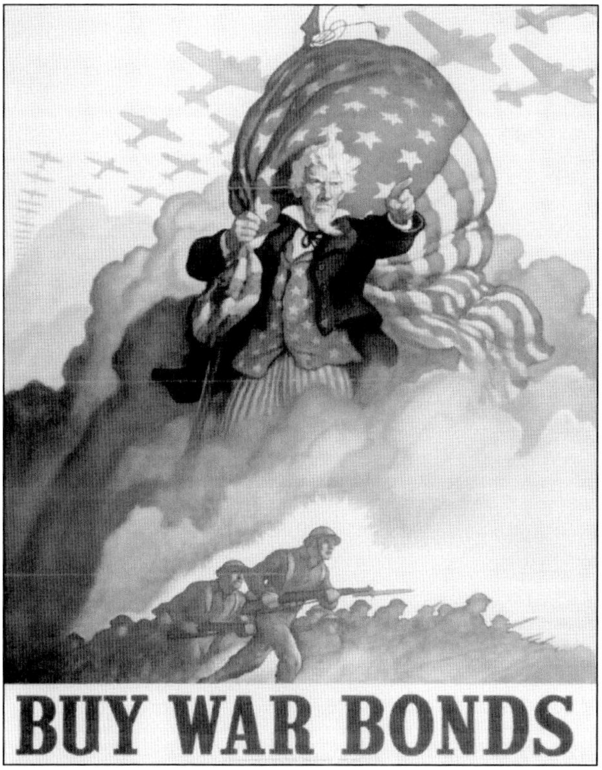

The residents of Sylvan Beach actively supported the effort during World War II. They hosted activities in the local school and churches to raise money. Part of the fiscal support given by these hardworking people was the promotion and sale of war bonds. Here is a poster typical of those that would have been on display at the pavilion during dances and picnics.

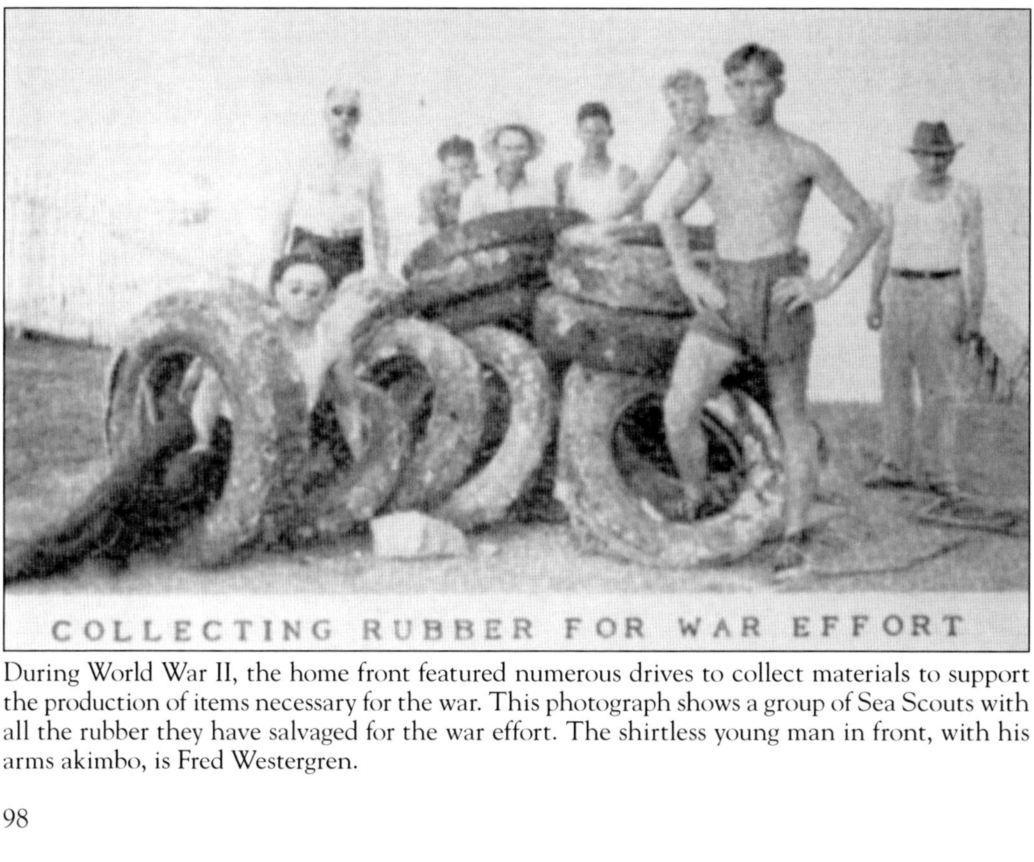

During World War II, the home front featured numerous drives to collect materials to support the production of items necessary for the war. This photograph shows a group of Sea Scouts with all the rubber they have salvaged for the war effort. The shirtless young man in front, with his arms akimbo, is Fred Westergren.

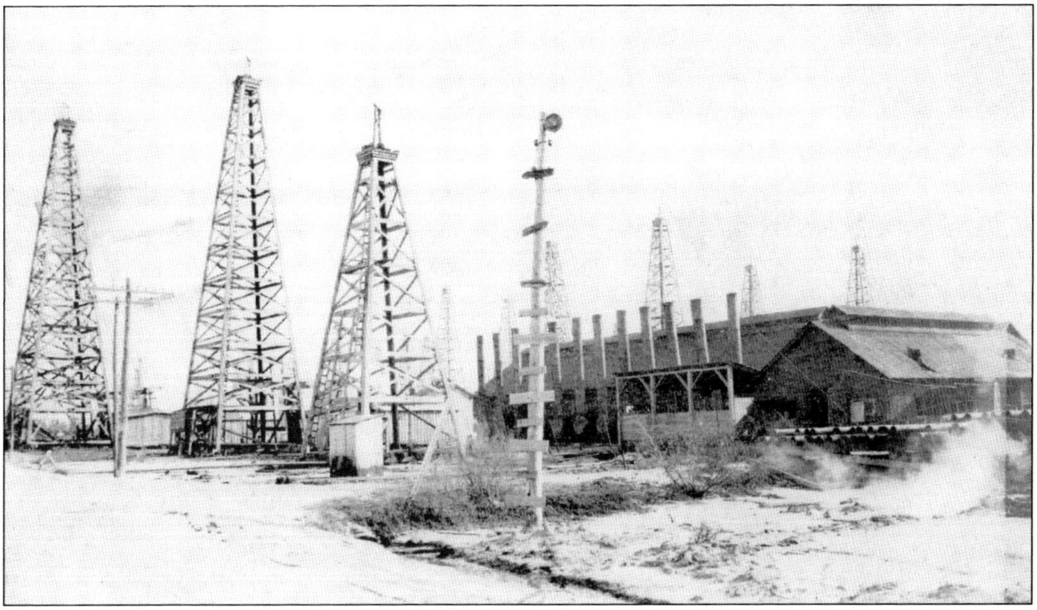

These are photographs of the Goose Creek Oil Field around 1916. Goose Creek, Pelly, and Baytown were once three separate towns. They were eventually merged into Baytown between 1945 and 1947. When the Goose Creek field was first developed, the wildcatters were not familiar with the trouble to the land that extracting oil could produce, and Baytown initially experienced significant subsidence. Humble Oil was deeply involved in Goose Creek, and Humble president (and future Texas governor) Ross Sterling built his home on Bayshore Drive just a few hundred yards from Sylvan Beach. From the bay side, it bears a striking resemblance to the White House. Sterling and his wife, Maud Abbie Gage Sterling, had come from a rural background, and local legend states that even after his mansion was built, Maud continued raising crops and chickens on their estate. Despite the couple's wealth, it was reported that once a month, Maud Sterling would have her limousine deliver her to Isensee's Grocery in downtown La Porte, where she would sell her chicken eggs.

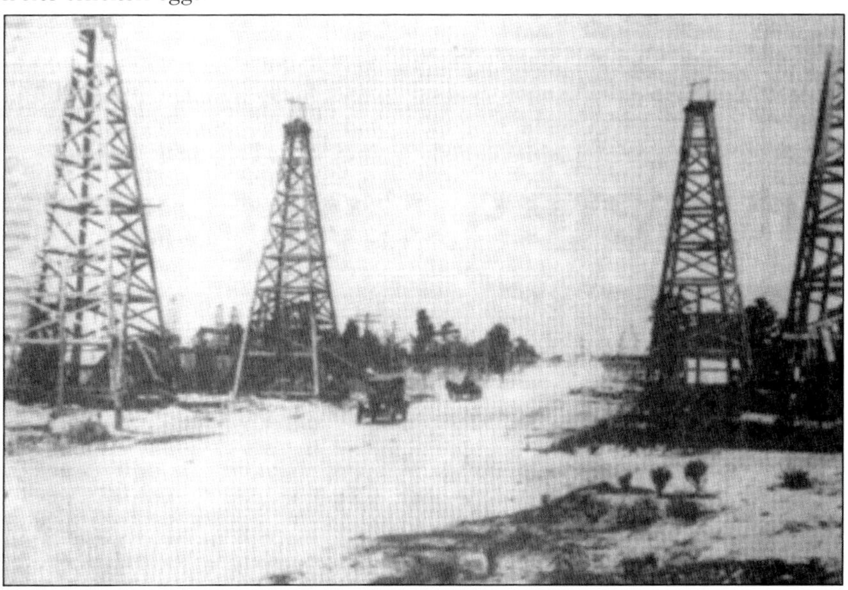

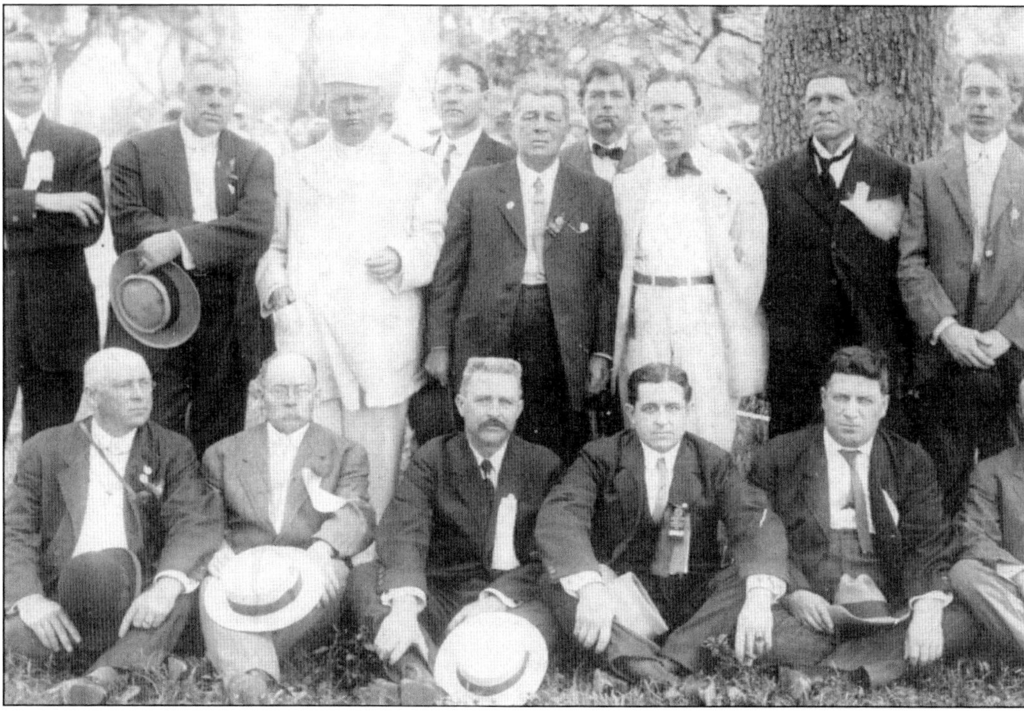

Pictured here at Sylvan Beach with some fellow Humble Oil directors, John Summerfield Bonner (third from left in the back row) is wearing a white suit. The handwriting on the bottom of the image reads: "Memories of the Golden Pack." Bonner had a wonderful wit and attitude. When Humble took a 20-year lease on the million-acre King Ranch in South Texas, he was quoted as saying, "A ranch of over a million acres was bound to contain at least a few oil fields." (Courtesy of Buck Bonner.)

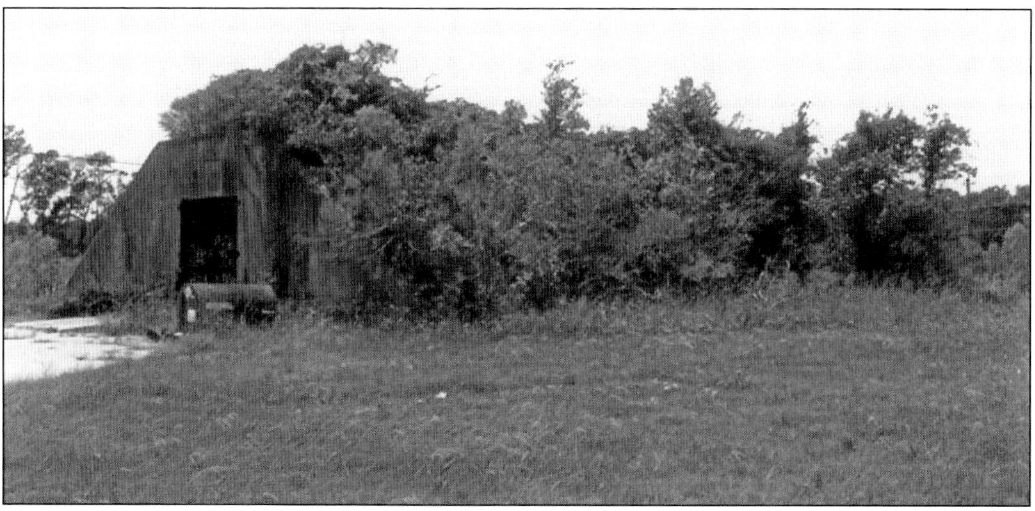

The San Jacinto Ordnance Depot was on the ship channel near Sylvan Beach. The depot supplied both the Army and the Navy. By December 31, 1945, it had received over 329 million pounds of ammunition and shipped over 208 million pounds. The depot continued to ship Army and Navy supplies between 1945 and 1950, but plans had been made for phasing out activities as soon as the decreasing need for war materiel would allow. (Courtesy of George Wolf Jr.)

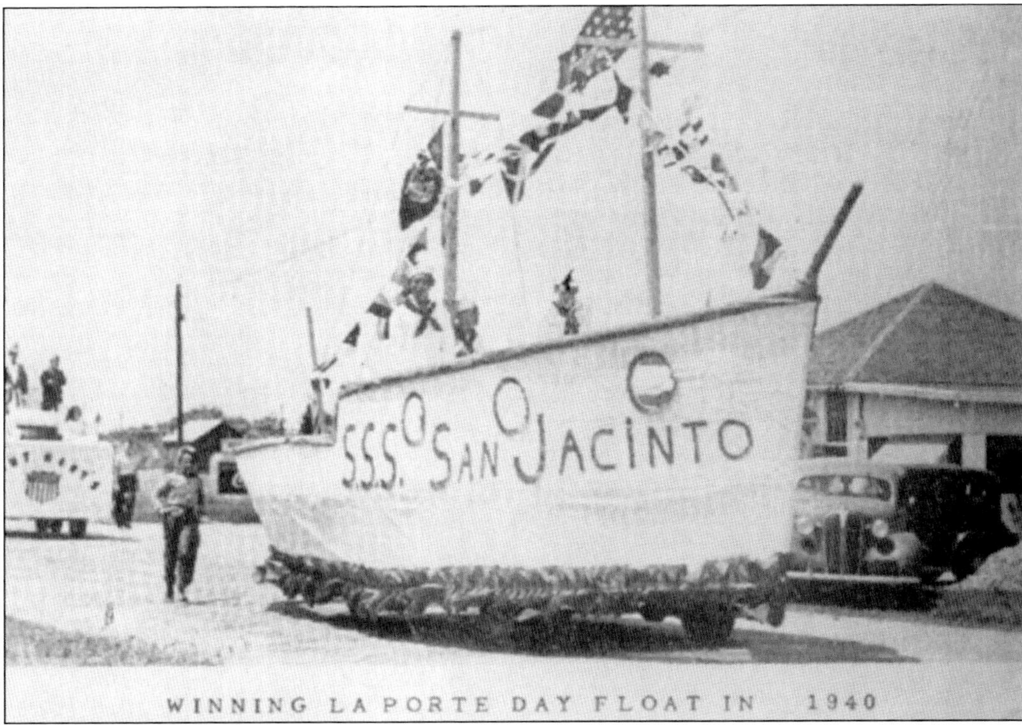

This is the Sea Scouts float at the La Porte Day parade in the 1940s. The St. Mary's Seminary float is just behind it. The Sea Scouts won for best float to aid the war effort. After World War II, several companies that had grown significantly during the war relocated to or near La Porte.

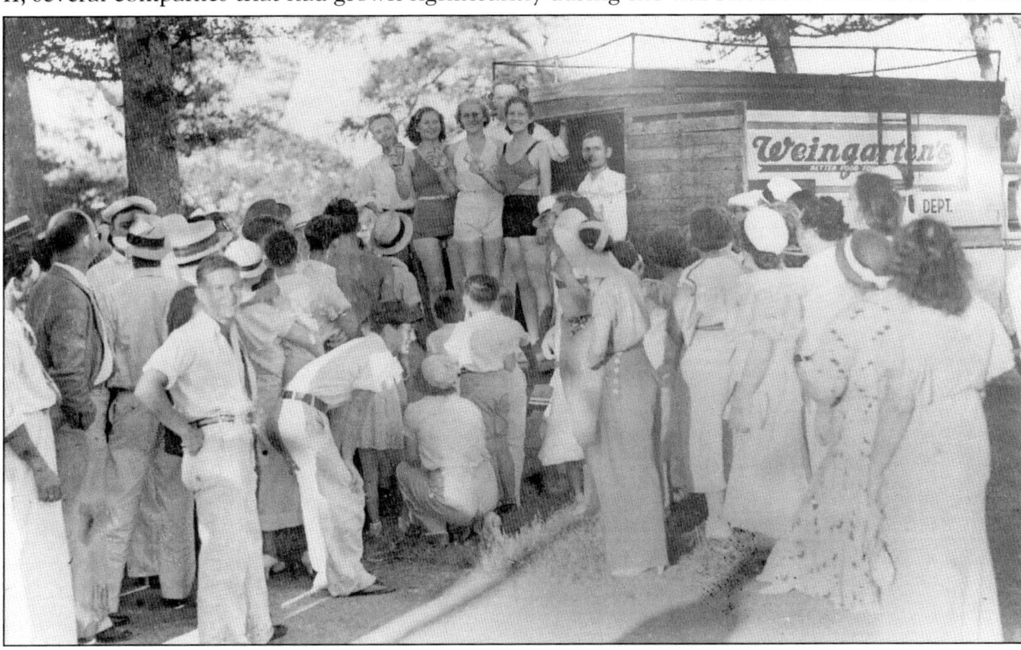

During World War II, the entire city of La Porte and surrounding areas took the war effort seriously, but that did not mean a lack of bathing beauty contests. Pictured here is the Weingarten's Truck with contestants in tow. (Courtesy of the Houston Metropolitan Research Center.)

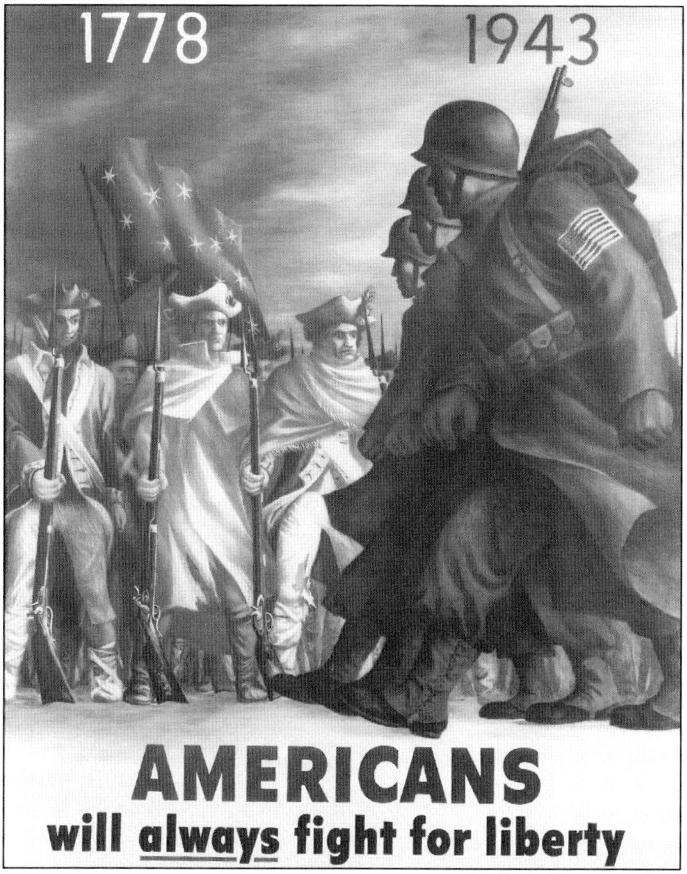

During the war years, La Porte and the surrounding residential communities grew steadily larger as the factories located on the ship channel were integral to the munitions and gasoline fuel of the war effort. The federal government published colorful and exciting posters aimed at inspiring more volunteerism, while the popularity and convenience of driving a private automobile continued to become more widespread. In the picture below, three families have joined at Sylvan Beach for an afternoon excursion, and their cars stand ready for action.

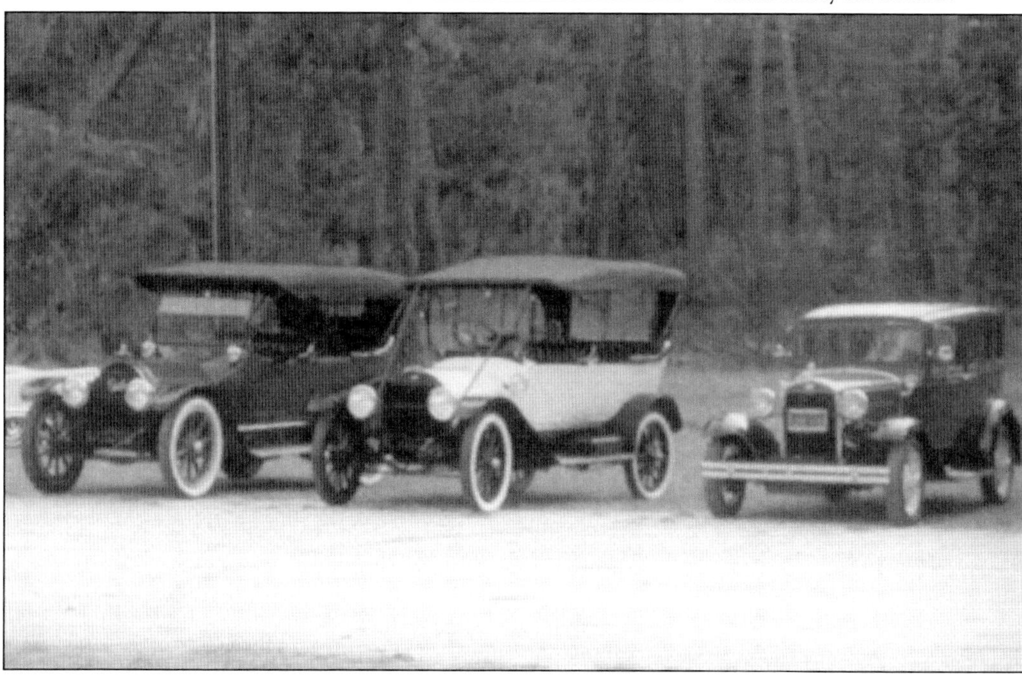

Seven

Decline and Renewal

Sylvan Beach was nearly destroyed by the great hurricane that struck the bay area in September 1943. At the height of World War II, with a large percentage of the American military's aviation fuel coming from nearby refineries, the well-being of the grand old park and its pavilion were subordinate to the war effort. The storm devastated the pavilion and the other structures in the park.

Most of the park structures had to be demolished thereafter because, at the height of the war, the will and money to repair them were just not there. Owner E.L. Crain had subleased the park in the late 1930s and passed away in 1951. Harris County purchased Sylvan Beach in 1954 and began construction on the new Sylvan Beach Park. The current pavilion was completed in 1956. The Sylvan Beach Festival—originally called La Porte Day—was started in 1956, although the park had hosted legions of festivals devoted to various causes and events throughout the years. The Sylvan Beach Festival continues to be an annual event, and the annual bathing beauty contest that started in 1924 continues to be a part of that event.

The next heavy blow to the park came when Hurricane Alicia hit in 1983. Afterward, the City of La Porte and other leaders, spearheaded by the La Porte Bay Area Heritage Society, took over management of the park. Bonds for restoring and improving the park were passed under La Porte mayor Norman Malone, who took office in 1985, and the renewal of Sylvan Beach began to gain momentum.

The vicissitudes of the bay's weather have sometimes rendered progress a matter of three steps forward and two steps back, and that has been the case with the renewal of Sylvan Beach and the pavilion. Much of the progress that occurred under the administration of mayors Malone and J.J. Meza disappeared in an instant when Hurricane Ike struck Sylvan Beach in 2008. Various well-meaning individuals proposed and sponsored plans for the renewal and improvement of Sylvan Beach, and it became a subject of much debate. La Porte citizen Ted Powell started a group to preserve the 1956 Sylvan Beach Park—Friends of Sylvan Beach Park & Pavilion—and the group was successful in its efforts. A combination of county, city, and private efforts led to the restoration, which was funded by Harris County.

Recently, in addition to the restoration of the pavilion, Sylvan Beach Park has also seen its beautiful pier rebuilt and the construction and installation of a sandy beach for sunbathing and swimming. Numerous other plans include improvements at Sylvan Beach Park and the reinstallation of artifacts from Sylvan Beach's past, a bandshell, and another Sylvan Beach hotel like the Sylvan Hotel or the Park View Hotel.

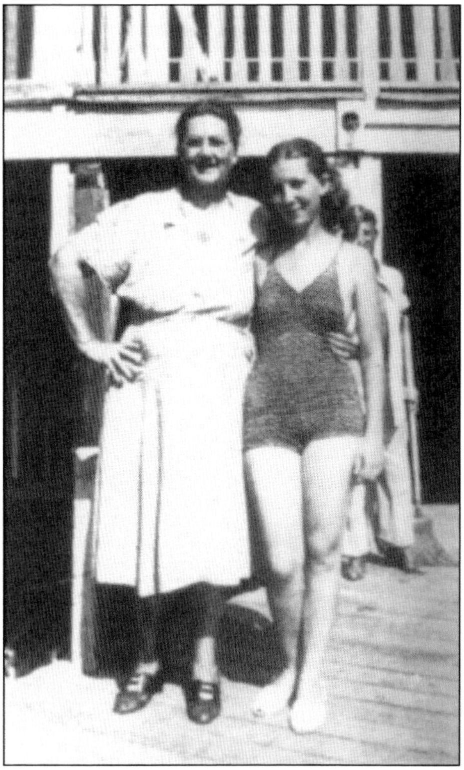

Mary Sullivan is pictured here on the left. She ran the bathhouse at Sylvan Beach from about 1920 until the 1940s. She looked after and was well loved by the girls who came to the park.

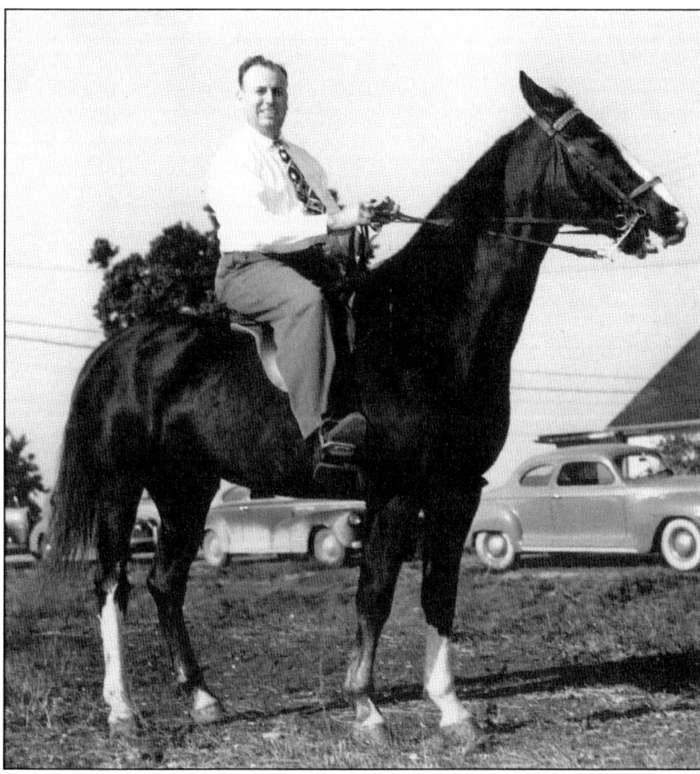

Cecil Sisson (pictured) stopped managing Sylvan Beach around 1925. The Great Depression was followed by a severe hurricane in 1930, and park owner Ed Eiseman soon left Sylvan Beach. Shortly thereafter, E.L. Crain took over. Crain spent heavily to develop Sylvan Beach and began looking for well-known national and local musicians to perform there.

In 1928, Donald "Dave" David and his wife, Lena, were on their honeymoon and traveling to Galveston from Port Arthur. As they came through La Porte and saw the crowds at Sylvan Beach, Dave got an idea. He purchased $15 worth of lumber and built this sandwich stand across from Five Points. Originally from New Iberia, Louisiana, he closed the stand after Labor Day and returned to Louisiana and relatives' farms, where he spent the winters butchering. The Davids returned the following spring and reopened for the summer before eventually finding a permanent space for Dave's Sandwich Shop.

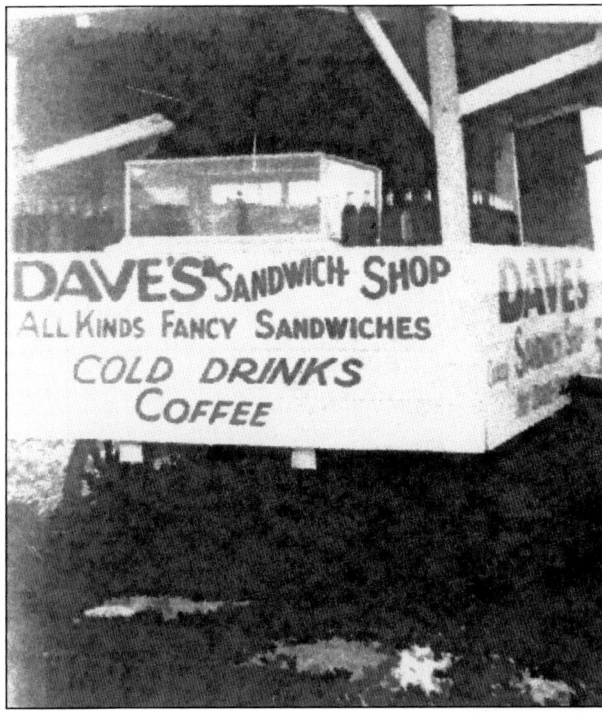

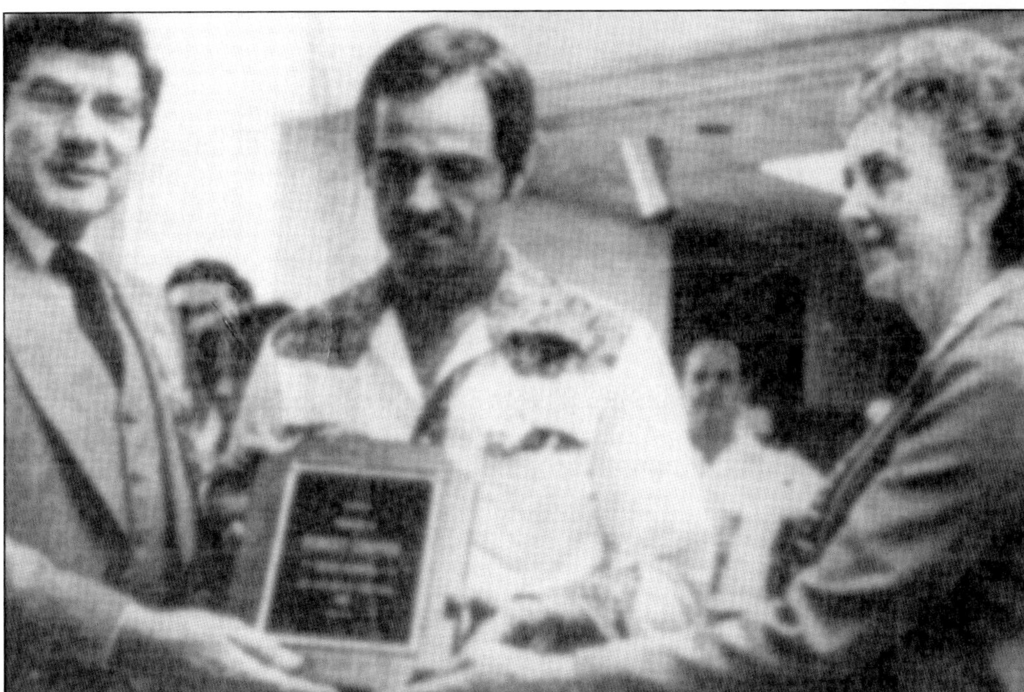

Bob Crippen (center) was an astronaut who made his home in La Porte and whose children attended La Porte schools. He was deeply involved in the community and even served as grand marshal of the Sylvan Beach Festival. J.J. Meza (left) was La Porte's long-serving mayor, and along with chamber of commerce president Lou Lawler (right), did much to preserve Sylvan Beach.

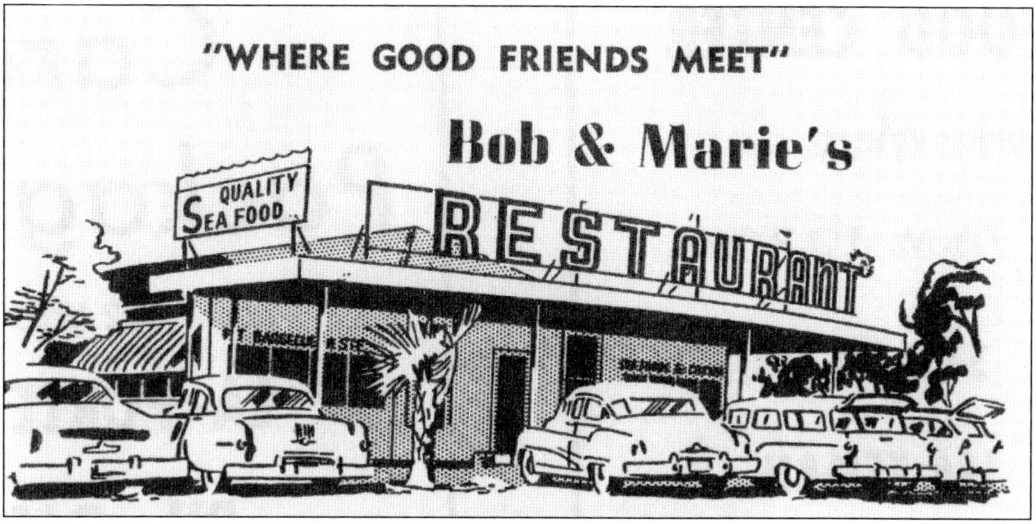

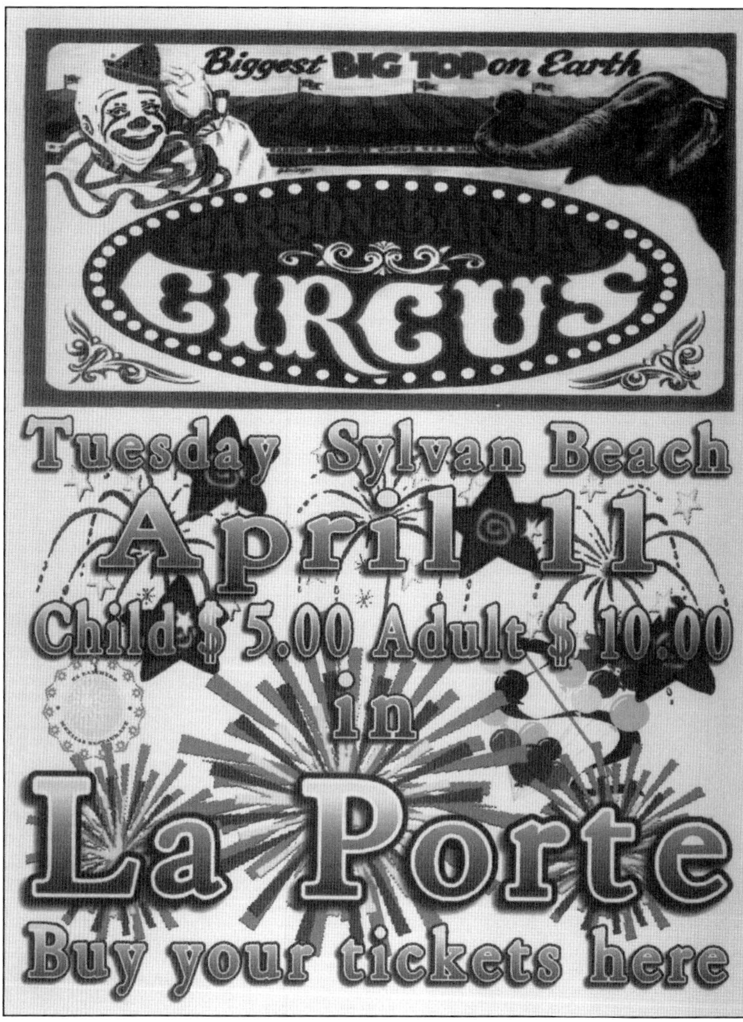

Bob and Marie's Restaurant was a Sylvan Beach fixture for many years. While some of the entertainment at Sylvan Beach was more seasonal, Bob and Marie's operated year-round.

Circuses have always loved Sylvan Beach as a venue. Even during the bleak period following the 1943 hurricane and World War II, when the park had no functioning pavilion, circuses would still occasionally set up at Sylvan Beach.

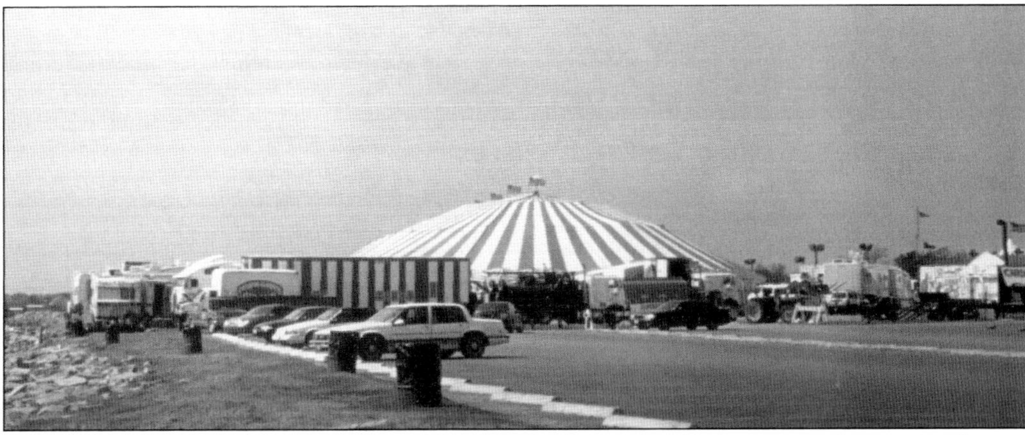

In 1943, when E.L. Crain owned the park, a terrible hurricane hit La Porte. The weather bureau called it a tropical depression, and the radio (the only popular widely used electronic mass communication of the time) gave scant warning because the armed services were worried about the Japanese knowing about a major storm hitting where most of America's aviation fuel was coming from. Circuses helped keep people coming to Sylvan Beach in the following years. In 1943, the pavilion was built on pilings almost over the bay; after the storm, the pavilion, pier, carousel, cabins, and most of the other rides and buildings were all destroyed. The last band to play at the pavilion had been Louis Armstrong and His Orchestra on Labor Day in 1941.

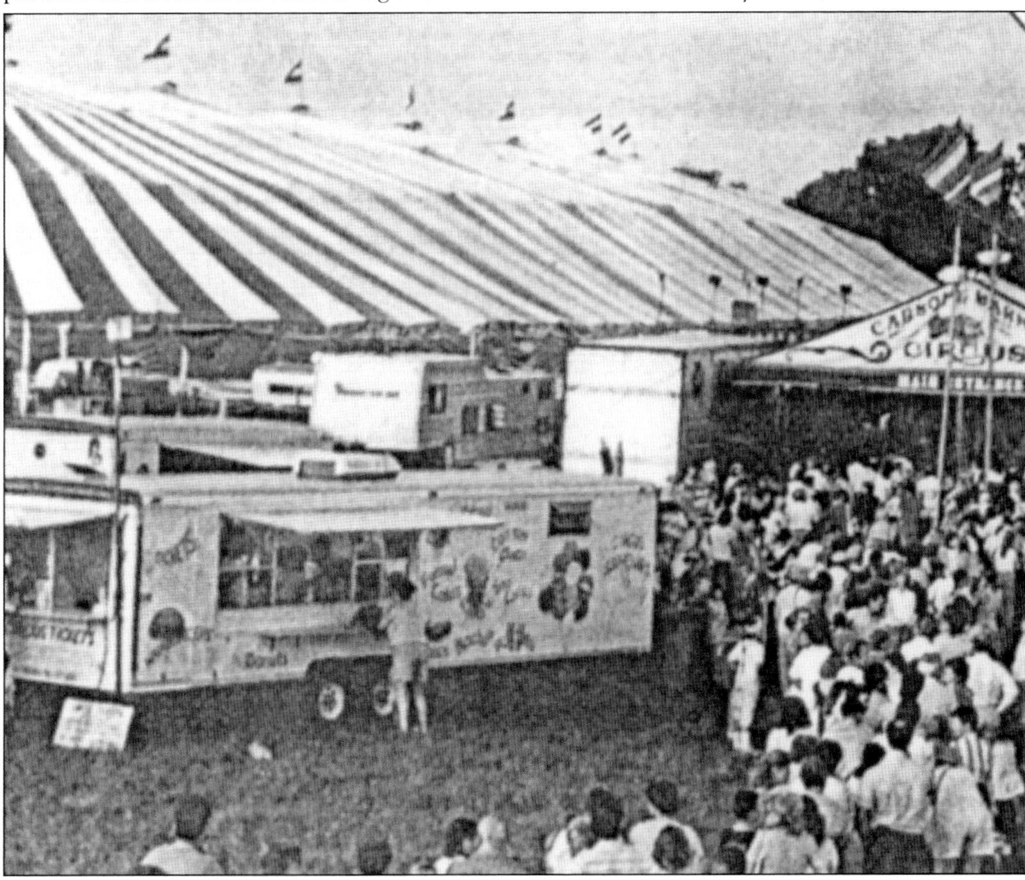

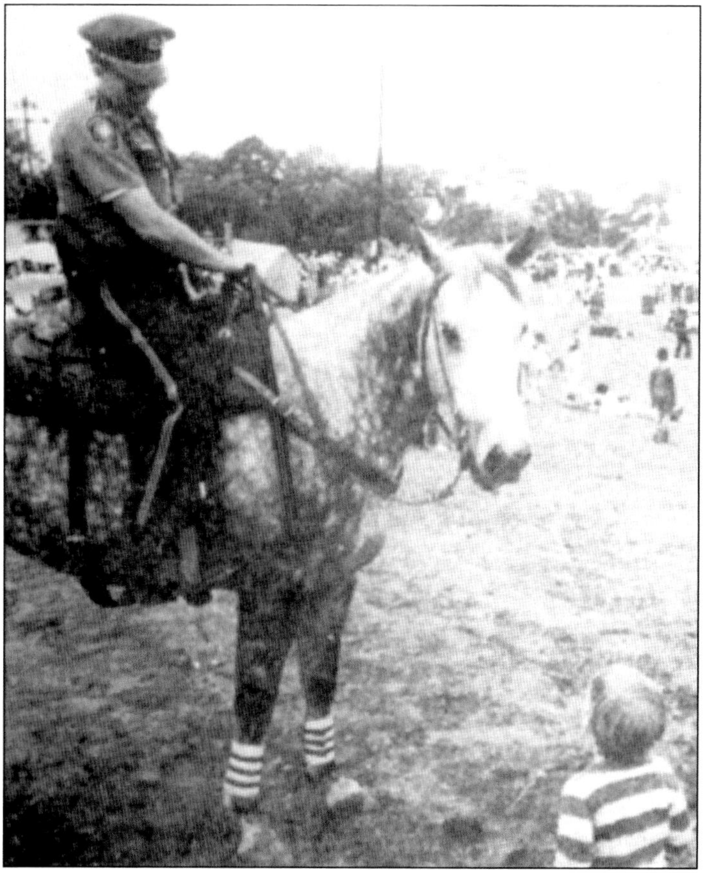

After Sylvan Beach was decimated by hurricanes in 1941 and 1943, owner E.L. Crain gave up management of the park and pavilion. In 1948, the City of La Porte began efforts to have Harris County take over ownership and management of the park; there was no longer a pavilion or other structures on the grounds. Between 1950 and 1954, Harris County took over the park, and in 1954 they began construction of the new Sylvan Beach Pavilion.

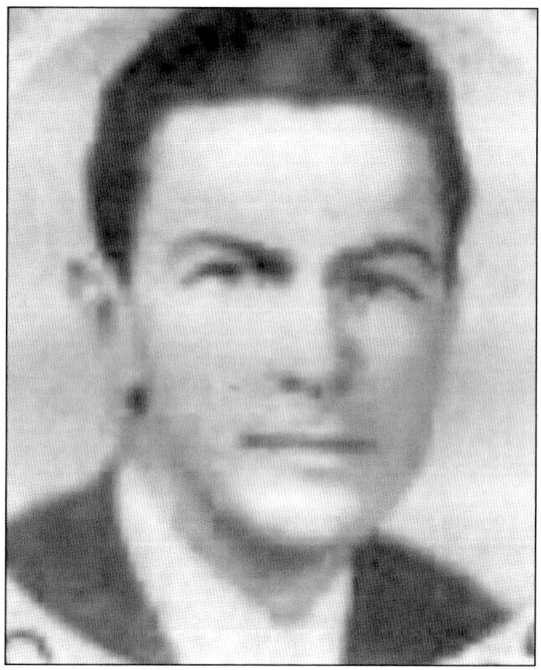

La Porte mayor M.D. Burgin declared May 12, 1956, as "La Porte Day," and Harris County Commissioners' Court judge Bob Casey (pictured at right) rode in one of the head cars in the parade celebrating the dedication of the park as a county park. Thereafter, Harris County took over peacekeeping responsibilities at the park; for a long time, this duty was carried out by Jake Bussey, and since his time, a long line of dedicated county sheriffs and constables (including the one pictured above) have kept peace at the park.

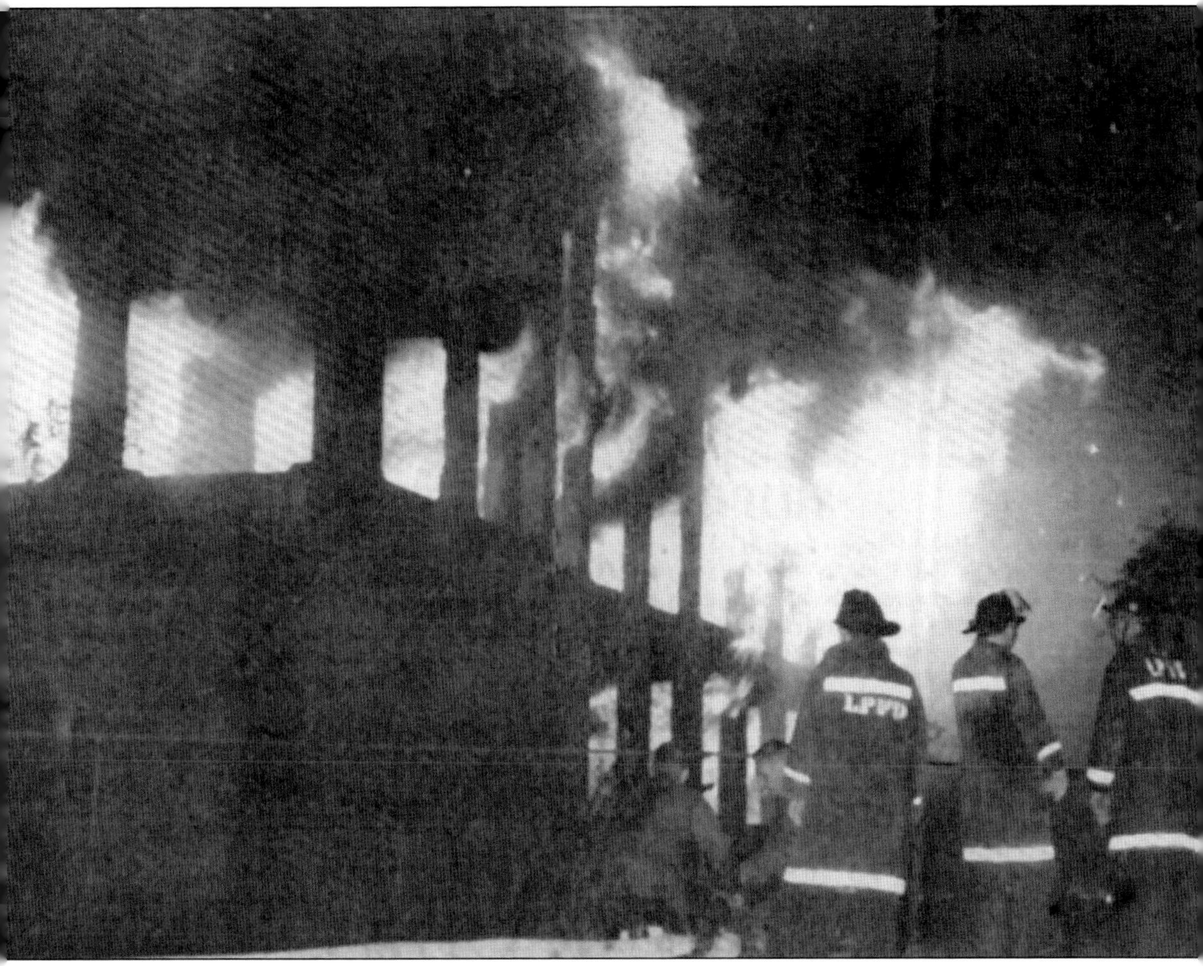

In 1892, between 14 and 22 acres were set aside by La Porte's developers for Sylvan Beach, originally called Sylvan Grove. In 1893, the Sylvan Hotel opened adjacent to the Park. It was four stories tall and wrapped with verandas. A 1,800-foot pier and the first Sylvan Beach Pavilion for dancing were built at Sylvan Grove before hotel and park visitors could disembark from vessels traveling down the bayou at the Morgan's Point pier. In 1894, the railroad was extended to (East) La Porte and the famous "Moonlight Excursion" train began to run from Houston. In 1898, the *La Porte Chronicle* ran an article referring to the land as "Sylvan Beach" for the first time in print. The Great Storm of 1900 heavily damaged the Sylvan Hotel; and in 1901, Bishop Nicholas A. Gallagher of the Catholic Diocese of Galveston bought it for St. Mary's Seminary, where it was used primarily as a dormitory. It stood as a part of St. Mary's Seminary until 1972, when it was destroyed by fire (pictured).

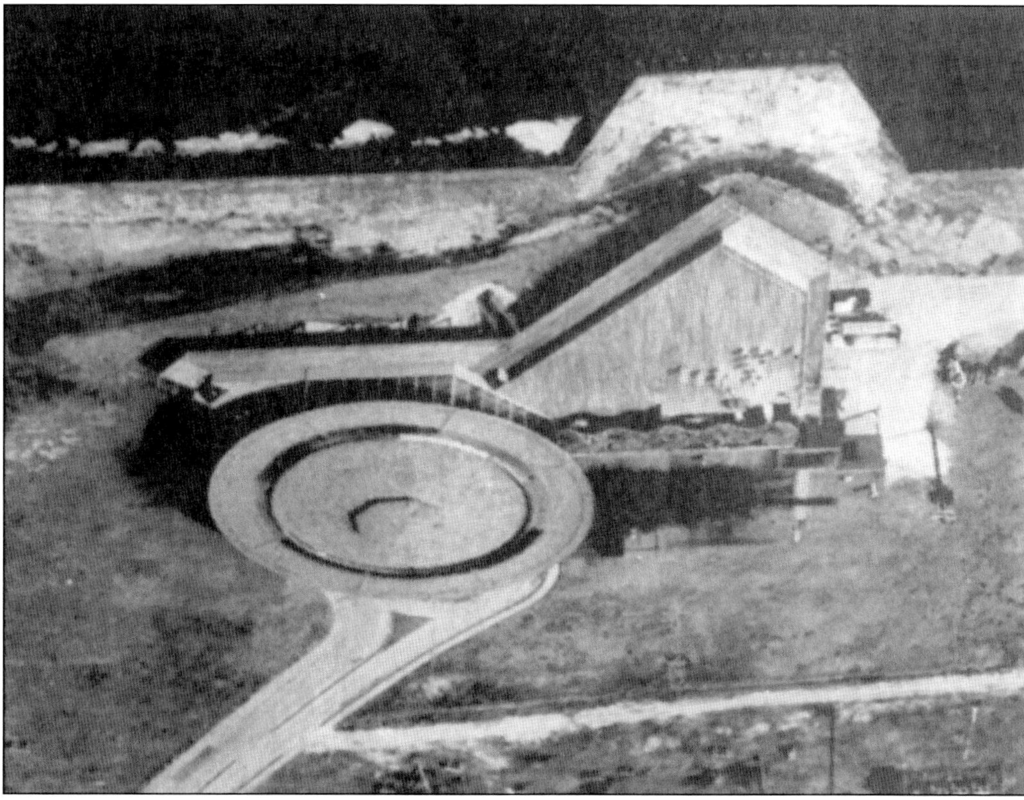

La Porte lobbied Harris County to take on Sylvan Beach as the county began stewardship of Sylvan Beach Park in 1954. The Sylvan Beach Pavilion was rebuilt and completed in 1956. These photographs show the Pavilion at that time—and the scarcity of surrounding structures. The circular pavilion houses the dance floor. The architects were Tom Greacen and Raymond Brogniez. Harris County brought the park for $1 million and spent another $500,000 to rebuild the pavilion and revive the park.

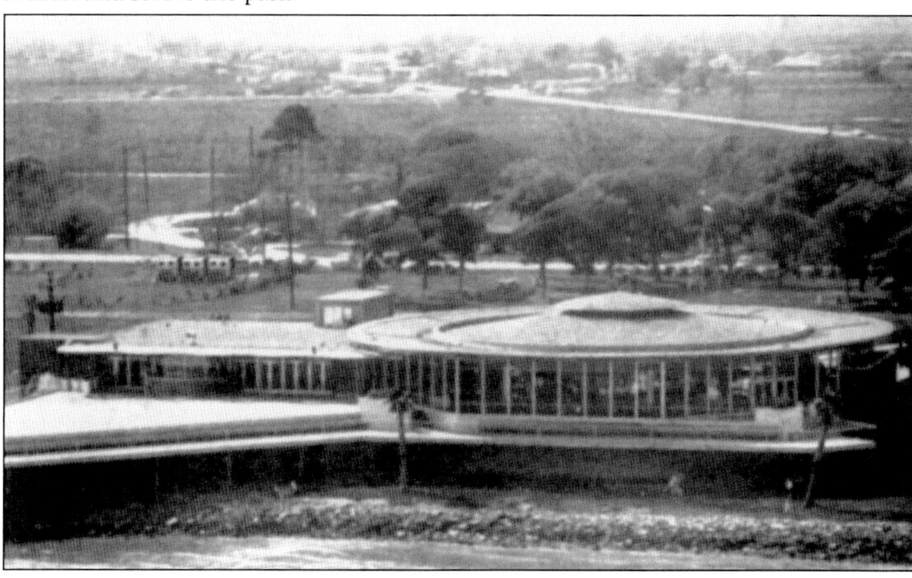

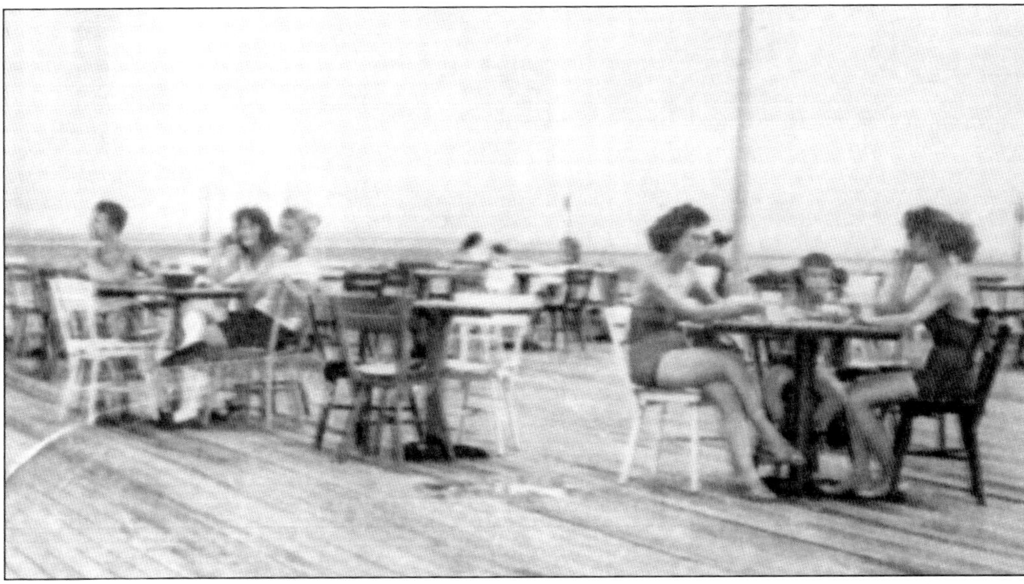

The deck outside the Sylvan Beach Pavilion was designed to give the impression of sitting or dining on the water as if sitting on the deck of ship. It has provided a romantic backdrop for many conversations since it was built.

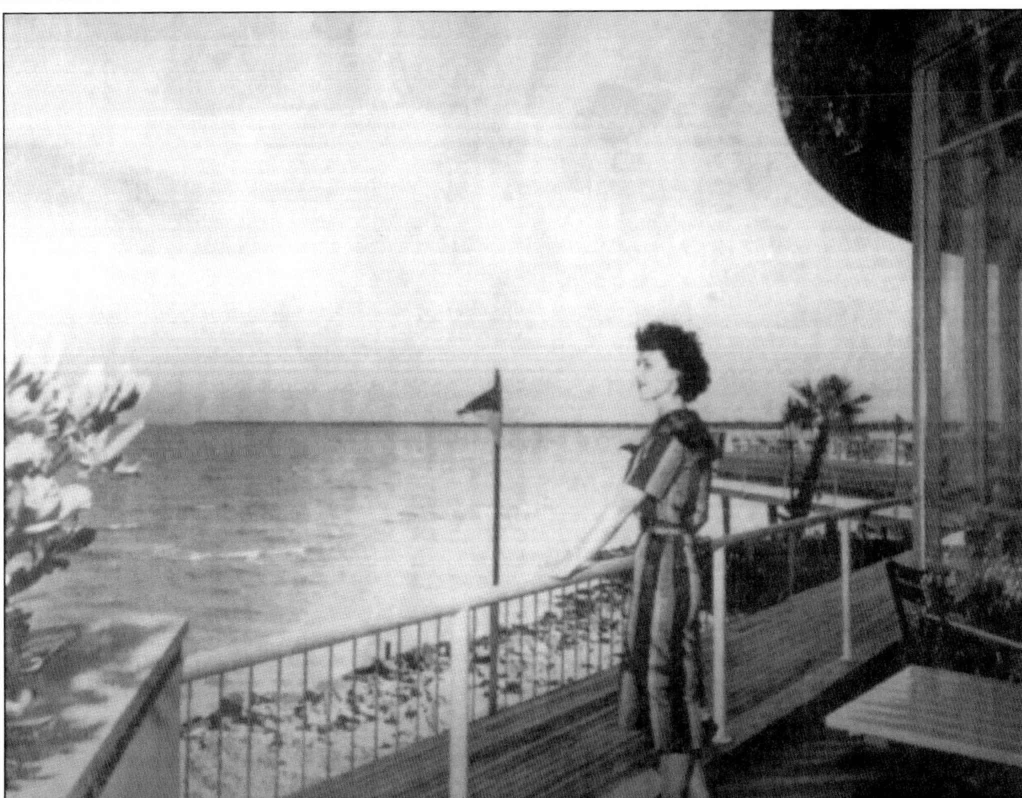

This photograph was taken to promote the pavilion. The Sylvan Beach Pavilion did well for the next several years; however, Hurricane Carla severely damaged it in 1961.

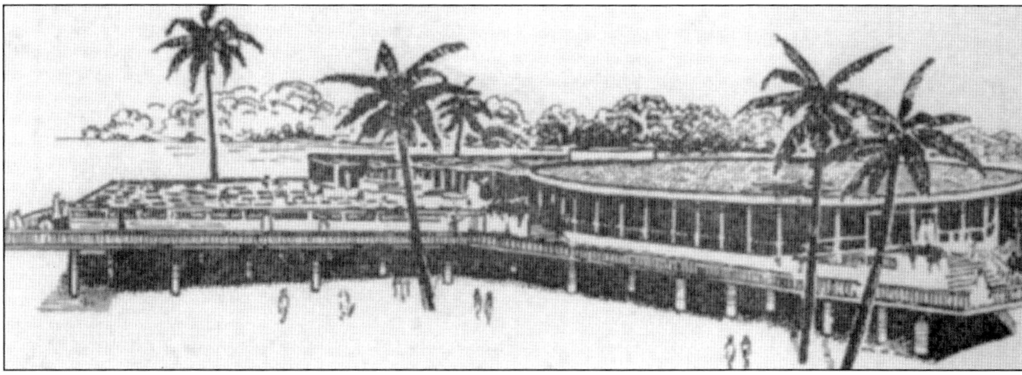

This is a sketch of the 1956 pavilion. The round pavilion is the dance floor. In the beginning, the bands would have, at various times, been set up in the center of the floor, but today there is a bandstand on the north side of the dance floor.

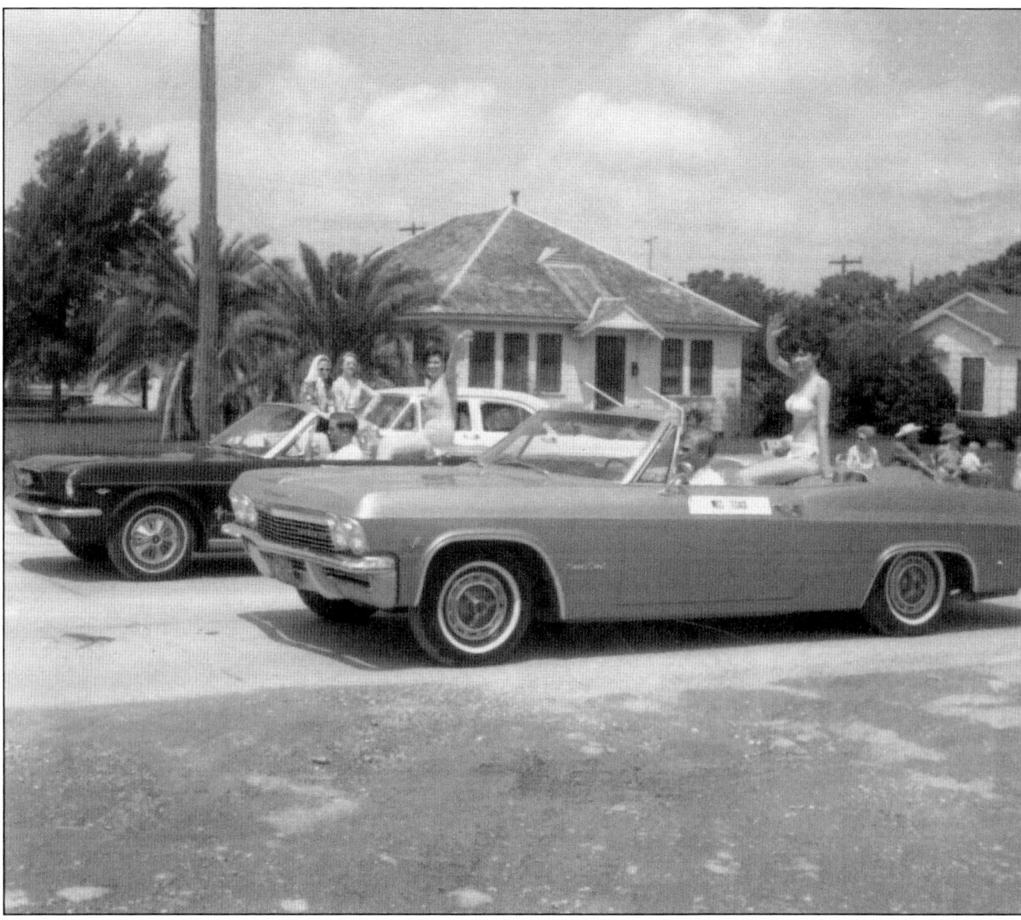

The Sylvan Beach Festival remained popular, as did the Miss Sylvan Beach Bathing Beauty Contest. Here, pageant contestants line up for the Sylvan Beach Parade around 1965.

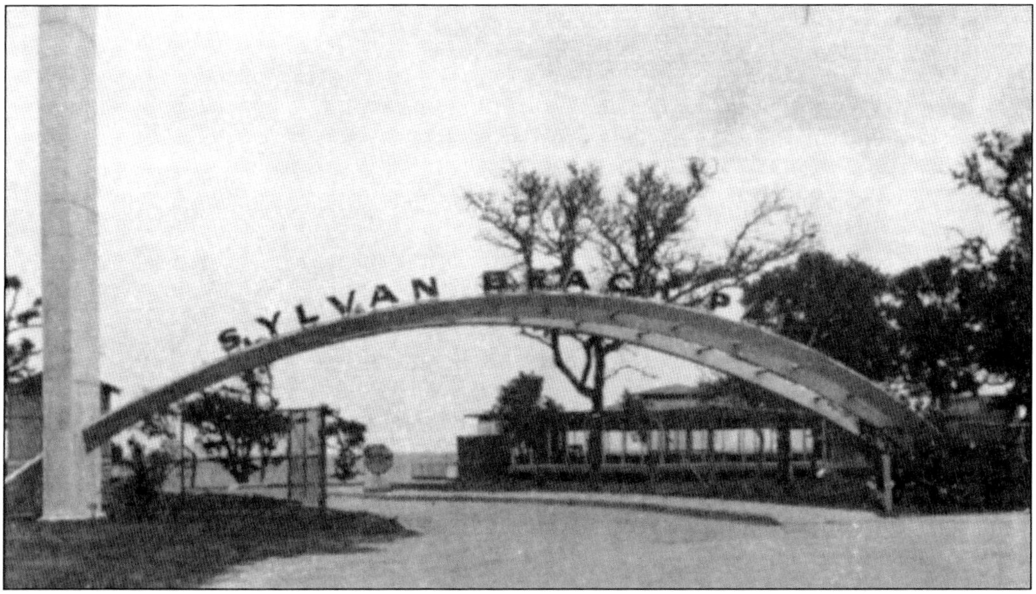

Yet another beautiful gate adorned the entrance to Sylvan Beach Park after it was refurbished by Harris County. This gate was destroyed by Hurricane Carla in 1961.

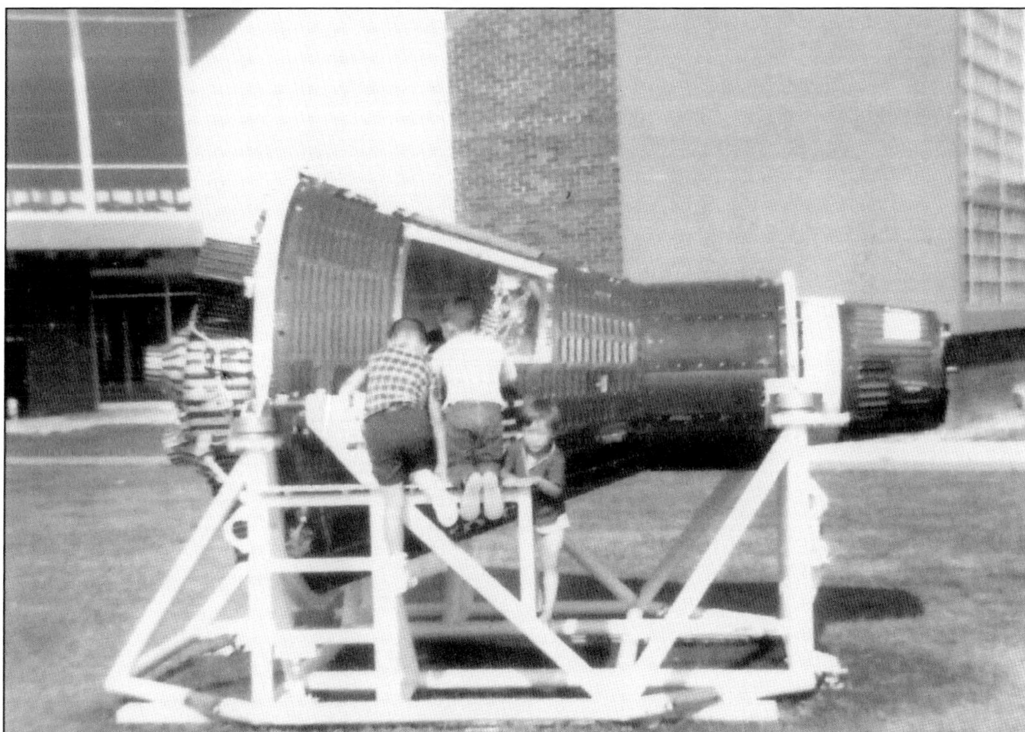

After NASA's Lyndon B. Johnson Space Center was constructed in Houston, Sylvan Beach Park was occasionally a site for displays associated with the space program. This photograph shows a Mercury space capsule on display in front of Sylvan Beach Park in 1964. In this image, local youths Chris Miller (left), Sean Garner (center), and Debbie Miller are giving it a close inspection.

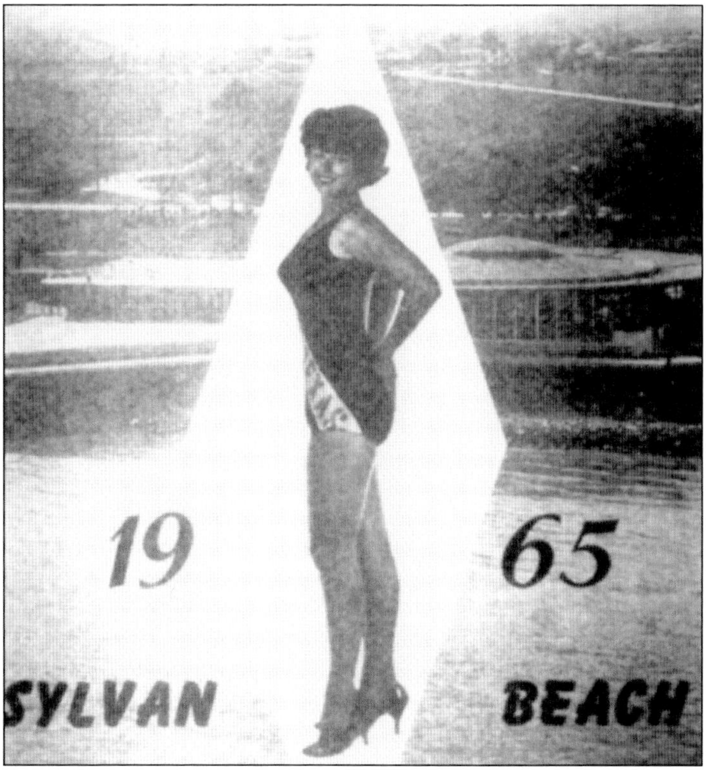

This photograph is of Miss Sylvan Beach of 1965. Winning the contest made the unidentified young lady a celebrity around La Porte, and the contest continues to this day.

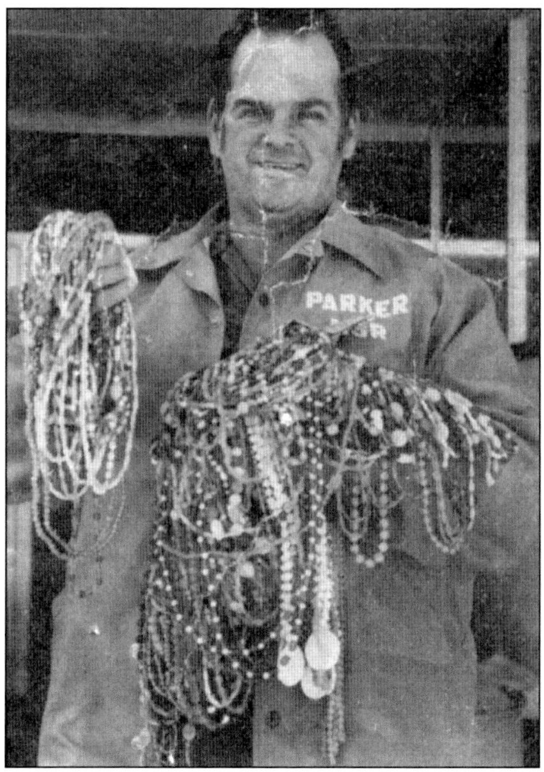

John Parker was the Harris County employee charged with managing Sylvan Beach. He became a good friend to the city of La Porte and was deeply involved in the festivals and events held at Sylvan Beach.

This photograph shows an unidentified woman, Lillian Gunderlach (center), and Lou Lawler (right). Lawler was president of the chamber of commerce and, for a time, also president of the La Porte Bay Area Heritage Society.

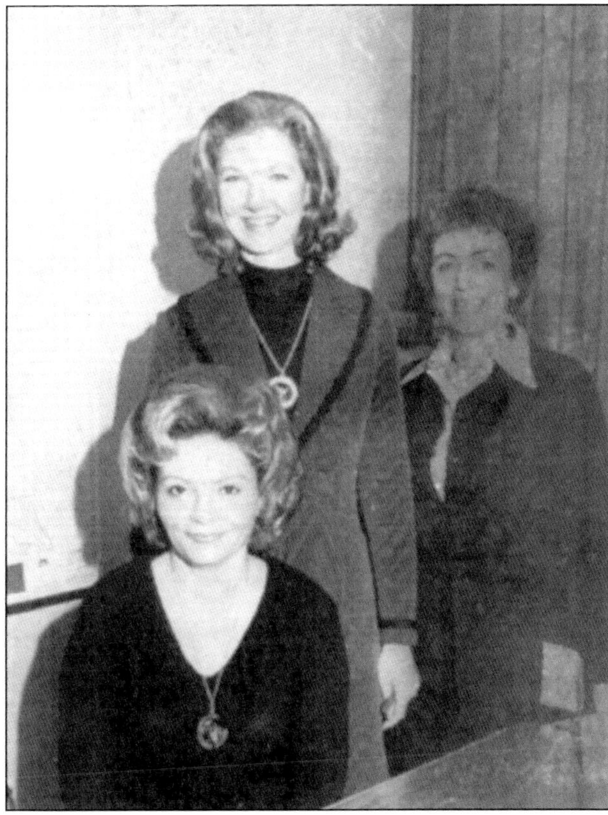

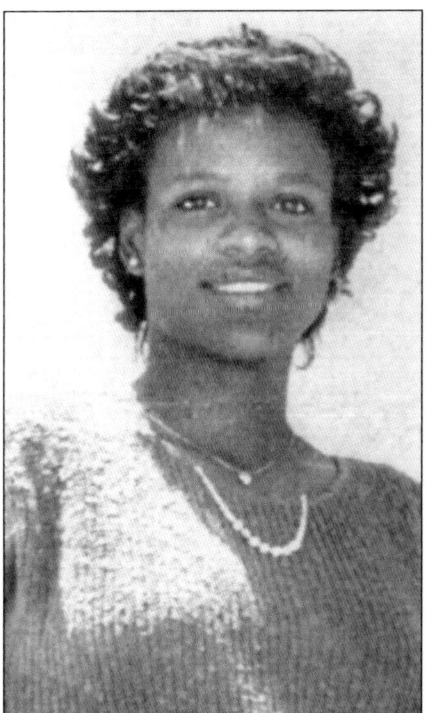

This is Pauline Monsegue (a La Porte High School student at the time) at the Miss Sylvan Beach Contest in 1985. For the first 70 years of its existence, Sylvan Beach was a segregated park, although there were some exceptions, such as the huge and successful Juneteenth celebration held at Sylvan Beach in 1956. In 1961, four black dentists filed suits after being denied entrance to the park, and in 1962, the park was finally desegregated as a result of the suit.

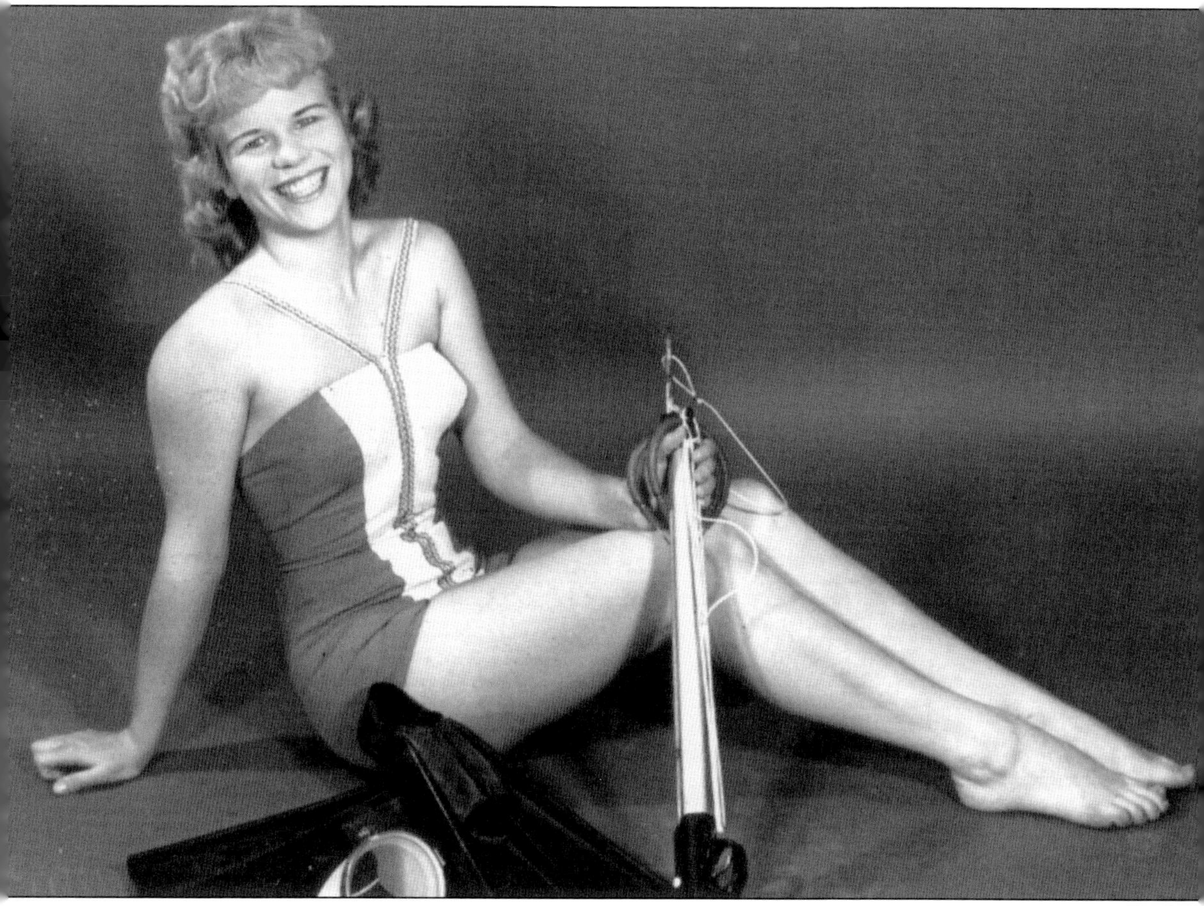

Here is one of the Sylvan Beach bathing beauty contestants from 1960. Maggie Anderson still lives in La Porte and owns the local newspaper *Around La Porte*. Anderson is a supporter of all things La Porte and Sylvan Beach.

The Sylvan Beach Day Parade is a huge local event. La Portians have always loved a parade. In the 1988 image at right, Ray Vandeventer and his wife are dancing the Cotton Eye Joe at a La Porte Bay Area Heritage Society dance at Sylvan Beach Pavilion. The image below shows a sample ticket from the 1991 festival.

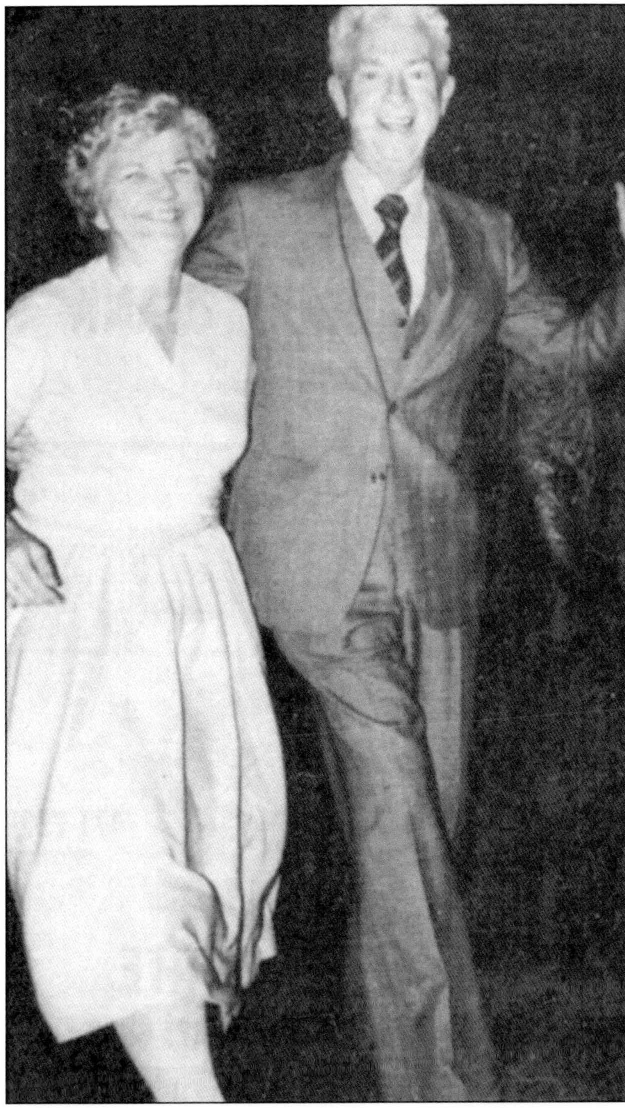

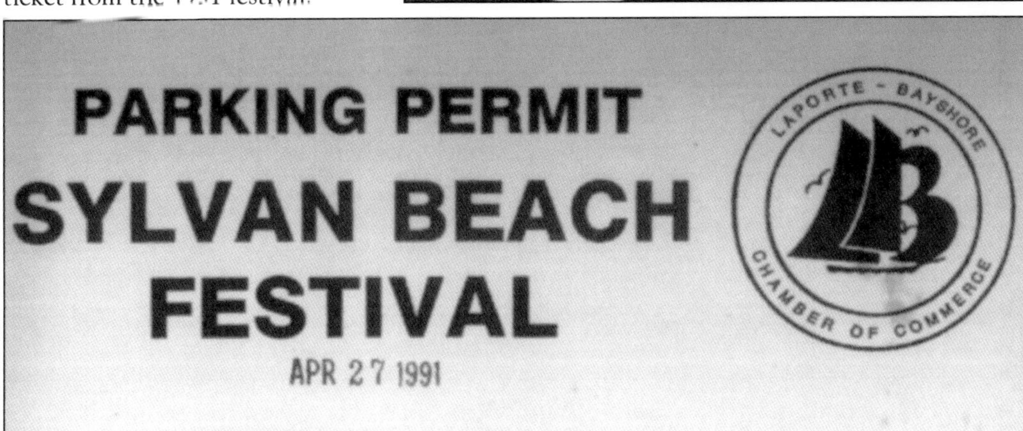

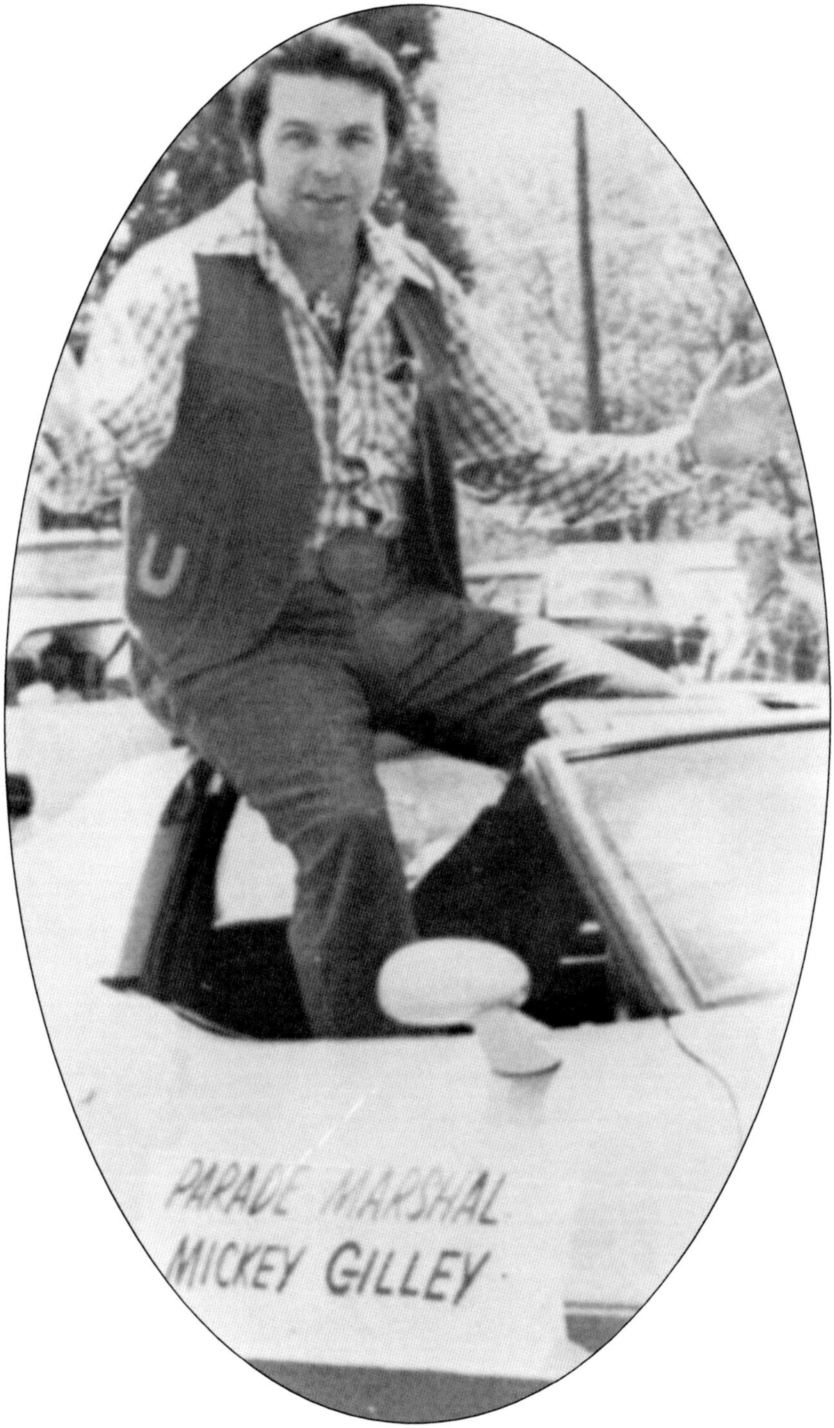

In 1978, Mickey Gilley served as the grand marshal for the Sylvan Beach Festival parade. His dance hall, Gilley's, was located about two miles down Main Street (aka Spencer Highway). Gilley's was made famous in the movie *Urban Cowboy*. Gilley's may have been a large hall, but the new Sylvan Beach Pavilion was also very large.

Sports announcer and newscaster Bob Allen is one of many local celebrities who has served as grand marshal for the Sylvan Beach Festival parade. Local celebrities such as Marvin Zindler have also served as judges for the Sylvan Beach Bathing Beauty Pageant.

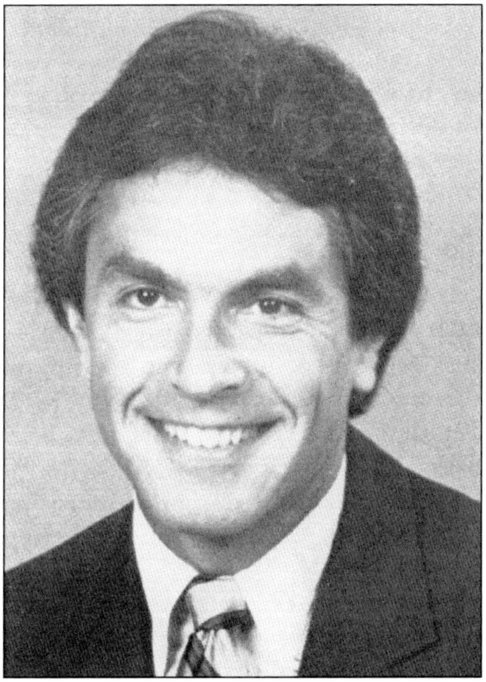

This is a promotional advertisement for the Sylvan Beach Pavilion when it was under the management of the City of La Porte. The capacity for the pavilion is 1,000 people.

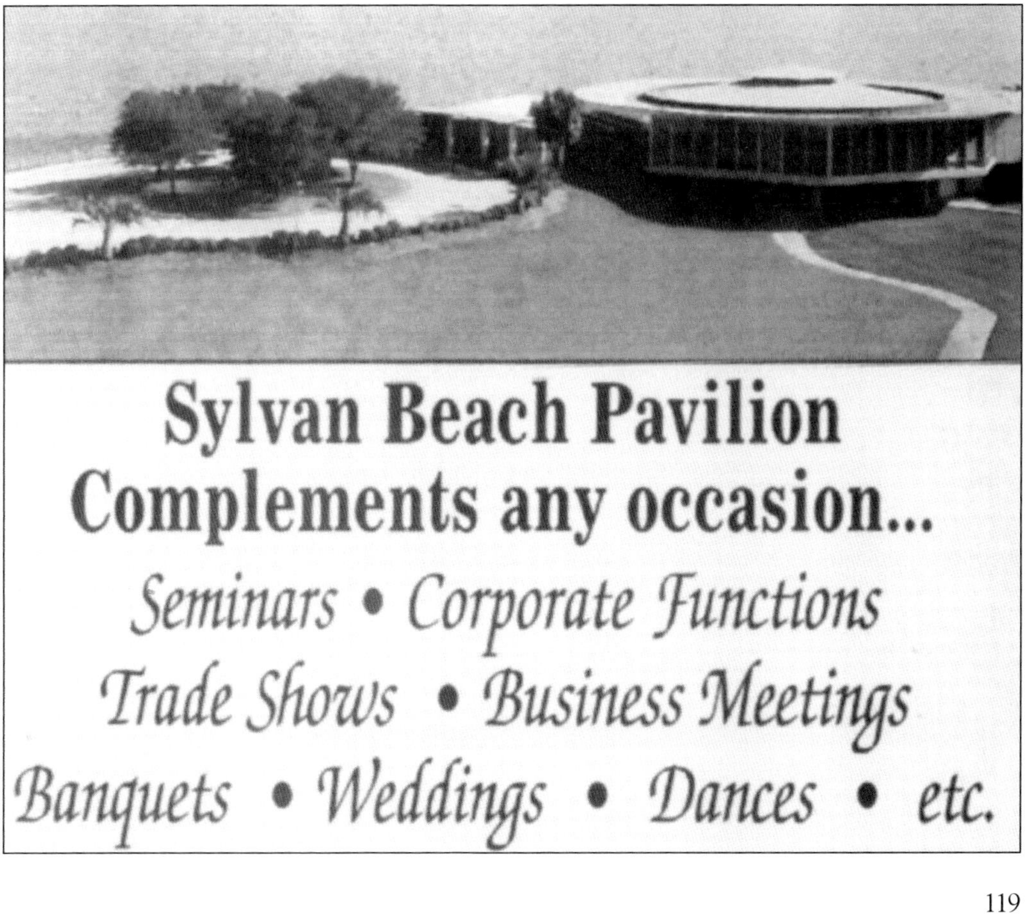

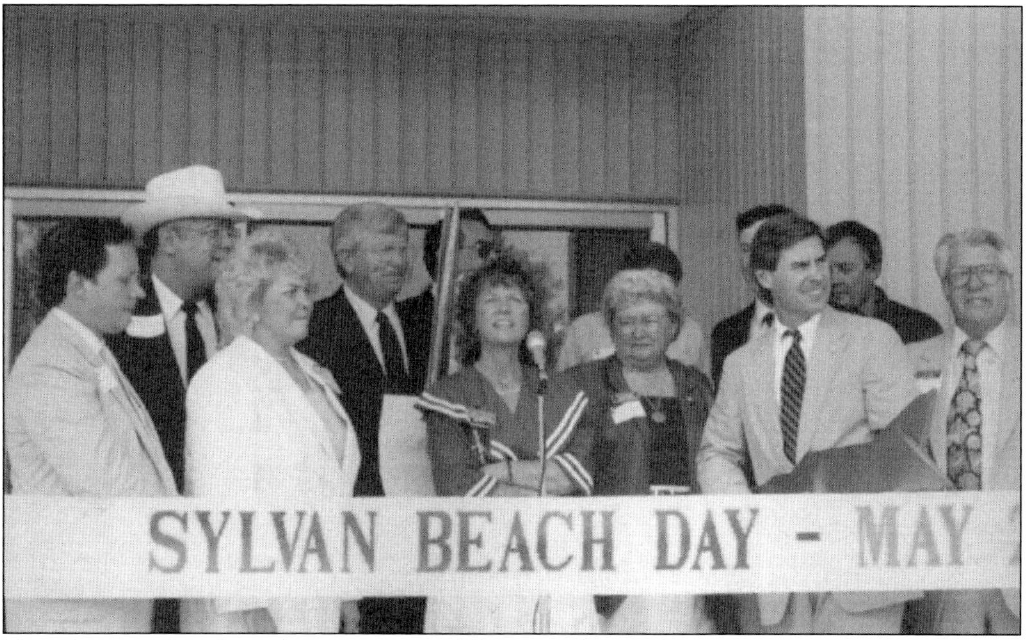

This photograph is from the reopening celebration of the Sylvan Beach Pavilion in 1987 after Hurricane Alicia severely damaged the building in 1981. It was a momentous occasion for the city of La Porte and Sylvan Beach. The then-governor of Texas, Mark White, honored the city by coming to help celebrate. Governor White and La Porte mayor Norman Malone are pictured here flanked by Harris County, local, and national dignitaries, including Texas state representative Mike Andrews, La Porte city manager Bob Herrera, and La Porte councilman B. Don Skelton.

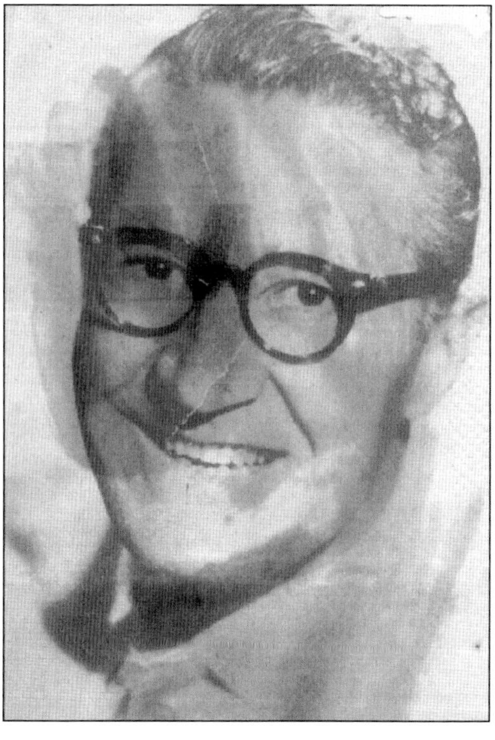

Ray McKinley was a local musician who was popular at Sylvan Beach. His band performed in the late 1970s at the La Porte Bay Area Heritage Society Dance at the Sylvan Beach Pavilion. McKinley is a native Texan who played with the Dorsey brothers and led the Glenn Miller Orchestra after Miller's death.